CL- 3rd ed.

An Economic History
of Argentina
in the Twentieth Century

The Columbia Economic History
of the Modern World
Stuart W. Bruchey, General Editor

An Economic History
of Argentina
in the Twentieth Century

Laura Randall

Columbia University Press / New York / 1978

Laura Randall is associate professor of economics
at Hunter College.

Library of Congress Cataloging in Publication Data

Randall, Laura Regina Rosenbaum.
    An economic history of Argentina in the twentieth
century.

    Bibliography: p.
    Includes index.
    1. Argentine Republic—Economic conditions.   I. Title.
HC175.R353   330.9′82′06   77-24388
ISBN 0-231-03358-3

Columbia University Press
New York and Guildford, Surrey

Acknowledgments

This book could not have been written without substantial help from several people and institutions. Financial support was provided by the Social Science Research Council and Hunter College of the City University of New York. The Institute of Latin American Studies of Columbia University generously provided an office. Research in Argentina was facilitated by the staff of the Central Bank, F.I.E.L., and the Ford Foundation. I am particularly indebted to Carmen Llorens de Azar, Mario Brodersohn, Reynold Carson, Marcelo Diamand, Alain de Janvry, Nita Rous Manitzas, Juan Carlos de Pablo, Julio Olivera, Lucio Reca, Jorge Sabato, Elias Salamma, Ruth Sautu, Haydee Gorostegui de Torres, and Javier Villanueva.

Research in the United States was aided by both students and colleagues: in particular, Roberto Agosti, Walter Bourne, Ed Goff, Richard Lissak, Vincent Mahler, Marianne Pietersen, Frantz Price, Constantine Soras, James Suarez, and Patricia Vega. Members of the Faculty Seminar at Lehigh University provided a helpful discussion of chapter 3.

January 1977

Contents

An Economic History
of Argentina
in the Twentieth Century

Chapter One: Introduction

TO THE EXTENT that Americans have thought about Argentina at all, our opinions have been sweeping, often ignorant, and more than a bit racist. At the beginning of the twentieth century, we thought of Argentina as the United States of South America. After all, the land was good and white people lived there. By the 1930s, the author of a confidential document reported that as long as Argentina produced cows, she would maintain her superiority, but if she tried to industrialize, "negro Brazil," with its larger market, might take over South America's leadership. In the early 1940s, Americans became convinced that Argentines were dictatorial, anti-Semitic, Nazi-loving fascists. By the 1960s, they seemed to comprise merely one more politically backward nation that was divided against itself in everything except xenophobia.

One might expect a book about Argentine economic history to be centered on the fate of gauchos dependent upon world markets for their livelihood. Yet the facts of Argentine economic history differ from this stereotype. For example, Argentina is not a dominantly agricultural country whose economic structure changed as a result of the breakdown in international trade during the Great Depression. In 1900, agriculture provided 32.2 percent of Argentine gross domestic product; by 1930, the percentage was 24.2; in 1969, Argentine agriculture accounted for less than 14 percent of its gross domestic product. Agriculture has not been larger than any of the other sectors of the economy since 1947 (see Tables 1.1 and 1.2).

Table 1.1 Percentage Distribution of Argentine Gross Domestic Product at Factor Cost, Based on 1935–1939 Price Weights, 1900–1955

Total (millions of 1935–1939 pesos)	Year	Agriculture	Stock Raising	Fishing	Mining	Manufacturing	Construction	Commerce	Transport and Communication	Other Public Services	Housing and Finance	Personal Services	Government Services
2,226	1900	15.6	16.6	0.1	0.3	11.0	3.3	14.6	4.8	0.3	16.2	9.8	7.4
2,433	1901	15.6	20.6	0.1	0.3	10.1	2.9	13.5	4.7	0.4	15.3	9.4	7.1
2,395	1902	13.9	19.5	0.1	0.3	10.9	2.7	13.6	4.8	0.4	16.1	10.1	7.7
2,733	1903	19.2	17.3	0.1	0.3	10.5	2.5	14.0	4.8	0.4	14.6	9.3	7.1
2,966	1904	20.9	14.9	0.1	0.3	10.6	3.3	15.4	4.9	0.4	13.4	8.9	6.8
3,248	1905	18.0	15.3	0.1	0.3	11.3	5.4	15.7	5.2	0.4	13.2	8.5	6.5
3,427	1906	18.3	14.1	0.1	0.2	11.2	4.8	16.9	5.9	0.4	13.0	8.3	6.5
3,449	1907	14.6	13.2	0.1	0.3	12.4	5.6	17.8	6.3	0.4	13.7	8.6	6.9
3,833	1908	18.4	12.9	0.1	0.2	11.9	5.0	16.7	6.5	0.4	8.0	5.0	6.7
3,959	1909	17.8	11.5	0.1	0.3	11.3	6.6	10.7	6.6	0.5	13.4	8.1	6.9
4,196	1910	15.7	10.9	0.1	0.4	13.1	6.9	17.4	6.7	0.5	13.4	8.0	6.6
4,265	1911	11.3	12.1	0.1	0.4	13.8	6.9	18.0	7.2	0.7	14.0	8.2	7.2
4,802	1912	19.1	11.5	0.1	0.4	11.6	4.6	16.9	7.4	0.8	13.3	7.4	6.8
4,875	1913	18.1	9.6	0.1	0.5	12.1	4.2	17.5	8.3	1.0	13.7	7.6	7.1
4,528	1914	18.9	10.3	0.1	0.5	11.9	2.6	15.4	7.8	1.2	14.9	8.5	8.0
4,668	1915	21.7	12.4	0.1	0.4	10.4	1.4	13.9	7.6	1.2	14.3	8.6	8.0
4,549	1916	17.5	13.5	0.1	0.4	10.9	1.2	14.0	8.2	1.4	14.9	9.4	8.5
4,213	1917	11.3	16.0	0.1	0.5	11.7	0.9	13.9	8.2	1.5	16.2	10.2	9.5
4,953	1918	18.2	14.6	0.1	0.4	11.8	0.8	13.3	7.8	1.4	14.1	9.1	8.3
5,120	1919	18.2	13.4	0.1	0.3	11.9	0.8	14.3	7.6	1.4	14.5	9.1	8.2
5,424	1920	19.9	11.2	0.1	0.4	11.7	1.5	15.0	8.1	1.4	13.7	8.9	8.0
5,534	1921	18.1	12.7	0.1	0.3	12.1	1.8	14.7	7.7	1.5	14.0	9.0	8.2
5,912	1922	15.2	14.4	0.1	0.3	12.5	2.2	15.3	8.0	1.5	13.8	8.7	7.9
6,431	1923	14.8	13.0	0.1	0.4	13.5	3.1	16.7	8.3	1.4	13.3	8.3	7.6
6,964	1924	16.9	12.6	0.1	0.5	13.1	2.9	15.6	8.8	1.4	12.6	8.1	7.3

6,938	1925	14.7	12.2	0.1	0.6	14.3	2.6	16.4	9.2	1.5	13.2	8.3	7.6
7,337	1926	17.4	11.7	0.1	0.6	13.5	2.4	15.8	8.9	1.5	12.8	8.1	7.5
7,761	1927	17.2	11.1	0.1	0.6	13.3	3.0	16.2	9.4	1.4	12.4	7.9	7.3
8,195	1928	17.0	10.3	0.1	0.6	14.1	3.1	16.5	9.9	1.4	12.1	7.7	7.2
8,513	1929	16.5	9.7	0.1	0.7	14.2	3.6	16.5	10.3	1.4	12.1	7.7	7.2
8,206	1930	13.9	10.3	0.1	0.6	14.6	3.6	15.8	10.4	1.6	13.1	8.2	7.7
7,906	1931	15.6	10.1	0.1	0.8	13.4	2.2	14.3	10.9	1.7	13.9	8.7	8.2
7,703	1932	17.1	10.8	0.1	0.9	13.0	1.6	13.2	10.3	1.9	14.1	9.1	8.6
8,027	1933	16.1	10.8	0.1	1.0	14.1	1.8	13.9	9.3	1.9	13.6	9.0	8.4
8,529	1934	16.2	10.5	0.1	0.9	15.1	2.4	14.1	9.2	1.9	13.0	8.6	8.1
8,976	1935	18.3	10.6	0.1	1.0	14.7	2.1	13.2	9.2	1.9	12.6	8.5	7.9
9,006	1936	15.3	10.8	0.1	1.2	15.6	2.2	13.4	9.5	2.0	12.8	8.6	8.4
9,561	1937	14.9	10.5	0.1	1.4	15.6	2.7	14.2	9.7	2.0	12.4	8.3	8.2
9,534	1938	12.5	10.6	0.1	1.5	16.0	3.0	14.3	9.7	2.1	12.7	8.5	8.8
9,989	1939	14.3	10.4	0.1	1.5	16.2	2.7	13.7	9.6	2.1	12.5	8.3	8.6
10,257	1940	15.3	10.5	0.1	1.7	15.8	2.3	13.2	9.5	2.1	12.4	8.3	8.7
10,780	1941	16.6	10.8	0.1	1.7	15.6	2.3	12.6	9.6	2.1	12.1	8.1	8.5
10,935	1942	15.7	11.0	0.1	1.7	15.6	2.2	12.4	9.8	2.1	12.3	8.3	8.8
10,335	1943	12.4	12.2	0.1	1.9	17.2	2.5	13.0	11.0	4.4	13.3	9.2	9.6
11,995	1944	14.8	10.8	0.1	1.7	16.8	2.6	11.8	9.7	2.2	11.9	8.3	9.3
11,642	1945	10.1	11.0	0.1	1.7	17.5	2.6	12.1	10.2	2.2	12.9	8.9	10.9
12,598	1946	10.2	10.1	0.1	1.5	18.2	2.5	12.9	10.6	2.2	12.7	8.5	10.5
13,926	1947	10.7	9.1	0.1	1.4	19.0	2.3	13.7	11.0	2.1	11.8	7.9	10.9
14,662	1948	10.4	8.5	0.1	1.3	18.3	2.4	13.8	11.4	2.2	12.1	7.9	11.2
14,567	1949	9.0	8.5	0.1	1.4	17.7	3.2	13.0	11.7	2.3	12.7	8.4	11.7
14,709	1950	8.2	8.2	0.1	1.4	18.1	3.3	12.9	12.0	2.4	13.0	8.5	12.0
15,241	1951	9.3	7.4	0.1	1.4	14.9	2.6	12.4	11.8	2.4	12.8	8.4	11.9
14,469	1952	7.4	7.0	0.1	1.3	17.5	2.8	11.5	10.3	2.2	14.2	9.1	13.1
15,383	1953	10.9	8.0	0.1	1.5	16.1	2.1	11.1	12.0	2.1	13.5	7.5	12.8
15,310	1954	10.5	8.0	0.1	1.5	17.5	2.8	12.1	12.3	2.7	14.0	9.3	13.0
16,532	1955	10.1	7.8	0.1	1.5	17.8	2.6	11.6	11.5	2.7	13.4	8.7	12.3

SOURCE: For derivation of this table, see explanatory note under Table 1.2, comparing ECLA's estimates and my own.
NOTE: Totals do not always add to 100.0 due to rounding of decimals.

Table 1.2 Percentage Distribution of Argentine Gross Domestic Product at Factor Cost Based on 1960 Price Weights, 1950–1969

Total (millions of 1960 pesos)	Year	Agriculture	Mining	Manufacturing	Construction	Commerce	Transport, Warehousing, and Communication	Electricity, Gas, and Water	Finance, Insurance, and Real Estate	Services
688,589	1950	18.0	0.5	27.9	4.8	19.5	8.5	0.9	4.1	15.8
715,330	1951	18.6	0.6	27.6	4.7	19.5	8.5	0.9	4.0	15.7
678,941	1952	16.8	0.7	28.5	4.6	19.1	8.3	1.0	4.4	16.7
715,819	1953	20.8	0.7	26.9	4.3	17.8	8.1	1.0	4.2	16.2
744,893	1954	19.9	0.7	27.9	4.0	18.0	8.2	1.1	4.2	16.0
798,133	1955	19.3	0.7	29.2	3.8	18.6	8.0	1.1	4.1	15.2
820,284	1956	17.9	0.7	30.4	3.6	18.9	7.8	1.1	4.0	15.5
864,467	1957	17.0	0.8	31.2	4.0	19.2	7.8	1.1	3.9	15.0
916,451	1958	16.7	0.7	31.8	4.5	19.0	7.8	1.1	3.9	14.5
856,934	1959	17.6	0.9	30.5	3.6	18.1	8.0	1.3	4.2	15.8
924,937	1960	16.6	1.1	31.1	4.0	18.9	7.9	1.2	4.0	15.2
990,865	1961	15.4	1.4	32.0	3.9	19.6	7.9	1.4	3.8	14.6
974,109	1962	16.3	1.6	30.7	3.6	19.2	7.7	1.6	4.0	15.3
951,236	1963	17.0	1.6	30.2	3.5	18.1	7.7	1.7	4.1	16.5
1,049,960	1964	16.5	1.5	32.5	3.3	17.9	7.7	1.7	3.8	15.1
1,145,594	1965	16.0	1.4	33.9	3.1	18.1	7.7	1.8	3.6	14.4
1,154,016	1966	15.3	1.5	33.9	3.3	17.9	7.7	2.0	3.6	14.8
1,183,197	1967	15.6	1.6	33.5	3.6	17.6	7.5	2.1	3.7	14.8
1,237,839	1968	14.3	1.7	34.3	4.1	17.7	7.6	2.1	3.7	14.5
1,335,868	1969	13.8	1.7	35.3	4.1	18.2	7.4	2.2	3.6	13.8

SOURCE: BCRA, *Origen del Producto y Distribución del Ingreso, Años 1950–1969*: p. 30.
NOTE: Coverage of industries is different in Table 1.1 from Table 1.2; differences in sector shares for 1950–55 in the two series reflect both different coverage and different price weights. It is not possible to reconcile the two series.

As a result, although changes in agricultural output have influenced production in other sectors, they have not been the only, or necessarily the most important, determinant of production in the rest of the economy. This stems in part from the fact that Argentine agricultural production has used land much more extensively than either labor or capital. As a result, changes in agricultural output have had little direct effect on employment. Nonetheless, there has been continuing concern about the impact of agriculture on the Argentine economy because agriculture provided virtually all merchandise exports at the turn of the century, and about 90 percent of them in the postwar period. Within this total, wheat, maize, and beef have dominated export production throughout the century. To rephrase the question of agriculture's impact on the Argentine economy, a crucial issue is whether, and to what extent, Argentine economic growth has depended on foreign exchange income earned by agricultural exports.

In an earlier book, I indicated that economically, Argentina was a part of Britain's unofficial empire until the beginning of World War I. The shock that changed Argentina's economic structure and transformed it from a supplier of raw materials to a semi-industrialized nation was World War I, rather than the Great Depression. Moreover, the transformation of the economy was inextricably bound up with a transformation of the importance and content of government economic policy. There are two main conclusions in the present book: (1) For the last fifty years, Argentina has not been part of any other nation's economic empire. It has been economically independent in all essentials. (2) The Argentine government's policies and the frequency with which they have changed have been the key variables in the explanation of the performance of the Argentine economy in the twentieth century. Indeed, since the domestic sector of the economy in the twenties was about three times bigger than the export sector, and rose to about ten times bigger than the export sector in the post-war period, it would take considerable ingenuity to show that any other nation determined Argentine economic history during the past half century.

The Argentine government policies that influenced Argentine economic performance often reflected policy makers' thoughts about how economic growth takes place; these opinions were frequently couched in the language of formal economic analysis. In chapter 2, accordingly, five explanations of economic growth are presented; Argentine economic policy makers are identified according to which explanation of economic growth they used.

The content of economic policies, and the timing of their adoption and implementation, were primarily the result of political forces. The greatest political changes in twentieth-century Argentina were marked by the winning of the presidency by Hipólito Yrigoyen in 1916, his ouster in 1930, and the increasing power, then presidency of Perón. These shifts in political control were followed by a shift in the rate of change of Argentine economic structure. Thus, a Marxist interpretation does not appear to fit the facts of the Argentine case. Similarly, the economic structure of Argentina was not altered by change in the ownership of the means of production: although the government created firms in strategic sectors, they never produced more than 2 percent of the gross domestic product.

The economic policy decisions taken by Argentine presidents before World War II reflected their need for support from regional and sectoral interest groups. The widening of the electoral base by World War II led the president to use economic policy to bid for the support of a new group, labor, in order to maintain himself in office. At the same time, increasing ideological acceptance of an active role of government led to adoption of policies designed to modify Argentine economic structure. The government's ability to carry out economic policy gradually increased; new institutions and techniques of control developed slowly, first during the Great Depression, and later under Perón.

Occasionally, economic actions were taken for personal reasons. For example, Perón expropriated the Bemberg agricultural holdings, allegedly because the Bembergs had snubbed his wife in Paris, while other large landholdings escaped untouched. Such incidents, however, were not frequent enough to modify my conclusion that the economic performance and structure of the Argentine economy was largely the result of government policies that strongly influenced profit opportunities in each sector of the economy. In chapter 2, it is shown that a policy cycle gradually developed in which various regions, sectors of production, and economic classes were favored in turn. As the impact of government economic policies on the distribution of real profits among all of the sectors is central to the explanation of any sector's ability to expand output, chapter 2 includes the presentation and testing of a model that shows the responsiveness of each economic sector to the changes in real profit opportunities in all of the sectors.

According to many economic theorists, the performance of an economy is heavily influenced by the distribution of income. Chapter 3 presents an analysis of the effect of Argentine economic policy on income distribution, and, in turn, the effect that shifting income distribution has had on the demand for consumption goods, sources of funds for investment, and sectoral profits, and, therefore, on Argentine economic performance.

The model described in chapter 2 provides a satisfactory explanation of the performance of each economic sector and of the performance of the economy as a whole. Government techniques of economic control, and policies toward the most important sectors, are therefore explored in the second part of the book. The overall functioning of the economy is regulated, in part, by macroeconomic policies which have been carried out by the government banks. The evolution of the Argentine banking system, and the steps that the Central Bank has taken to regulate the economy, are described in chapter 4. Chapters 5 to 7 are devoted to the history of the government policies toward, and the performance of, the agricultural, manufacturing, railroad, and petroleum sectors.

The analysis of Argentine economic policy and economic history presented in the first seven chapters is consistent with the assertion made at the beginning of this book that Argentina has been economically independent for the last fifty years. The relationship between Argentine economic policy and per-

Chapter Two: Economic Theory
and Argentine Economic Growth

ARGENTINA HAS CONTROLLED her economic growth through her own policy decisions since the 1920s. The stated reasons for choosing a given policy, and criticisms of the choice by Argentine and foreign economists, were frequently couched in terms of academic analysis selected from among five theories: classical, monetarist, structuralist, Keynesian, and Harrod-Domar. Although the names that identify these theories are those used in the post-war period, they really refer to different emphases in Argentine economic thought throughout the twentieth century. These theories are presented and analyzed in this chapter.

Statements of reasons, however, do not necessarily explain why a policy is adopted. Therefore, I also emphasize what seems to me the underlying fact that the choice of economic policy was determined by the scramble for income and wealth by competing groups who influenced government selection of policies which implicitly determined the profit level of each sector. Profits for each sector are important because profit-conscious businessmen invest in those sectors in which profits are greater than those which could be earned in other sectors, and disinvest in sectors in which profits are lower than those which could be obtained elsewhere. Cumulatively, this explains both the level of investment and changes in that level in each sector.

It must be stressed that profits, rather than prices, determine economic activity: if prices received by producers rise, but costs increase more than receipts, profits fall. The analysis presented in this chapter differs from earlier studies in its use of changes in profits rather than changes in prices. For example, for the output of each sector, the effect of changes in real profits in each of the nine sectors of the economy, and the previous year's input of the sector, are examined for 1950–69, as adequate data are available for those years.

In the course of the analysis, it will be shown that the various sectors of the economy differ from each other both in the length of time it takes them to respond to real profit opportunities, and in the characteristics of their response. One result of this phenomenon is that after World War II, the adoption of a policy to favor one sector almost necessarily forced the adoption of a policy favoring a different sector in a subsequent period. The policy cycle adopted, and its consequences, are presented in the third section of this chapter.

Five Explanations of Economic Growth

The most persistent conservative criticism of the Argentine economy is that Argentine economic institutions and economic policies differ from those based on classical British economic analysis.

The merits of classical economic analysis have been debated by Argentines since the nineteenth century. Its assumptions were that in the absence of a banking system, savers and investors are identical; prices are flexible; there are many producers and consumers in a market; labor and capital are mobile, both within nations and across national boundaries; and currency devaluation increases export sales sufficiently to increase the supply of foreign exchange.

These assumptions are at least partially descriptive of the Argentine economy at the beginning of the nineteenth century. By the end of the century, a banking system had developed, and had financed considerable growth, often by using illegal methods. Prices were flexible downward as well as upward, at the cost of falling real wages for Argentine workers and considerable labor unrest. This led, in the twentieth century, to a process of unionization that limited downward price flexibility.

Although there were many producers and consumers in manufacturing and services, the ownership of agricultural land was notoriously concentrated. International labor mobility was evident in the large number of immigrants who came to Argentina before World War I; international capital flows have been maintained to this day. Within Argentina, both labor and capital have been highly mobile.

The classical economists argued that when world conditions were close to those assumed in their analysis, the government should not intervene in the economy, so that production would reflect the choice of individuals. Similarly, they advocated free trade under the gold standard. There were two exceptions to the policy of nonintervention. The first was protection in matters vital to national defense. The second was the temporary protection of economic activity for infant industries in those cases in which it was believed that after these industries grew up, protection would be removed, and the mature industries would survive international competition. Argentine presidents and their ministers of economy mainly adhered to this view from 1900 through 1935, defending actions taken in opposition to the prescription derived from classical theory as "temporary actions that would be reversed when conditions returned to normal." Classical economic doctrine was then abandoned until after the overthrow of Perón, when it was espoused in the 1960s by Economy Ministers Pinedo and Alsogaray.

One of the reasons for the decline of acceptance in Argentina of classical economic analysis was the fact that the British classical economists usually ignored the fact that since income and wealth were unequally distributed, only those with large incomes and wealth would strongly influence the functioning of the economy. Consequently, the free play of the market benefited them more than other groups. Similarly, the classical writers thought that economic growth at a desired rate would be ensured by the market system. The question of who paid for or benefited from growth was not strongly emphasized. Argentines who advocated policies based on classical British economic analysis were therefore thought either to enjoy privileged and powerful positions within the Argentine economy, or to be associated with foreign interest groups. Since many of the Argentine elite were exporters, they were accused of advocating policies originated by the British, which benefited them and their British trade partners, rather than the Argentine nation as a whole.

A case in point is devaluation of the Argentine currency, which was urged by exporters and British importers as a remedy for Argentine trade deficits. For reasons that will be discussed later, this resulted in an increase in cattle herd size rather than an immediate increase in Argentine cattle slaughter, agricultural exports and therefore in foreign exchange earnings (see chapter 4). As a result of the apparent difference between the classical economists' predictions and Argentine economic performance, few Argentines currently urge the use of classic British economic analysis. Instead, schools of thought that are descended from classical analysis, but differ from it, are used to justify policy prescriptions. Two such schools of thought are the monetarist and structuralist theories, which analyze economic growth using the quantity theory of money as a starting point.

In its simplest form, the quantity theory states that gross national product is equal to the quantity of money multiplied by its velocity, which is defined as the average number of times it is spent each year. It is also equal to the volume of production multiplied by its average price. The monetarists assume that this identity can be used to show causality. Price rises are attributed to excess demand, made possible by an increase in money supply, which in turn leads to balance of payments difficulties. The monetarists' remedy for inflation and balance of payments difficulties is a policy package of a reduction of the money supply, devaluation, and a wage (and sometimes a price) freeze.

This analysis breaks down in both theory and practice, because the quantity theory cannot be used to establish causality. An increase in money supply would be certain to lead to inflation only if velocity and the physical volume of goods produced were constant. Since an increase in money supply could be accompanied either by a change in velocity, an increase in goods produced, or by a long-run price fall, no causal statement is possible. Moreover, the quantity theory is valid only if resources are homogeneous, and all sectors respond to a price increase with an identical percentage increase in quantity supplied. In this case, a given increase in money supply would lead to a predictable increase in price and quantity, no matter how the money was spent. When resources are not homogeneous, an increase in money supply yields a different increase in price and quantity supplied in each sector: the weighted sum of the responses of each of the sectors is needed to predict the response for the country as a whole.

The failure to distinguish between sectoral responses leads the monetarists to differ from classical economists, who argue that in a market system that ensures optimal economic growth, entrepreneurs invest where profits are highest and consumers purchase where their satisfaction is greatest. Monetarists emphasize the effect of price, rather than profit, on average economic behavior. Yet, prices rise at different rates throughout the economy, with the result that profits in each sector change. Investment is directed to the most profitable sectors. The distribution of investment, in turn, determines the growth rate. Thus, because the distribution of money supply affects the distribution of prices and profits, not only the level, but also the distribution, of money supply is a determinant of economic growth.

The policy prescription of the monetarists is not very helpful: if the government had been able to limit the money supply or to control wages and prices, it would have done so. The advice to "be different" cannot be carried out, while a devaluation will not necessarily improve the balance of payments position.[1] In practice, post-World War II devaluations were accompanied by refunding Argentina's debt. The creditors imposed the acceptance of monetarist policies recommended by the I.M.F. as a condition of refunding the debt and extending new loans in the late 1950s and early 1960s. The resulting domestic credit shortage harmed the Argentine economy. Many Argentines therefore reject monetarist analysis and prescription.[2]

Structuralists view economic difficulties as originating in world trade structures that favor rich countries, and in incomplete domestic economic structures that inhibit the economic development of poor countries from agricultural to manufacturing nations. The first well-known Argentine structuralist in the twentieth century was Alejandro Bunge, who urged the government to aid manufacturing growth so that the intense difficulties resulting from the cutoff of foreign supplies during World War I would never be repeated. To some extent, the Argentine government attempted to improve the nation's infrastructure during the late 1930s, and strongly intensified these efforts under Perón.

The formal working out of structuralist theory is associated with the writings of Raúl Prebisch in the 1950s and 1960s. Since much of Argentine economic policy has focused on fighting inflation, structuralist economic theories necessarily present an explanation of inflation. It states that inflation is less the result of excess demand than of the inability or unwillingness of producers to increase supplies in response to price signals.[3] Structuralists believe that there are several different conditions that can lead to a limited increase of quantity supplied in response to a price increase, and, therefore, to inflation. They feel that appropriate policies to end inflation must reflect the specific cause of limited supply response in each nation. For example, if large landowners limit production to maintain prices and income, a land reform will yield many small producers, none of whom can afford to keep land idle. If production in manufacture or services does not increase in response to steep price rises, the state can establish its own enterprises to increase the supply; indeed, many radicals recommend nationalization of existing firms. If supply bottlenecks are ended by an increase of firms in the private sector, credit must be extended to the new firms. Short-run inflation is a concomitant of growth, as the money supply must be increased in the short run to improve the market structure and end inflation in the long run.

Structuralists also argue that the ability of the economy to expand output is limited by the need to import items not available from domestic producers. Imports require foreign exchange, which can be earned only if developed nations are willing to buy less-developed nations' exports. Unless developed nations grow rapidly, and have favorable tariff policies, demand for less-developed nations' products will not increase. External constraints on international trade were blamed for unsatisfactory growth rates until the late 1960s, when the Viet Nam War increased the demand for the raw materials products; at the same time, competing industrial nations were increasingly concerned about securing continuing supplies of raw materials.

During the 1950s, structuralists argued that, because of labor unions' strength in rich countries, productivity increases are almost matched by increases in wage payments, so that prices do not fall by the extent warranted by the productivity increase; while in poor countries, the unlimited supply of labor prevents wages from rising when technological improvements occur. As a result, an increase in productivity in poor countries yields a fall in the prices of their exports, and rich importing countries capture the largest part of the gains of poor countries' technological progress. Thus, because of the difference between rich and poor nations in internal institutional structure and in international bargaining power, the rich nations appropriate the lion's share of the gains from trade.[4] This line of reasoning was central to structuralists' analysis until the improvement of trading conditions in the late 1960s, when it became less plausible to blame foreigners for a low growth rate. Concern therefore shifted from increasing the growth rate to maintaining employment and improving the regional distribution of growth.

Structuralist highlighting of the wealth and power that underlay domestic supply responses and bargaining in international trade led to a discussion of the political determinants of inflation. Each sector is viewed as trying to increase its wealth and power through price rises, and the resulting inflationary spiral is less destructive than open sectoral clashes in politics, which might result in civil war.[5]

Although structuralist theory is not narrowly economic, its policy proposals are intended to yield a market structure close to the competitive ideal of the classical economists. Both classical economists and structuralists are concerned with varying sectoral opportunities. The structuralists, like the monetarists, concentrate on response to price signals, whereas the classical economists more realistically discuss alternate profit opportunities. Thus, it is the concerns of the structuralists, rather than their analytical technique, that have been adopted by recent Argentine economic policy makers.

Keynesian economic analysis has influenced Argentine policy makers since the 1930s. Keynes' writings were translated by Raúl Prebisch, who was a prominent government adviser in the 1930s and early 1940s. Keynesian analysis underlies much of the technical analysis of the Argentine economy that was undertaken in the 1960s. Yet evaluation of the application of Keynesian analysis to the Argentine economy is made difficult by the continuing debate about "what Keynes really meant." The version of Keynesian analysis that is best known in the United States centers on two statements: that market forces may lead to an equilibrium at less than full employment, and that the government can counteract a depression through fiscal policy. The discussion of appropriate fiscal policies is conducted in general terms; in many nations, however, the impact of spending differs not only among income classes, but also among geographical regions and economic sectors: special, rather than general policies are required. A further difficulty is that in some cases, government spending may frighten investors into spending less as government spending increases, thus defeating government attempts to increase total spending.

Keynesian analysis of fiscal policy prescriptions rests on the fact that private consumption and investment expenditures depend, in part, upon expectations about the state of the nation in general, and about the outcome of a given investment in particular. However, as Shackle points out, Keynes states that "we simply do not know" what expectations depend upon.[6] Thus, neither expectations, nor private investment spending, nor overall economic performance, can be completely controlled. In econometric applications of Keynesian analysis, expectations about future conditions are measured by the interest rate; they are assumed to have a major influence on investment and total spending. Yet, when measured by the interest rate (see Table A.1), expectations have little influence on the structure or level of Argentine real gross domestic product. This occurs because capital is mobile between nations, and the rate of interest consequently often reflects international rather than national economic conditions and expectations.

In order to capture the effect of expectations about the Argentine economy in this analysis, a variable other than the interest rate is needed. In the model described in Chapter 8, expectations are included by using who was president as a proxy for expectations about the state of the nation in general. Although there may be some variation in economic policy and in business confidence within presidencies, the variables for presidency significantly affect the percentage change and level of real gross domestic product (see Table A.1), which suggests that control of the presidency is a partial determinant of economic performance.[7] Since Keynesian models cannot be sufficiently tailored to the Argentine economy, both for conceptual reasons and for lack of adequate data, they are not explored at length in this book.

A more general economic model, which has been frequently used in the analyses of the Argentine economy prepared by the Economic Commission for Latin America and by the National Development Council (CONADE), is the Harrod-Domar model. The advantage of using a Harrod-Domar model to analyze Argentine economic growth is that it makes no assumptions about institutions or causal behavior, but instead clarifies technical relations. In its simplest form, the model centers on the need to obtain capital in order to generate economic growth. It states that if all funds saved are invested, the amount of extra income generated will equal the amount invested divided by the number of years (called the payback period) needed to generate income equal to the value of investment. Thus, if ten dollars are invested and the payback period is five years, two dollars of income are generated each year. The more invested, the greater the growth; the shorter the payback period, the greater the immediate growth. Similarly, the higher the share of savings and investment in national income, the higher the growth rate.

Savings and investment are divided into Argentine private, Argentine government, and foreign components. The Harrod-Domar model provides a framework for evaluating the effect of policies designed to increase the level of a component of savings or investment on the other components, and therefore of the net impact on total savings and investment.

The theoretical payback period of an investment is calculated on the assumption that equipment is used in optimum conditions: all economies of scale are realized, and machines never lie idle. Realized payback periods are longer than theoretical ones if equipment is operated at less than full capacity. In a more advanced form, the Harrod-Domar model includes a correction coefficient which converts the theoretical to the actual payback period. By including a correction coefficient, the model implicitly highlights policies which improve utilization of equipment: better training of the labor force, an end to strikes and lockouts, maintenance of demand for the product to ensure production at full capacity, and better physical maintenance of equipment. Thus, the Harrod-Domar model implicitly emphasizes policies important at the level of the firm.

While the Harrod-Domar model highlights the determinants of economic growth for the economy as a whole, it ignores differences between sectors. It is complementary to, rather than inconsistent with, analyses stressing alternate profits and expectations.

That alternate profits and expectations explain Argentine economic growth is well known to businessmen. Yet, this explanation lacks the elegance of many economic theories, which neither assume Argentine economic institutions nor predict Argentine economic behavior. Thus, for reasons of elegance—and sometimes belief—the five theories described are offered by Argentines as apologies for the adoption or criticism of economic policy. They do not, however, adequately explain the determinants of Argentine economic growth.

A Model of Argentine Economic Growth, 1950–69

Argentine economic growth in the twentieth century has been determined by expected alternate profit opportunities; because it takes time to adjust output to expected alternate profit opportunties, and past practice influences current practice, the production of a sector for any year also depends upon the level of inputs utilized in the preceding year.[8]

"Alternate profit opportunities" refers to the difference in the ability to earn a given rate of profit in one sector of the economy rather than another. This, rather than the general level of profits, determines the pattern of investment among economic sectors. The form that investment takes depends upon expectations. Investment in heavy capital equipment to increase the productive capacity of the sector takes a long time to produce enough income to cover the initial cost of investment. If it is thought that the pattern of alternate profit opportunities will hold for an extended period of time, then it will be profitable to invest in capital goods. If alternate profit opportunities are expected to shift, then capital should be invested in projects that pay for themselves in a short time, so that the funds can be reinvested in another sector, when it becomes more profitable than the sector in which the capital was initially employed. If there is great uncertainty regarding the future pattern of alternate profit opportunities, then investment in stocks of finished goods, or in foreign exchange and other highly liquid assets, rather than in expansion of productive capacity, becomes the most rational form of investment.

A great deal of modern technology is capital intensive, requires a large initial investment, and has a long payback period; it can be adopted only if entrepreneurs expect that the alternate profit patterns will be stable. The corollary is that instability leads to failure to adopt new techology. For example, the rapid shifts in Argentine economic policy led investors, after the war, to concentrate on projects that had a maximum payback period of three years, and, when inflation was severe, of one year.

For the economy as a whole, profit expectations are linked with the presidency. The long term growth rate depends significantly upon who is president. Yearly changes in output, however, depend upon changes in the level and distribution between sectors of money supply, government spending, and foreign exchange, which affect alternate profits and expectations. Changes in expectations, when the president continues in office, are reflected in two ways: the first is the number of years of economic behavior that businessmen take into account in making their decisions; the second is the level and term structure of interest rates.

If policies are expected to continue unchanged, then businessmen will use average conditions over the past several years as a guide to future behavior. If conditions are changing rapidly, then only current conditions are taken into account. For example, in the case of beef cattle production, Dr. Lucio Reca has found that from 1923 to 1947 conditions were relatively stable. "Product prices changed basically as the result of the operation of market forces," and the expected price used in decisions concerning the size of herds was formed by the seven past annual prices. In contrast, "for most of 1945–1965 ... policy ... introduced a considerable amount of uncertainty through the frequent manipulation of prices." The expected price included only one past price.[9] Further, the absence of technological progress in the beef cattle industry—despite calving rates 19 percent below those of the United States, and a refusal to improve natural pasture, which would more than double the carrying capacity of the land[10]—is consistent with a refusal to tie up funds in long-term projects when there is considerable uncertainty.

Dr. Reca's observations can be modified and extended to all of the Argentine economy. Instead of examining the effect of past prices on output, I examined the effect on output of changes in real unit profits for each sector.[11] This change in each sector is referred to as the change in real alternate profits. This amount was calculated for agriculture, mining, manufacture, electricity, construction, commerce, transportation, finance, and services. The decline in the usefulness of information about past price patterns noted by Dr. Reca is seen to have been carried even further when alternate profit patterns are examined, and more recent years included. When businessmen are accurate in their judgment about current profit patterns, their estimates of profits is measured by those which actually prevailed. The belief that businessmen could easily predict profit patterns during the year is based on the knowledge that alternate profits are heavily influenced by government activities, and government policies are known. For example, regression analysis indicates that the best estimate of the output of the construction sector is that obtained by using changes in real alternate profits that take place during the year that output changes (see Appendix A). Current output of the agricultural, mining, and service sectors is determined by changes in real alternate profits which took place last year and by last year's output. The output of the gas, water, and electricity, and of the financial services sectors, is determined by the changes in real alternate profits which occurred two years ago and last year's output. The output of the manufacture, commerce, and transport sectors is determined by their output in the previous year and the weighted sum of changes in real alternate profits for the previous five years. An analysis of the economic model used to obtain these results, and an estimate of the time needed for each sector of the economy to adjust to alternate profit opportunities, is presented in Appendix A. The average length of time needed for the economy to adjust to changes in alternate profits is two and a half to three years, reflecting the length of time needed to install an advanced technology, bottlenecks in supply, and institutional rigidities. There is, consequently, little reason to believe that the government could achieve desired changes in the economy faster than the private sector. This is one reason that direct ownership of the economy was not a major feature of any government's plans before 1970.

It must be stressed that this model focuses on actual, rather than on potential, growth. It indicates how business responded to profit signals, but does not explain why governments' policies affecting profits were adopted. It also accepts technology available to the Argentine economy as given at any particular time; however, the model is consistent with changing technology, and consequently with changing capital and labor requirements over time. The details of the forms that capital takes, whether infrastructure, improved land, capital equipment, buildings, inventories, or investment in people, are explored in the chapters of this book outlining the economic history of each sector. It is worth noting in passing that Argentine businessmen, when possible, pressured the government into providing the physical infrastructure and educational system best calculated to serve their needs. The model does not consider sociological factors, such as the cultural composition of the nation, the attitude towards and number of entrepreneurs, and so forth, which are analyzed, when relevant, in the subsequent chapters.

The Argentine Economic Policy Cycle, 1950–69

It has been shown that changes in alternate profits are central to an explanation of Argentine economic growth. Since changes in sectoral profits depend upon the rate at which a sector's prices rise relative to those of all other sectors, the most important policy area for the government is its setting of sectoral prices, whether by direct controls or by other policy instruments. In a recent study of the effect of government policy on agricultural and manufacturing prices, the American economist Huntley Hedges Biggs suggests that the prices received by Argentine food producers differ from world agricultural prices in large part because of devaluations and export taxes. Prices received by food producers in turn are a statistically significant determinant of food prices; similarly, food prices largely determine wage rates, and wage rates strongly influence product prices.[12] Product prices in turn affect prices food producers pay, and therefore the profits they make.

The ability of food producers, laborers, and manufacturers to pass on their increased costs through price increases has varied considerably (since post-war government policy has not consistently favored one sector). It can be described as a policy cycle: between 1945 and 1964, government policy repeatedly favored first agriculture, then services, and finally manufactures, a sequence triggered by a shortage of foreign exchange which led to a devaluation. (That the government favored a given sector, so that its profits increased, did not necessarily mean that the sector's profits reached the average level of profitability which prevailed in the rest of the economy. See Appendix Table A.2.) In order to prevent inflation from offsetting the results of the devaluation, the government limited increases in money supply. In the short run, inflation continued, real money supply was reduced, and real interest rates rose. In the long run, inflation increased beyond anticipated amounts, and real interest rates were negative. Nonetheless, since the future rate of inflation was not known, investment appeared unprofitable. The situation was made more difficult to the extent that the government obtained funds that otherwise would have been available to the private sector.[13] Thus, the reduction in money supply described above was not adequate to counteract a cost inflation generated by rising import prices, and it generated unemployment, which resulted from illiquidity in real terms.

The next step in the policy cycle occurred when, faced with both inflation and unemployment, the government felt compelled to spend its way out of a recession, and to maintain or increase tariff protection. In the course of this expenditure, the pre-1964 sectoral policy pattern emerged.

When the peso was devalued, the government hoped that the increased domestic value of foreign exchange would stimulate agricultural exports. These, in turn, would increase the supply of foreign exchange and help to maintain the exchange rate. The anticipated exchange increase did not materialize,[14] because an increase in cattle prices led cattle owners to build up herds in hopes that the offspring would command high prices.[15] As a result, cattle slaughtered and exported decreased, and foreign exchange receipts declined correspondingly. This is particularly important because cattle products are Argentina's single most important export.

The rising prices of agriculture and livestock obtained by devaluation resulted in an increase in the share of agriculture and livestock in gross domestic product, which includes inventories. It did not result in an increase in marketed production. Popular hostility towards agriculture and livestock raising increased because whenever policies to promote agriculture and livestock via devaluation were adopted prior to 1964, they were accompanied by policies to restrict imports, limit inflation, and attract foreign exchange. Because of the shortage of supplies and credit which resulted from these policies, whenever the share of agriculture and livestock in the national economy increased, gross domestic product fell.

The consequently reduced tax base was further eroded by inflation, which made postponement of tax payments profitable. As a result, the government lacked funds and did not feel able to invest in long-term, expensive projects. Instead, it avoided massive unemployment by spending on labor-intensive services and construction. As recovery spread to manufactures, the government increased credit to the private sector. Since imports are required as inputs for expanded economic activity, and the marginal propensity to import is apparently greater than the marginal propensity to export, balance of payments troubles followed. The policy cycle came full circle with the next devaluation.[16]

The government attempted to break this policy cycle after 1964. On various occasions, it limited the cattle price increase associated with devaluation by taxing agricultural exports. It limited the increase of domestic food prices following devaluation by taxing exports and by regulating sales for domestic consumption. It limited wage increases by government-influenced wage settlements which were made possible, in part, by government subsidies and price controls on goods and services essential to workers' standard of living. Finally, it limited the increase of product prices by giving special benefits to producers who maintained prices.

The pre-1964 policy cycle had been adopted in response to political pressures; an attempt to change the cycle implied either immunity to those pressures or conditions so bad that individual interests were temporarily abandoned in the national interest. To some extent, both of these conditions obtained in the post-1964 military governments, but precisely because of the success of the post-1964 policies, it was impossible to maintain them in the late sixties. As economic conditions improved, individual interest groups were no longer willing to forgo possible increased benefits. As the military contemplated returning the government to civilians, increased concessions to class, regional, and sectoral interest groups became necessary to influence the future course of politics.

The inflationary system of division of economic gains was reestablished, but with a different credit policy, so that in the late 1960s, inflation was accompanied by growth. This situation lasted until the return of Perón (1973), when a fresh burst of confidence led to a temporary dramatic drop in inflation accompanied by continuing growth.

The pattern of Argentine economic growth during the twentieth century is typical of dominantly capitalist economies. Expectations determined private spending. Although expectations are difficult to predict, they are easy to analyze. Who is president is the most important determinant of expectations of economic events, by virtue of both the economic actions directly taken by the president, and the investments made or withheld by businessmen in response. Once expectations are evaluated, the details of economic policy conform: as described in chapter 8, external forces such as war and drought are more important than some aspects of domestic economic policy in determining Argentine economic performance. Argentine economic policy was more influential than foreign economic policy in determining Argentine economic growth.[17] The following chapters explore the development of institutions and policies that enabled the government to control the distribution of profits and economic growth.

Chapter Three: Income Distribution, Consumption, and Investment

IN THE SECTORAL analysis of the Argentine economy I will focus on the ability of each sector, faced with complex historical situations, to supply goods. In particular, the net impact of government policy will be emphasized. I will include in the analysis the effect of changes in labor relations and the cost of labor insofar as they affect both the ability to produce, and profits earned from production. In the analysis of the manufacturing sector, the effect of changes in labor income on the demand for certain goods will be considered. In this chapter, the analysis is extended to the economy as a whole, and the effect of the distribution of income between workers and entrepreneurs on the demand for real private consumption, and for investment goods, is considered.

The most politically sensitive question in studies of economic growth is: what is the optimal relationship between the distribution of income and wealth, and economic growth? The rich often diversify their assets, so that it is not easy to know the total wealth of an individual, or the distribution of wealth for a nation. For this reason, the analysis presented in this chapter makes only brief reference to the influence of the distribution of wealth on Argentine economic growth, and focuses on the relationship between income distribution and economic growth in Argentina from 1914 to 1969.

I shall begin by discussing income distribution in other nations, in order to evaluate the possibility of utilizing their experience to judge that of Argentina. I shall then proceed to examine the relationship between increases in workers' and entrepreneurs' income and increases in investment, as an economy will grow only if investment takes place. Moreover, because funds spent on private consumption cannot be invested, and because much economic analysis has taken the form of examining the relationship between changes in income and changes in consumption, the relationship between changes in income and changes in consumption will be examined for Argentina. This examination will be carried out for several catagories of income, and take into account the ways in which inflation and ownership of some categories of wealth enter into an explanation of the relationship between changes in income and changes in consumption.

One way of exploring the relationship between income distribution and economic development in Argentina is by comparing Argentine experience to that of other nations. The best-known study of the relationship between income distribution and economic development is that of Simon Kuznets, who received a Nobel Prize for his work. One aspect of this study revealed that poor nations had relatively egalitarian income distribution before contact with richer, more modern countries. After investment by foreigners who used new techniques, enclaves of high-income activities were created. This increased the inequality of income distribution, a process that continued until the level of income per capita reached $400 in 1950 dollars. Thereafter, continued investment in all sectors of the economy decreased the inequality of income distribution.[1]

Kuznets' findings raised the question of whether income inequality was needed for growth. There was and is little agreement about whether inequality of personal income is necessary for economic growth because to some extent, the relationship between income distribution and growth that is "best" is a matter of social convention, and differs among countries and centuries. This is the implicit assumption of classical economists, whose models assume that income distribution, at least initially, is a result of the free play of market forces, so that the most efficient entrepreneurs and workers receive the highest incomes. The best income distribution, in their view, is that which results from the free play of the market, since this encourages efficiency. Note that the goods produced, or services sold most profitably, may differ at various times and places. Comparison of "efficient" income distributions between countries and across centuries is therefore quite difficult. Similarly, personal income distribution also reflects social agreement on the division of national income. Redistribution of income to a desired egalitarian pattern, in the absence of underlying socio-political agreement, will not necessarily create the type of economy of which an egalitarian income distribution is as much a symptom as a cause. For example, Britain had a more egalitarian income distribution in the 1960s than did Chile. Redistribution of Chilean personal income in the late 1960s and early 1970s did not produce a social agreement underlying an egalitarian society, but instead led to breakdowns in production and to civil war.

Both economic and political reasons make cross-country comparisons difficult. For this reason, a more useful statement of the problem is: for a given nation at a specific time, what will be the economic effect of a given change in personal income distribution? This question can be subjected to statistical analysis using data from a country which has experienced strong shifts in personal income distribution. Argentina is such a country: the share of workers' real wages income in total real gross domestic product fell dramatically from 37 percent in 1914 to 20 percent in 1918; it rose to 28 percent in 1919, and reached 42 percent in 1928. By 1930, the share was only 38 percent of a falling national income (see Table 3.1). From 1931 to 1939, the wage share was roughly stable at 42 percent; it fell until 1942, and stood at 37 percent in 1947. It rose to 47 percent in 1954, fell to 35 percent in 1959, and rose to 42 percent in 1967.[2]

In the Argentine case, as in that of other nations, there are technical as well as political reasons for inequality of income distribution. On the question of supply, higher than average income is usually needed to elicit the highly skilled laborers and entrepreneurs needed for modernization. If, however, work can be redesigned so that new techniques requiring fewer skills performed by a large labor force can produce as much output as a small skilled labor force using large amounts of capital— which the Chinese claim to have done in agriculture—then

Table 3.1 Real Wages as a Share of Real Gross Domestic Product, 1914–1934

Year	Percent	Year	Percent	Year	Percent
1914	36.5	1921	33.6	1928	41.7
1915	31.2	1922	35.8	1929	39.6
1916	27.7	1923	36.1	1930	37.7
1917	24.0	1924	35.2	1931	40.8
1918	20.1	1925	37.0	1932	42.8
1919	27.7	1926	36.5	1933	39.5
1920	27.6	1927	39.4	1934	40.8

SOURCE: Departamento Nacional de Trabajo, *Estadísticas de huelgas* (Buenos Aires, 1940), pp. 20–21; *Revista Económica Argentina* (1942), p. 218; Murmis and Portantiero, *Estudios Sobre Orígenes del Peronismo,* p. 85; Ministerio de Asuntos Económicos, *Producto e ingreso de la República Argentina* (Buenos Aires, 1955).

neither highly skilled labor nor highly unequal personal income distribution are necessary for economic growth. Similarly, if people respond to nonmonetary incentives, then a "new man," based on unique educational and motivation schemes, can be brought into existence, whether by the Church, anarchists, or revolutionaries; and monetary work incentives, along with income inequality, can be substantially reduced.

Argentines have not attempted to redesign work; nonmonetary incentives are not heavily emphasized. Argentine personal income distribution has resulted from the bargaining strength of various labor and employer groups, and their ability to obtain special laws from the administration in power. The result has been a personal income distribution that attracts more than enough workers into professional and liberal arts education, but too few into technical professions and middle-skill occupations.[3]

The effect of unequal income distribution on demand for goods produced within the nation is complex. Sismondi and Luxemburg argued that Britain did not need to pay high wages to workers for them to buy back British goods and ensure full employment because Britain exported goods, and did not rely on British workers' demand. Similarly, Edel argues that the Latin American Common Market is a device that ensures a market for Latin American manufactures without requiring the redistribution of income in any one country.[4] Thus international trade, which was very important in Argentina until

World War I but much less important after World War II, weakens the effect, in the case of a single nation, of income distribution on demand. When trade breaks down, as Keynes noted, the ability of workers to buy back the goods they produced is far more important. At first glance, it would seem that, as a consequence of the decline in the importance of international trade, workers' income would increase in importance as a determinant of demand. Statistical examination reveals that there was a slight nonsignificant increase in the relationship between real wages and personal consumption from 1935 to 1954 and 1950 to 1969. In the former case, a 100 percent increase in real wages was associated with a 41 percent increase in real private consumption; in the latter case, a 100 percent increase in real wages was associated with a 48 percent increase in real private consumption (see Table 3.2).

The lack of statistical significance[5] of the increase may be explained by the increasing share of government in gross domestic product, which broke the direct link between wages and consumption spending because the government taxed the workers. Moreover, Morley and Smith[6] have recently shown that in Brazil, the rich buy goods requiring a great deal of labor in production, while the poor buy goods requiring capital-intensive techniques of production, so that a possible effect of income redistribution from the rich to the poor is that many of the poor will lose their jobs. Because a number of factors influence the relationship between income inequality and economic development, and the importance of these factors has changed, the same degree of inequality of personal income distribution can have very different effects at different time periods, and appears to have done so in Argentina in the twentieth century. This is clearest in the rate at which the rich and the poor spend additions to their income, and in the relationship between personal income distribution and investment spending.

It is often asserted that the rich are entrepreneurs, and save a larger share of additions to their income than do the poor, who are workers. Therefore, to encourage savings and with them, investment, which is needed for economic growth, it is necessary to give the lion's share of national income to

Table 3.2 Determinants of Consumption and Investment, Argentina 1914–1954 and 1950–1969

Dependent Variable	R^2/SEE	Log Real Wage	Log Real GOS	Constant	Durbin Watson	Years
LR private consumption	.9777*	.4062*	.4600*	1.614*	.94	1935–54
(t)	.2703	12.51	6.369	3.508		
LR private consumption	.9841*	.4801*	.5191*	0.4850*	1.49	1950–69
(t)	.0275	8.582	13.83	9.939		
		Log Real GDI				
LR private consumption	.9850*	.9897*		−.2268*	1.39	1950–69
(t)	.0260	34.33		−3.534		
		Log Real Wage				
LR investment	.7339*	1.144*	.2972	−4.951	.69	1914–35
(t)	.3364	3.557	.3777	−1.062		
LR investment	.6216*	.7298*	.2157	−1.320	.81	1935–54
(t)	.1946	3.123	.4148	−0.3984		

NOTE: Logarithms are used to obtain percentage change in variables. Thus the regression weights refer to the percentage change in the dependent variables associated with the percentage change in independent variable. See text for examples.

*Significant at the 5 percent level of probability.

LR   Log real
GOS   Gross operating surplus
GDI   Gross domestic income

entrepreneurs. Yet, phrased as this was, the assertion is misleading: people's spending habits are set in relation to their income, not in relation to their income category's share of national income. For this reason, the assertion is recast, and the question examined is: what are the relationships between a 1 percent change in workers' and entrepreneurs' income, and real private consumption and real investment; and do these relationships significantly differ from each other?

From 1914 to 1935, a 100 percent increase in real wages was associated with a 114 percent increase in real investment;

from 1935 to 1954, a 100 percent increase in real wages was associated with a 73 percent increase in real investment (see Table 3.2). The difference in the relationship between the two periods can be explained in either of two ways. The first is that there were more immigrants in the labor force in the first period. Immigrants presumably obtained less income in their country of origin than in Argentina. It is likely that their spending habits were set in relation to the income to which they were accustomed, rather than the new, higher income which they received, and therefore that they saved (and made available for investment) a higher share of income than native-born Argentines. The second is that both wage share and investment share are the result of government policy,[7] which shifted between the two time periods.

An examination of Table 1.2 indicates that an increase in real entrepreneurs' income (called gross operating surplus) is associated with an increase in real investment in a way that is not significantly different statistically from the relationship between an increase in real wages and an increase in real private consumption. Although at first glance the relationship between an increase in real entrepreneurs' income and real investment appears different from the relationship between real wages and real investment, especially from 1914 to 1935, when they are subjected to statistical testing, the two relationships do not differ significantly from each other for two reasons. First, there is a great variation over the years in the relationship between an increase in real entrepreneurs' income and real investment. Second, the largest component of entrepreneurs' income is the income of the self-employed, who range from highly paid professionals to small business men. As a result, the entrepreneurial category includes many poor and partly employed persons with low income. A change in income of entrepreneurs can increase the income of either rich or poor entrepreneurs. If there are differences between them in the share of additions to income they spend on investment goods, then there would be a great variation in how increases in entreprenurs' income was related to investment spending, depending upon which group of entrepreneurs' income increased. This point is more important for entrepreneurs' than workers' income because income distribution among entrepreneurs is more unequal than among workers.[8] Consequently, "entrepreneurial income" is not a satisfactory substitute for the category "income of the rich" or "income of entrepreneurs in the modern sector."

Despite the above evidence and arguments, a great deal of Argentine discussion of income distribution assumes that the category of economic service for which income is received is directly related to the way in which income is spent. This assumption can be justified on the grounds that rentiers and entrepreneurs are rich, while workers are poor, so that functional income distribution is a reasonable substitute for income distribution by decile (for which Argentina has information for selected years from 1953, but lacks a complete time series) in economic analysis. Accordingly, the functional income distribution concepts were refined so that the relationship between a 1 percent increase in the income of each category and a change in personal consumption and national investment could be explored.

I shall begin by modifying the textbook example that there are two factors of production, and that workers supply all the labor, while entrepreneurs supply all the capital. This is misleading. Part of the income received by entrepreneurs is a return to their own labor, and should be excluded from the entrepreneurial income category. Although estimates of net investment which are made using adjusted entrepreneurs' income, or using profit or dividend income alone, predict actual investment well, this is because of their effect on investment climate, rather than because of the unique behavior of recipients of these kinds of income. For example, when adjusted entrepreneurs' income and other income is regressed against real private consumption, there is no significant difference between the effect of adjusted entrepreneurial income on private consumption and that of other income. However, when adjusted agricultural entrepreneurs' income and other income is regressed against real private consumption, there is a significant difference between the effect of adjusted agricultural entrepreneurs' income on private consumption and that of other income (see Table 3.3).

Table 3.3 Percentage of Change in Real Private Consumption and Adjusted
Entrepreneurial Income, and Adjusted Agricultural Entrepreneur's Income

		1950–1961		
1 LRPRICON	R^2/SEE	LRC	LRO	Constant
OLS	0.9642*	0.2429*	0.7337*	0.4469
DW = 2.28	0.0276	7.913	6.233	0.4857
2 LRPRICON	R^2/SEE	LRAP	LRQP	Constant
OLS	0.9659*	0.0872	0.9374*	−0.2456
DW = 1.74	0.0269	1.315	11.16	−0.4299

SOURCE: Data from ECLA, *Economic Development and Income Distribution in Argentina;* BCRA, *Origen del Producto y Distribución del Ingreso.*
NOTE: All figures on second lines indicate *t.*
LR   Log real
Pricon Private consumption
C   Entrepreneurial income, net of income attributable to personal service, all
        entrepreneurs
O   All income other than C
AP   Agricultural entrepreneurs' income, net of income attributable to personal
        service
QP   All income other than AP
    *Significant at the 5 percent level of probability.

The unique case of agricultural entrepreneurs probably
reflects their holdings of wealth, compared to other groups of
income recipients, rather than atypical patterns of spending
and saving. Evidence on the effect of wealth (in the form of
property ownership) on consumption patterns is presented on
pages 36–38 and 41, and suggests that holders of real estate save
a larger share of their income than do other income recipients.
The regression analysis is consistent with popular Argentine
belief that agricultural entrepreneurs are far wealthier than
other entrepreneurs and average income recipients.

We have already seen that changes in workers' and entrepreneurs' income have different effects on investment at different times. Greater insight into these relationships can be
obtained by subdividing entrepreneurial income into its components, which include interest, rent, and net income, net
profit of stock companies and public enterprises, and net profit
of personal enterprises. This distinction reflects the fact that as
economies develop, public and private corporations in capital-

ist (and in some socialist) societies replace family firms. Thus, because entrepreneurial income includes that of individuals and firms, an analysis of the differences in relationship between workers' income and spending and entrepreneurs' income and spending is not a comparison between comparable groups of individuals. It is, instead, a comparison between the spending habits of a group of individuals (workers) and those of a group which includes corporations (entrepreneurs). For this reason, a detailed examination of the relationship between changes in the level of various categories of entrepreneurial income and changes in personal consumption will be presented in the following pages. These relationships will be explored in the answers to these questions: what is the effect of a 1 percent change in real income (of each category of income) on real personal consumption? Is the effect of each one (of these income categories) on real personal consumption significantly different from that of any other income category?[9]

In studying the relationship of various categories of real income to real personal consumption, we would ideally wish to have disposable income figures. The only adjustment that it was possible to make, by category of income receipt, however, was the exclusion of contributions to social security.[10] Further, the estimates presented here differ from those of earlier investigators because personal consumption is calculated as a residual: I have revised the estimates for investment spending, so that personal consumption estimates change in consequence.[11]

The relationship between real income distribution by economic sector and by economic function, and real personal consumption between 1950 and 1969, is indicated in Table 3.4. The "t" tests for groups of real income whose change is significantly related to a change in real private consumption indicate the lack of significance in the difference in spending patterns for the various groups.

For example, an increase in real agricultural income is associated with a greater increase in real private consumption than is an increase in real urban income, but the difference in spending patterns is not significant. The similar lack of significant difference in the relationship between various groups of gross operating surplus and real private consumption, and

Table 3.4 Percentage Change In Real Private Consumption And Percentage Change In Real Income Received According To Economic Function, 1950–1969

DW	R²/SEE	RAGW	RMNW	RMFW	RCNW	RCXW	RTNW	RCSW	RUTW	RFNW	RGOS	Constant
2.45	.9960*	-.002	-.072	-.108	.098	.563*	.295	-.020	.135	-.155	.632*	-7.812*
	.0189	-.033	-.841	-.723	1.263	3.920	2.019	-1.261	1.242	-1.357	6.547	-11.805

DW	R²/SEE	RAGG	RMNG	RMFG	RCNG	RCXG	RTNG	RCSG	RUTG	RFNG	RWAGE	Constant
3.45	.9930*	.062	-.059	.237	.069	-.025	.233*	-.024	.009	.055	.369*	-4.664*
	.0251	.588	-1.205	2.202	.858	-.191	2.458	-1.706	.229	1.210	2.879	-4.119

DW	R²/SEE	Total Agriculture	Total Urban	Constant
1.58	.7018*	.5154*	.4259*	-5.579
	.1190	2.427	2.635	-4.655

NOTE: All figures on second lines indicate t.

W	Wages
G	Gross Operating Surplus
R	Real
DW	Durbin Watson
SEE	Standard Error of Estimate
AG	Agriculture
MN	Mining
MF	Manufacturing
CN	Construction
CX	Trade
TN	Transportation
CS	Community Services
UT	Utilities
FN	Finance

*Significant at the 5 percent level of probability.

between groups of real wages and real private consumption, supports my belief that the relationship between income and spending is associated with levels of income and wealth, rather than with the economic function performed in order to receive income. Moreover, the lower level of significance of the relationship between changes in income received according to category of economic function and changes in real private consumption than between changes in real gross domestic income and changes in real private consumption also supports this view.

Workers' and entrepreneurs' spending habits can be examined by estimating the percentage change in consumption which accompanies a percentage change in income. For the Argentine economy as a whole, a 100 percent change in real income yields a 98.97 percent change in real consumption. This estimate is basically the same as that estimated by Simon Kuznets for the United States for long periods of time.[12] For 1950–69, the difference between Argentine workers' and employers' spending patterns was not statistically significant. Although the regression equations are statistically significant when based on data for 1950–69, when they are tested for subgroups of five years within this period, they are not always significant, both because of the small number of years included, and in particular because the relationship between income and consumption shifts during the business cycle. Five years is too short a period to include the same phases of the business cycle in each of the five year groups.[13]

As the rate of inflation varied considerably between subperiods, it was introduced into the regression. This did not significantly improve the regression results for the twenty-year period, although there was a significant improvement in the estimate for the 1960–64 period. Estimates of percentage increase in real private consumption were not significantly improved by using estimates of percentage change of the inflation rate, or by using the deviation of the inflation rate from an anticipated average rate. This was true for estimates of a percentage change of real private consumption using a percentage change of real gross domestic income, of real wages, and of real gross operating surplus. There was no significant difference between the spending patterns of workers and entrepreneurs when inflation was introduced into the estimates.[14]

Since the spending patterns of workers and entrepreneurs do not differ significantly from each other, it is necessary to reexamine the reasons for expecting them to differ. One reason might be that entrepreneurs were richer than workers; however, as noted above, many small entrepreneurs earn lower incomes than highly skilled and well-paid managers and technicians. The functional distribution of income is therefore not a perfect substitute for personal income distribution by decile. Nonetheless, many people believe that entrepreneurs and workers behave differently from each other. Evidence on this point is available from studies of other nations which indicate that income whose receipt is uncertain is more likely to be saved than income whose receipt is certain, or viewed as "permanent."[15] Thus, entrepreneurs who undertake great risks in investing would be expected to save a larger share of their income than workers. For example, in England in 1688, the share of additions to income spent was virtually the same for rich and for poor, with one exception: merchants by sea.[16]

Entrepreneurs are rewarded for risk taking, and foreign trade in a sailing era, when communications were poor, is a highly risky business endeavor. Only merchants in foreign trade saved and invested a larger-than-average share of income, because the size and timing of payment was uncertain. Since income from rent or interest was at least as certain as payment of wages, it was spent in much the same way. Similar development patterns hold in the United States, where the early textile industry was financed in significant part by New England merchants in foreign trade, and in Japan, where savings are the highest in the world. The high Japanese savings rate occurs in large part as a result of higher-than-expected bonus payments, which were based on profit sharing in an economic growth that was consistently greater than that forecast by the government in the post-war period.[17] The high Japanese savings rate, which is in part the result of a large transitory income component in total income, and the high savings by merchants in foreign trade, who also experienced a large transitory income component in total income, suggests that uncertainty of payment, rather than the economic activity for which payment is made, is an important element in the explanation of savings behavior. A recent study of United

States savings makes a similar point by suggesting that only proprietors' income and dividends should be included in "risky" entrepreneurs' income, with rent and interest, as safe income, added to the wage share.[18] In Argentina, this pattern is modified because rapid inflation (25 percent per annum from 1950 to 1969) makes employers and workers rapidly spend any kind of income they get, for fear that the money received will lose its value. We have seen that the rate at which workers spend additions to their income does not differ significantly from that of entrepreneurs. The next step is to examine the ways in which expenditures of subgroups of income vary from each other (see Table 3.5). Detailed information is available for the years 1955–61.[19]

In general, a 1 percent increase in any subcategory of real entrepreneurial income is not significantly related to an increase in real personal consumption. There is one statistically significant exception: an increase in real dividend income is associated with a significantly smaller than average increase in real private consumption, confirming the importance of uncertainty of payment in influencing spending patterns. Interest income, unexpectedly, was spent significantly differently from other categories of income; the relationship between

Table 3.5 Percentage Change In Categories Of Real Gross Operating Surplus And Percentage Change In Real Private Consumption, 1955–1961

	R^2/SEE	LRDIV	LROD	Constant		Durbin Watson
LRPRICON	.9730*	.2346*	.7041*	−6.055*		2.17
(t)	.0240	5.626	6.377	−7.970		
		LRREN	LRUREN	LOREN*	Constant	D.W.
LRPRICON	.9755*	.1697	−.078	.9138	.2352	1.37
(t)	.0146	2.059	−1.316	8.064	.2175	
		LRIN	LR13	Constant		D.W.
LRPRICON	.9530*	−.0607	.9058*	−5.841*		2.29
(t)	.0175	−.8808	5.419	−5.289		

LR	Logarithm of real	OREN	Income other than rent
PRICON	Private consumption	UREN	Urban rent
DIV	Dividends	IN	Interest
OD	Income other than DIV	13	Income other than IN
RREN	Rural rent		

*Significant at the 5 percent level of probability.

Table 3.6 Public Enterprise Profits, Stock Company Profits, and Other Determinants of Log-Real Private Consumption 1955–1961

	R^2/SEE	LRPUB	LR14		Constant	Durbin Watson
LR PRICON	0.9423*	0.00009699	0.007554*		−0.04994*	1.84
(t)	0.0001935	0.4747	7.917		−5.798	
		LR15	LRST			
LR PRICON	0.9502*	0.009747*	−0.0003759		−0.06702*	2.40
(t)	0.0001798	3.113	−0.4422		−2.818	
		LRPUB	LRPWA	LZ		
LR PRICON	.9591*	.01301	−.009092	.8903*	.7142	2.08
(t)	.0188	.6516	−.6302	5.443	.4940	

LR	Logarithm of real
PUB	Public enterprise profits
14	Income other than that of PUB
15	Income other than ST
ST	Stock company profits
PWA	Stock companies withheld profits
Z	Income other than PUB or PWA

*Significant at the 5 percent level of probability.

changes in real interest income and changes in real private consumption was not, however, significant. It is possible that in Argentina's highly inflationary situation, the real return on lending is uncertain, so that interest income is spent, in this case, in the same way as other income the receipt of which is uncertain. Alternately, this relationship may indicate that the contractionary policies associated with increased interest rates decreased real private consumption, and that riskiness of interest income does not provide a full explanation of the relationship.

Although a smaller share of increases in income received from rent is spent on increases in real private consumption than is the share of increases in income received from other categories, the relationship between rental income and private consumption is not significant. However, the fact that rental income is spent somewhat differently from other categories suggests that its recipients have sufficiently above-average wealth for this to affect their consumption patterns.

An examination of other categories of entrepreneurial income indicates (see Table 3.6) that an increase in real withheld profits is associated with a small, nonsignificant decrease in real private consumption; the increase in real public enterprise profits is associated with a smaller increase in real private consumption than is the increase in other income, but the relationship between public enterprise profits and consumption is not significant. Nonetheless, we note that the relationship between a 1 percent change in withheld stock company profits and the change in real private consumption is not significantly different from the relationship between a 1 percent change in public enterprise profits and the associated change in real private consumption; both withheld stock company profits and public enterprise profits are significantly different in their relationship to real private consumption from other categories of income. In both cases, corporations are able to withhold net income from the spending stream to a degree that affects the rate of real private consumption. Gross profits, however, are not significantly different in their relationship to a percentage change in real private consumption from all other groups of income, as part of gross profits enter the spending stream via dividend payments to individuals.

The above relationships are consistent with the fact that since personal monetary income received is spent rapidly in inflationary Argentine conditions, savings and investment are possible only when funds can be diverted from personal income to public and private corporations. As mentioned earlier in this chapter, there is evidence to support this: when the relationship of single variables to net domestic capital formation is examined, undistributed profits predicted 97 percent of net domestic capital formation from 1955 to 1961.[20] This indicates the importance of undistributed profits in influencing expectations about business conditions, and, consequently, investment, as well as their importance for the size of investment, because the size of undistributed corporate profits, although increasing, was lower than their predictive value for net domestic capital formation. During this period, undistributed corporate profits, together with undistributed profits of personal enterprises, rose from one-quarter to two-thirds of net investment funds. This compares with about 73 percent of investment accounted for by internal finance in United States firms.[21]

The increased reliance on internal finance was brought about by credit restrictions that had been imposed to combat inflation. Even without these restrictions, it would have been difficult for firms to raise funds, as inflation had made investment in inventory more attractive than long-term investment. Investment in inventory gave a fairly predictable return in the immediate future, while the dynamics of inflation were such that the government's policies favored each sector in sequence, so that entrepreneurs in any one sector were well aware that their current relatively favorable profit position, compared to other sectors, would not be maintained.[22] They were therefore hesitant to undertake long-term investment.

The pattern of relying on internal finance held for personal enterprises as well as stock companies. A United Nations study states that personal enterprises less well known on the market used their current profits to cover their financial requirements.[23] However, the rate at which entrepreneurs spent their net real income after allowing for a return to their own labor services does not differ significantly from the rate for any other category of spending. This implies a lower rate of reinvestment in personal enterprises than in stock companies.

Although undistributed corporate profits explain the bulk of investment behavior, it did not make sense for all firms to invest in themselves. Profits varied widely according to economic activity. For example, the share of private enterprise profits for stock companies in industry divided by their share of value added by private enterprises at factor cost was 123 percent of the average for all stock companies from 1955 to 1961. In services, this ratio was 64 percent, and in agriculture, 40 percent, of average. This is consistent with evidence presented in Table A.2 that investment in industry was more profitable than in agriculture. Under these circumstances, we would expect agricultural and service firms to invest some of their funds in industry, and note that the change in distribution of unit profits among sectors explains 98.6 percent of the level, and almost as much of the distribution of Argentine economic activity.[24] This occurred both because of the rational response of private entrepreneurs to profit opportunities and because of government allocation of investment funds through the banking system under Perón. The government manipulated relative prices, and consequently profits, so that activities to which investment was directed were also highly profitable.[25]

Although undistributed corporate profits predict investment, and changes in profits explain the level of production, labor income does enter this final analysis of consumption and investment behavior because labor costs influence profits. All sectors of the Argentine economy reduced the share of income paid to labor. In part as a result of government policies, physical output per percentage of income paid to labor increased by 46 percent in manufacture, but by only 35 percent in agriculture.[26] Either labor income would have to be depressed, or productivity in agriculture increased, for investment in agriculture to become attractive. The Argentine government has been more willing to depress agricultural wages than to permit increased mechanization of agriculture through the importation of needed equipment, for the reason that it would obviously damage the interests of the dominant manufacturing sector, which produced high-cost agricultural equipment under government protection against competing imports.[27]

The implication of this analysis for the relationship between income distribution and investment and economic growth in an inflationary situation is that investment will increase if income payments are diverted from individuals, regardless of economic function performed, to corporations.[28] If inflation is not an overwhelming factor, investment will also increase, to some degree, along with an increase in the share of personal income whose receipt cannot be predicted with certainty. Further, if income is redistributed to landowners, savings will increase, because holding great wealth influences spending patterns. There are no data available for Argentina about the ways in which ownership of differing amounts of wealth affect consumption spending of the various groups analyzed here. It is possible, but not certain, that a redistribution of wealth would have a significant effect on the share of savings and consumption in Argentine gross domestic product. On the other hand, as long as there is no significant difference between the share of additional monetary income spent by workers and that spent by entrepreneurs, and the government's concern is obtaining increased investment, then proposals for either radical redistribution of income to the workers or for increases in the share of national income paid to industrial and technocratic elites must rely on political rather than economic justification.

This conclusion stands when additional elements are introduced into the analysis. The discussion that follows describes the probable effect of several factors on the conclusions; the information described was not available for enough years to include these factors in the statistical analysis. The first possible modification is that in addition to income received by entrepreneurs and workers for work currently performed, transfer payments for social security and retirement were made and received by them. The net effect of such payments is to redistribute 1.7 percent of family income from the top decile to remaining families. I have already excluded income contributed to the social security system from my analysis; such contributions were regressive in impact. On the other hand, payment from the system was not included in my analysis, and transferred about 2.5 percent of family income from the top 10 percent to the remaining families.[29]

The second possible modification is the effect of government taxes and expenditures on income receipts. Direct taxation of income led to a transfer of about 2 percent of family income from the top decile to the remaining families. However, the regressive effects of indirect taxation on production cancelled out from 40 to 80 percent of the progressive effect of direct taxation. As a result, less than 1 percent of total income was transferred by taxation, and when inflation was great, and direct taxes consequently declined, the percentage transferred was almost negligible.[30] Public funds are spent on goods and services more heavily used by the poor than the rich; in addition, various goods are subsidized. The result was a transfer of 0.7 percent of income to the bottom 90 percent. In combination, fiscal and welfare programs redistributed about 3 percent of family income from the top 10 percent to the families in the lowest 90 percent of income earners in Argentina.[31]

An extension of this analysis to earlier periods of Argentine history indicates that indirect taxes were strikingly more important before than after 1941. The heavy taxation of workers' goods made the imposition of these taxes quite regressive, and meant that the workers' real income decreased more than that of entrepreneurs. As a result, the effects of changes in workers' and in entrepreneurs' income on consumption were even closer to each other than the regressions in Table 3.2 indicate.

A third possible modification is that prices of goods bought by workers changed at a different rate from those purchased by entrepreneurs. Poor people in Argentina spend more of their income on food and utilities than rich people, who spend more of their income on durable goods, ownership and maintenance of cars and housing, and on services. In general, workers are poorer than entrepreneurs, and suffer more from increased food prices. An examination of budgets by income class indicates that although food prices, compared to those of manufactures and services, are more favorable to the poor in Argentina than in most of Latin America, the overall impact of changes in relative prices reinforced the changes in wage shares: the middle classes bore a higher-than-average share of price increases from 1950 to 1955, while the lowest and highest income groups bore a less-than-average price increase. From 1955 to 1963, the lower the income class, the higher the share of price increases.[32]

The most detailed of my statistical analyses covered the years 1955 to 1961, when relative price movements decreased workers' real income below that used in my data, and, conversely, increased that of entrepreneurs. On the other hand, fiscal and welfare programs benefited workers at the expense of entrepreneurs. Rough calculations using the distribution of workers and entrepreneurs in various income classes indicate that the effect of relative price changes roughly cancels out the effect of fiscal and welfare programs on transfers of real income between wage earners and entrepreneurs.

A final modification might result from the introduction of the effects of foreign ownership of investment on spending patterns of entrepreneurial income, and of the availability of imports on investment spending. The former point is not examined in detail because foreign investment was a trivial share of total investment in Argentina during the period for which detailed statistical analysis is presented in this chapter. A brief examination of the latter point indicates that the relationship of a percentage increase in either imports or in machine imports to net domestic capital formation is weaker than that between withheld profits and net domestic capital formation.[33]

However, the larger question of the relationship of the Argentine to the world economy during the twentieth century remains, as does the question of what forms economic dependence took during the periods in which it was an important factor in Argentine economic development. These questions are explored in detail in chapter 8.

foreign owned, and did not subscribe to the Argentine national banking system.

This type of problem was not unique: a number of state-chartered banks in the United States did not join the national banking system after the Civil War. Similarly, in both Argentina and the United States, entrepreneurs' needs for credit, combined with many bankers' desires to expand loans beyond legal limits, and thus increase their income, led to fraudulent practices in a number of banks. The section that follows describes the law, if not all of the practices, of Argentine banking at the beginning of the twentieth century.

Turn-of-the-century banking structure was the result of banking difficulties in the early 1890s.[1] At that time there were no nationwide banks; the post office, therefore, performed banking functions and was often required to send quite small sums to the provinces. In 1891, the creation of a new official bank was proposed. This bank, the Banco de la Nación, began as a mixed enterprise, and was converted to a government bank in 1904. The bank's capital doubled in 1907, and it took over clearing-house functions in 1912. According to Raúl Prebisch, who presided over Argentina's first Central Bank, the Banco de la Nación Argentina in effect loaned to banks by rediscounting and moreover loaned to the Treasury, carrying out the primary functions of a financial agent. All this was at the expense of the resources that it had to carry out its specific functions as a commercial, agricultural, and industrial bank.[2] For example, from 1905 to 1914, one-quarter of the bank's funds were unavailable for loans to the private sector (see Table 4.1.) Foreign banks filled credit needs that could not be met by the Banco de la Nación; British banks preferred to limit themselves, where possible, to relatively secure commercial loans, avoiding long-term credit risks.[3] The association of British banks with the Argentine exporting elite gave an impression of foreign dominance of the banking industry that was reinforced by the fact that each of the banks tended to specialize in the activities that it financed. For example, the Anglo Sud-americano, at one point, monopolized the Patagonian wool and meat market. In addition, grain exports were sometimes financed on London banks.[4] It seems likely that credit was also available through trade channels.

Table 4.1 Percent Distribution Of Credit By The Banco De La Nación
1894–1930

Year	Agriculture	Cattle	Commerce	Industry	Banks	Other
1894	10.7	19.2	45.5	11.0	—	5.7
1905–09	9.1	25.5	32.9	7.0	—	25.3
1910–14	8.5	24.1	36.5	6.9	—	23.8
1915–19	7.5	27.2	23.2	4.9	—	37.2
1920–24	4.0	28.1	23.6	4.2	—	40.0
1925–29	5.3	14.3	23.9	7.6	32.5	16.5
1930	7.5	14.5	20.4	7.5	39.0	11.1

SOURCE: El Banco de la Nación Argentina, *El Banco de la Nación en su Cincuentenario*, fol. 257.

In addition to providing credit, the Banco de la Nación attempted to influence the level of economic activity in Argentina, first by maintaining convertibility, and later by the active use of rediscount policy. From 1900 until the onset of the Great Depression, the first priority among various economic objectives was given to the maintenance of convertibility at a fixed exchange rate. This was governed by the Conversion Law of 1899, which was established when the exchange rate was appreciating. The government succeeded in its aim of stopping the appreciation of the peso by adopting the gold standard, fixing a ratio according to which redemption of paper money was to be made in specie, accumulating a metallic reserve for this purpose, and maintaining the specie/paper ratio by adding a bureau to the Caja de Conversión (the Exchange Office) to act as a regulator of the currency, increasing or decreasing the amount of paper in circulation according to the amount of gold deposited.[5] The government promised to redeem paper money at the rate of 227.27 (44 centavos gold for a paper peso), which was equal to a premium of 127 percent.[6]

In practice, the Conversion Fund operated only in bills of exchange, and it succeeded in stabilizing the exchange rate. The Caja de Conversión absorbed the effects of gold flows through changes in its outstanding note issue emitted against gold, against commercial paper, and against government paper. The Treasury managed, moreover, an incipient exchange fund in order to regulate exchange through the Banco de la Nación. The Oficina de Control de Cambios, aside from its relations with importers and exporters, controlled the foreign exchange trade of banks.

In principle, the dispersion of monetary control among the Caja de Conversión, the Banco de la Nación Argentina, the Oficina de Control de Cambios, and the Tesoro Nacional should have made control of the money supply difficult. In fact, this difficulty was avoided: whenever outflows of gold would have required the Caja de Conversión to reduce the money supply by converting paper to gold, it stopped functioning, rather than conflict with the policy of the Banco de la Nación of offsetting trade deficits by expanding the money supply. For example, the reasons that the Caja ceased functioning in 1914 are described as follows:

At this time, European investors, especially in Argentine real estate, tried to repatriate their capital. The value of land fell. As capital was repatriated, and the harvest was poor, the money supply fell, and it was consequently difficult to pay back bank loans; the government tried to cut its budget to match its reduced revenues. Moreover, the reduction in international trade further reduced government income. Foreign sources of credit were cut off. In 1914, payment in gold was prorogued for as long as the Caja de Conversión was closed. The Banco de la Nación was allowed to use the conversion fund in exchange operations. The Caja de Conversión was to rediscount commercial documents with the Banco de la Nación, emitting bills of the kind already in circulation, so long as the metallic guarantee of paper was not less than 40 percent.[7] Thus, the Caja functioned effectively from 1903 to 1914 and from 1927 to 1929.

Although the government offset the effect of trade deficits, it was unwilling to sever its connections with international financial markets. This was emphasized in the 1917 Annual Report of the Treasury, which stated: "In our country, external loans have always provided, with rare exceptions, the sums demanded by the public treasury,. . . . The flotation of internal loans has failed because the people prefer the advantage of other investments. Favorable external offers have always made internal efforts unnecessary."[8]

To maintain its credit standing abroad, despite the closing of the Caja in 1929, the Government continued to export part of its gold to take care of its service on public debt held abroad. Also, gold was shipped abroad in the beginning of 1931 in an unsuccessful attempt to contain the depreciation of money. Prebisch has stated that

> When gold was exported in this manner, the emission of money diminished parallelly, and bank reserves were sensibly affected, bringing them to a highly critical point. Because of this, in 1931, the Government decided to apply the old law of rediscount of commercial paper which had never been used before because of fear of inflation; and the Caja de Conversión emitted, for the first time, money against said paper. Rediscounting was used moderately to reconstitute bank reserves, and not to make new loans. In 1932, ... an emergency law permitted the Caja to issue new money against government paper in order to pay the urgent bills of the Treasury.

The money supply was also expanded by authorizing deposit of gold in Argentine legations abroad and the issue of currency in Argentina (against this gold) at the usual legal ratio,[9] thus ending the operation of the gold standard in Argentina.

As I have noted, from 1900 until the onset of the Great Depression, the Argentine government gave first priority among its economic objectives to the maintenance of a fixed exchange rate under the gold standard. Second priority was accorded to the offsetting of the impact of gold flows on the economy. In order to achieve this goal, the Banco de la Nación both borrowed in international markets and extended rediscounting facilities. For example, during the 1914 panic, the bank was able to counteract the effect of gold flows on the money stock; from 1909 to 1934 the Banco de la Nación increased its rediscounts to commercial banks during periods of gold outflows (see Table 4.2). The bank cushioned, but did not eliminate, the effects of international trade on the economy: the correlation coefficient between trade balances and the money supply is 0.4, significant at the 5 percent level. This is consistent with my finding in chapter 8 that foreign exchange is less significant than either government spending or money supply in determining Argentine income.

The fact that the Banco de la Nación compensated only for gold outflows, and did not use rediscount policy to compensate

Table 4.2 Banco De La Nación Rediscount Policy, Gold Flow, And Money Supply, 1913–1934

Change in	Constant		Net Gold Flow[a]	R^2
(1) Rediscount	11.5625*	–	.1973*	.6096
	(5.9363)[b]		(.0362)[b]	
(2) Money supply	127.5754*	+	.6906*	.3004
	(39.6253)[b]		(.2418)[b]	

Source: Halperin, *The Behavior of the Argentine Monetary Sector*, p. 142.
*Significant at the 5 percent level of probability.
[a]At average market exchange rate.
[b]Standard deviation.

for domestic economic fluctuations, probably strengthened private bankers', opinion of the Banco de la Nación as a competitor within the domestic market. This was reinforced by the precedence of debts to government banks over debts to other banks. As we will see below, intermittent attempts to maintain employment were shaped by political needs rather than by economic ideology. Yet, even if there had not been an element of competition in the relations between the Banco de la Nación and the private banks, it would have been difficult to influence the Argentine economy strongly by use of monetary policy both for institutional reasons and because of various policymakers' adherence to inadequate and inaccurate economic ideas, which lessened the ability of the government to control the economy.

The fact that the Argentine government gave third priority in monetary policy to the regulation of economic activity reflects the institutional peculiarities of the Argentine banking structure and banking practices. In other nations in the twentieth century, monetary authorities have influenced economic activity by changing required reserve ratios, by using rediscount policy, and by buying or selling government securities issued in the domestic market. In ordinary times, Argentine banks were reluctant to use rediscount facilities, as this was regarded as a sign of weakness.[10] For this reason, banks held large cash reserves, despite the lack of legal reserve requirements on private banks. (The Banco de la Nación was subject to a reserve requirement of 25 percent on total deposits.) The general practice of other banks was to keep a reserve of 25 percent against demand deposits, and 10 percent against time deposits.

In normal conditions, reserve requirements above 25 percent on total deposits are not needed to ensure the safety of depositors' money; reserves above that level would probably restrict the operation of the economy. Given the ample average level of reserves, it is unlikely that the government could have made effective use of changes in the reserve requirement, even if it had had the legal power to do so. The difficulties of using changes in the reserve requirement would have been compounded by two elements: first, there would have been a differential impact of such policy in favor of foreign banks because bank practice differed strikingly by bank category. In Prebisch's view, the domestic banks, excluding the Banco de la Nación, were characterized by a lack of forecasting, an excessive confidence, and a marked speculative spirit, while, on the other hand, the Banco de la Nación and foreign banks followed cautious policies.[11] An Argentine economist, Ricardo Halperín, found that the responsiveness (called elasticity)* of bank reserves with respect to the business failure rate was lower for domestic banks than for either the Banco de la Nación or for foreign banks, thus supporting the above analysis.[12]

Yet even if there had been no differential impact of reserve policy to worry about, it would have been difficult to use reserve policy to compensate for domestic economic fluctuations because of sharp fluctuations in the rate at which money

---

*"Elasticity" refers to the responsiveness of one variable with respect to a change in another variable. For example, if a 1 percent increase in the business failure rate is associated with a more than 1 percent decrease in the banks' reserves, then bank reserves are elastic with respect to the business failure rate; their elasticity is measured as greater than one in the formula:

$$-\frac{Br_1 - Br_2}{(Br_1 + Br_2)/2} \Big/ \frac{F_1 - F_2}{(F_1 + F_2)/2}$$

where

Br_1 Bank reserves in time period 1
Br_2 Bank reserves in time period 2
F_1 Failure rate in time period 1
F_2 Failure rate in time period 2

which is used to estimate elasticity. If a 1 percent increase in business failure rate is associated with a 1 percent decrease in bank reserves, they are "unit elastic" and their elasticity is measured as 1; if a 1 percent increase in business failure rate is associated with a less than 1 percent decrease in bank reserves, they are inelastic with respect to business failures and their elasticity is estimated as less than 1.

was spent (called the income velocity of money). Therefore, Argentine authorities would probably have been unable to use changes in the reserve requirement to influence the money supply and, with it, the level of economic activity.

Intellectual, rather than institutional, reasons prevented the use of rediscount policy to influence the money supply and economic activity. Argentine bankers operated under the commercial loan theory, according to which credit was extended when commercial paper was rediscounted; similarly, credit contracted as acceptable paper declined, thus accentuating business cycles.

This was offset, to a slight extent, by the government's use of credit that would otherwise have been made available to commercial banks to create jobs for its unemployed supporters, especially if elections were to be held in the near future. This tended not to occur very strongly before 1912 because middle-class job seekers were not enfranchised before the Saenz Peña law was passed in that year. The new voters elected the Radical Party candidates to the presidency in the 1916, 1922, and 1928 elections. As a result, the government responded to their need for jobs, and the share of the government in total credit extended by the Banco de la Nación increased from 24 percent from 1905–14 to 39 percent from 1915–24. However, the need to obtain foreign credit, and fear of the effect that devaluation would have on credit availability, led to a reduction in government absorption of credit from the Banco de la Nación in the remaining years of Radical Party administration, despite a flurry of job creation in 1930.[13]

An additional difficulty afflicting Argentine credit policy was that no provision was made for seasonal changes in the need for credit. In their use of the commercial loan theory to determine banking practices, Argentine banking practices at the beginning of the Great Depression resembled those of the United States at the turn of the century, before the establishment of the Federal Reserve System. A Federal Reserve System official wrote in May 1931:

> Perhaps the most striking feature of Argentine Banking is the lack of a direct connection between bank credit and the cur-

rency. Although the Bank of the Nation is the official central bank, it has not yet been fully endowed by law with the powers and mechanism for the rediscounting of commercial paper, so that the Argentine currency system is rigid and inelastic as was that of the United States before the establishment of the Federal Reserve System.

Although the banks can predict with considerable certainty when the period of heavy demand for funds to be used in moving the crops will commence, no adequate banking mechanism exists for effecting an expansion in the volume of money. The functions of the "Caja de Conversión" are merely to convert paper currency to gold and vice versa and to act as a storehouse for the gold stock of the country while the Bank of the Nation, until last week, has rediscounted only by treating the banks availing themselves of the facility like ordinary customers with no actual expansion in the volume of money. The natural result of this inelasticity is that there is usually a period of tight money at harvest time. The greater part of the additional money required for moving the crops during the height of the export season from about December to April is obtained in the exchange market. . . .[14]

Even if the government had abandoned the commercial loan theory, and decided to use rediscounting in an attempt to increase the credit available to private industry during an economic depression, it would have been difficult to implement rediscount policy because the government did not require honesty from private bankers: "The commercial banks of the country were, for all practical purposes, unregulated, uninspected, allowed to do business without adequate protection to depositors and to the country's credit."[15]

Even assuming adequate supervision of commercial banks, it would have been difficult to use rediscounting to aid them during a depression because the government competed with them for funds from the Banco de la Nación. According to Federico Pinedo, the Banco de la Nación could not lend to the Central government beyond a given limit. A subterfuge was adopted: other banks lent to the government and then rediscounted their loans at the Banco de la Nación. As the Banco de la Nación could only lend its excess reserves, bank financing of the deficit was limited.[16]

During the Great Depression, banks attempted to call in loans because the 50 percent fall in agricultural prices led to a decline in the value of commercial paper available for rediscounting. Yet even if the banks had been able to do so, there would have been continuing problems of bank credit. Raúl Prebisch points out that banks were also in trouble since funds were tied up in long-term loans to commerce and industry, and could not restrict credit as capital, reserves, and public deposits fell. These banks turned for help to the Banco de la Nación, which, in turn, was forced to resort to the Caja de Conversión. The Banco de la Nación also had its funds tied up in long-term loans, loans to the government to cover the deficit, and loans to banks. Moreover, the Banco de la Nación often "resorted to its portfolio" in order to aid firms since the other banks restricted credit. As a result, the Banco de la Nación itself required help from the government.[17] Thus, the government lacked the legal means, institutional arrangements, and economic ideas needed to counteract a depression by use of discounting.

The government also was not able to influence economic activity by buying and selling domestic securities. The Treasury precariously placed its bills and notes in order to attend to the payment of its debt service directly.[18] The government had relied on foreign loans for much of its finance; there only was a very limited market for government paper. Pinedo wrote that until August 1933, various treasury papers had no prestige, carried the same rate of interest as long term paper, 5½ percent, and were bought only when they were rediscountable. This permitted banks and other companies to buy such paper with money borrowed at lower rates from the Banco de la Nación, keeping the difference between the interest that the State paid for the papers and that which the Banco de la Nación charged for the rediscount.[19] Thus, before 1935, the Argentine government, unlike modern governments, could not influence the money supply by buying and selling securities, rediscounting, or changing reserve requirements.

The government could, however, influence the nation's economic structure by favoring one sector or another with bank loans. If the Banco de la Nación was initially conceived as a source of agricultural credit, this conception of the bank's lending role was modified as other banks and traders filled agricultural credit needs and new businesses clamored for credit. Although credit allocation by government banks among various economic sectors in part reflects these sectors' differing abilities to generate their own funds, or to obtain credit from other sources, it also reflects government priorities. A measure that can be used to indicate government policy is the bank credit coefficient, which relates the share of bank credit allocated to an industry to its share in gross domestic product. Favored industries receive a larger than average share of government bank credit in relation to their share of gross domestic product (bank credit coefficient greater than one); industries that are not favored receive a smaller than average share of government bank credit in relation to the share of gross domestic product (bank credit coefficient less than one).

The movements of the bank credit coefficient are consistent with our knowledge of Argentine economic policy (see Table 4.3). Before World War I, large-scale operations such as cattle raising and commerce were favored; small-scale operations such as agriculture and manufacture were not. During the war all of the private sectors' bank credit coefficients declined as the government increased its share of the Banco de la Nación's resources. Despite the government's continuing reliance on the Banco de la Nación in the immediate postwar period, the bank credit coefficient of the cattle sector regained its prewar levels. In the late twenties, however, this pattern was reversed: the bank credit coefficients of agriculture and manufacturing increased at the expense of cattle, commerce, and government as the government's desire for an increase in manufacturing and diversification of economic structure

Table 4.3 Bank Credit Coefficient, 1905–1909 to 1925–1929

Years	Agriculture	Cattle	Manufacture	Commerce
1905–09	52.3	190.3	60.3	210.9
1910–14	51.2	221.1	55.2	214.7
1915–19	43.1	194.3	43.4	166.9
1920–24	23.5	219.5	33.9	152.3
1925–29	31.9	130.0	54.7	146.6

SOURCES: Tables 1.1 and 3.1.

became apparent. These moves coincided with shifts in political alliances with the Radical Party, but also reflected the economic analysis of Argentina's leading economist, Alejandro Bunge.[20]

The level as well as the distribution of economic activity became one of the objectives of governpient policy during the Great Depression, when the government was gradually forced to take responsibility for Argentine economic performance; effective action was delayed because many members of the government based their opinions on inaccurate data and inaccurate definitions of money, which resulted in a misunderstanding of the relationship between money, foreign exchange, and Argentine economic activity. In an economy with a developed banking system, money is defined as demand deposits plus currency held by the public. In Argentina at the beginning of the twentieth century it was generally accepted that bank deposits were part of the money supply. However, in estimating the money supply a distinction was not always made between demand deposits and other categories of deposits. There was some justification for including savings deposits in the money supply. Small customers—households, for example—were able to open savings accounts in commercial banks, which paid interest at lower than market rates and which were, in practice, convertible on demand.[21] Demand deposits were held by firms as a condition of obtaining a loan; banks were reluctant to extend credit to small firms. There was a slight difference in the behavior of savings and demand deposits: the volume of savings deposits changed in response to economic conditions about three months earlier than did demand deposits. Banks did not levy charges on demand deposits; the interest they paid on savings deposits was sticky, so that price changes affected savings deposits more than demand deposits, although there is no consistent relationship between the direction of price change and the share of savings deposits in M2 (M2 is the broad definition of money supply, which includes currency in the hands of the public plus demand deposits plus savings accounts in commercial banks), as other factors intervened. For example, when World War I broke out, rapid inflation led people either to stockpile goods or increase their investment in savings deposits, which paid interest. After World War I, deflation made the unchanged interest rates more attractive. The share of savings deposits in M2 increased from 18.5 percent in 1909 to 50.5 percent in 1921. The high level of savings deposits compared to M2 continued to 1940. From then on, persistent inflation accompanied a continuing shrinkage in the ratio of savings deposits to money supply (M2).[22] The Argentine economist Halperín believes that these differences are not great enough to warrant exclusion of savings deposits from the definition of the money supply. Time deposits (defined to exclude savings deposits held at commercial banks), however, are excluded.[23]

The definition of money is important, since an inadequate definition would hinder the government's ability to either analyze or control the economy. The first published estimates of Argentine money supply were seriously defective. One of Argentina's leading economic analysts, Alejandro Bunge, published estimates of national money supply. It was stated that his figures for means of payment included money in circulation and bank deposits, and excluded gold held in banks. Although this appeared to conform to traditional definitions of money in circulation, his figures in fact included savings deposits and currency held by banks. Thus, Bunge's estimates of means of payment differed from that used in standard practice.[24]

The Sociedad Rural Argentina distinguished between cash held by banks and that held by the public, but did not publish figures corresponding to the narrow definition of the money supply (M1, defined as currency in the hands of the public plus demand deposits). The published figures included items normally included in the broad definition of money (M2), which, given the differences in timing of response of savings and demand deposits to economic stimuli, probably impeded the government's attempts to solve the banking problems of the Great Depression. Some idea of the intellectual climate regarding money in 1931 was given by Federico Pinedo, who wrote:

> As Marx said sixty or seventy years ago, circulation is only the superficial part of the economic structure of the nation, and it is not possible to find in this superstructure the cause which

determines the crisis and the cause which determines the economic distress in a given moment. Nothing will be settled by money. . . . An increase in money supply does not increase economic activity.[25]

On a later occasion, Pinedo explained that the benefit of the system of the Caja de la Conversión was that money was only made in exchange for gold; this system was rigid and automatic; money could not be issued simply because it was needed. When borrowing or rediscounting schemes were used to issue money, the various money issuing systems were not well meshed, and the old system of the Caja de la Conversión lost its virtue. In a panic, only gold stems it.[26]

Was Pinedo right in interpreting the role of money? His opinions are not consistent with economic behavior before the Great Depression, when the correlation between real gross domestic product and nominal money supply (M1) (.96) was significantly greater than it was from 1929 onwards (.86). After the Great Depression, however, real gross domestic product was significantly more strongly correlated with real than with nominal money supply. The difference in response to the money supply is at least in part explained by the availability before 1929 of capital goods and other imports needed to expand supply; as imports fell after 1929, businessmen were less able to expand output in the short run when the money supply increased.

Pinedo also stated that the increase of money in the form of cash had no repercussion on the increase of money in the form of bank deposits, which he believed to be the most important factor in determining the volume of credit. Pinedo, who was a former Socialist, cited Marx as an expert on monetary theory, saying that "as a simple substitute for metallic money, paper money, conforming to the laws that are appropriate to it, can be perfect if it is limited in its quantity to the minimum sum that is always necessary, and requires metallic cover only to permit the retirement of the quantity which by the shortage of necessities can be made superfluous. Banknotes or bank deposits, as part of the nation's circulatory system, are ruled by totally distinct laws, and it has been an error in theory and a fiasco in practice to wish to submit them to restrictions that limit the emission of notes in their function as substitutes for metallic money." Pinedo noted that President Justo tried to discuss only paper money, treating it separately from credit extended by the banking system.[27]

The actual relationship between cash and demand deposits in Argentina is indicated by the fact that the public held half of the money supply (M1) in the form of demand deposits. Loans obviously depended on the amount of money that the public was willing to hold in the banking system, instead of in cash, as well as the banks' willingness to lend. Although Pinedo's views would have hindered him if he had attempted to revive the economy by use of monetary tools, he did not try to do so. His actions appear to have been based on the assumption that continued access to international money markets was the key to Argentine economic revival. He thought that maintenance of the exchange rate and avoidance of inflation were essential for obtaining foreign funds and domestic recovery. A partial result of this view was that he saw little difference between a budget deficit and expenditures covered by loans. During Pinedo's ministry (1933–35), government policy was directed to the maintenance of its credit standing and the flow of funds to Argentina by regularizing the position of insolvent banks and maintaining the value of Argentine currency. For example, Pinedo thought that both of the 1932 measures which permitted the issuing of new money against both government securities and gold in Argentine legations abroad were inflationary. He said that as a result, the exchange rate went to the devil, and he therefore put an end to this during his Ministry.[28] At this time the Argentine government was, in fact, able to obtain foreign funds.

The government met its financial needs in 1933 by means of an "unblocking loan" negotiated as part of the Roca Runciman agreement. British firms had been unable to obtain as much foreign exchange as they desired for remittance to the United Kingdom under Argentine exchange control. The Argentine government issued twenty-year, 4 percent sterling bonds at par in exchange for the peso balances awaiting sterling exchange for remittance. The government accepted internal credit bonds and Treasury notes for under 10 percent of the subscription; the interest rate on Argentine government paper fell to 1.5 percent as a result of its greatly eased cash position.[29]

Once the immediate needs of the government were attended to, it was able to relieve private banks. I believe that the private banks' greatest need was a lender of last resort; the government, however, perceived its requirements to be the regularization of insolvent banks and the maintenance of the value of currency. The Central Bank was created to achieve the latter aims.

The drafting of the central bank law reflected the views of money and banking described above, the existing Argentine bank structure, and the need to obtain British approval of Argentine financial developments. Banking reform had been proposed at various times in the twentieth century. In 1932, Argentines wrote a draft of a central bank law; at the same time, a British expert, Sir Otto Niemeyer, came to Argentina. Many of his suggestions were incorporated in the 1935 Central Bank Law. The invitation of a foreign expert was criticized in the Senate. The Finance Minister, Alberto Hueyo, answered by saying,

> The Executive Power must declare, Mr. Senator, that it does not believe that the country lacks technicians who could be occupied in drawing up a modification of this nature; this is proved by the numerous projects which have been outlined and which could constitute the base of a new organization, but not one will deny that it is necessary for the prestige of a new institution that foreigners understand well that which is done in Argentina, and in this sense the cooperation of the Bank of England appears of the greatest importance.[30]

Hueyo continued that the United States Federal Reserve System had been unable to prevent bank failures during the depression, while the Bank of England had faced it without a single bank failure.[31]

Pinedo wrote that

> there was excessive partiality in favor of the British draft, from which we adopted not only many ideas, but also the phraseology, when it seemed to us that there was no serious

inconvenience in it, even though we believed that at times a better text could be adopted. And we did this because we did not wish to create useless inconveniences in the approval of these projects and we knew that by a curious modality of the collective spirit, in this moment the adoption of these government projects would be facilitated if we could present them as largely coinciding with the advice of the foreign expert.[32]

Pinedo went on to state that although in the case of many government measures affecting the economy, decrees or resolutions were issued, and Congress was given an explanation after the fact; in contrast, measures concerning bank reform and the creation of a Central Bank were sent to Congress for action.[33]

The ownership, objectives, and management of the Central Bank have been criticized, and defended, virtually since the bank was founded. The Argentine government reserved four of the fourteen places on the Board of Directors. The other ten were elected by shareholder banks. This meant that foreign-owned banks could influence Argentine Central Bank policy. The first manager of the Argentine Central Bank was Raúl Prebisch, who had criticized the unsound practices of nationally owned Argentine banks (see the forgoing), many of which had issued false balance sheets. Prebisch had served on the Roca Runciman mission and was well aware of the nation's dependence on foreign funds. According to Prebisch, the Banco Central de la República Argentina was thought of as an orthodox tool, not so much to maintain economic activity as to maintain the value of money. This is reflected in the law that created the Banco Central de la República Argentina. The Bank was created for a duration of forty years. The object of its establishment is stated as:

a) the concentration of enough reserves to moderate the consequences of the fluctuation of exports and foreign investment on money, credit, and commercial activities, in order to maintain the value of money;
b) the regulation of the quantity of credit and of the means of payment, adapting them to the real volume of business;
c) promoting liquidity and well-functioning bank credit, applying the provisions for inspection, verification and rules of banks established in the bank law;

d) acting as financial agent and counselor of the Government in its domestic and foreign credit operations and in the emission and service of public loans.[34]

This view of Argentine needs was held despite the nineteenth-century experience that showed that investment funds flowed to Argentina as long as economic activity expanded, along with a decline in the exchange rate, which occurred when the government was faced with a shortfall of earnings on trade account. Those who wrote the Central Bank Law believed that foreign loans depended on a stable exchange rate, and they were terrified of a domestic inflation.[35]

Prebisch believed that the draft law initially presented by Sir Otto Niemeyer was insufficiently adapted to Argentine conditions. For example, it did not provide for the regularization of the position of illiquid banks, nor for inspection of member banks, beyond examining the balance sheet. The Niemeyer project made no reference to crop cycle credit needs. It permitted the Central Bank to hold unlimited foreign exchange, while the Argentine draft permitted exchange to be equal to only 20 percent of gold and foreign exchange. Only half of the 20 percent exchange could be counted in the calculation of the legal reserve of the Central Bank.[36] This measure reflected Argentine distrust of all paper money, including foreign exchange. Sir Otto Niemeyer objected to this provision. In response, the Argentine Finance Minister wrote, "I agree that the project may be excessively conservative in this respect but I do not believe there can be any hindrance for removing this clause, sometime hence, when the principal countries of the world return to monetary stability and the facts make it desireable to do so."[37]

The Niemeyer project would have limited the discretion of the Central Bank by imposing a modified Gold Standard: an increase in the rate of rediscount at the Central Bank would have been required when the monetary reserve with respect to notes was less than 33 percent. The Argentine projects required fewer signatures to rediscount paper than did the Niemeyer project, which also excluded industrial paper from rediscount. In addition, the Niemeyer draft did not discuss the exchange fund or exchange control.[38]

Although the money supply was not linked to gold and foreign exchange reserves, neither was counter-cyclical "Keynesian" policy adopted, because President Justo believed that "expansion is only justified if it is meant to meet an increased volume of general business, since the means of payment respond to no other purpose; the duty of the Central Bank is gradually to adapt the note circulation to the real requirements of business."[39]

Under the 1935 law, the Central Bank regulated the money supply, monitored the commercial banks, and acted as financial agent for the government. In regard to regulation, the Central Bank was granted both monopoly power over note issue and partial use of two of the three major instruments of monetary policy. The Bank was permitted to engage in open market operations, subject to limits on its holdings of government bonds (gold and foreign exchange could not drop below 25 percent of the note issue outstanding), and to change the discount and other related rates. It could also adopt rediscount rationing policies. In general, however, it could not change bank reserve requirements, which were set at 16 percent for demand deposits and 8 percent for time deposits, although it could grant temporary exemptions from reserve requirements to individual banks. As a result of these restrictions, the Bank's ability to control the money supply was limited.

The Central Bank also oversaw the soundness of the commercial banks. Limitations on portfolio composition were determined by the law, but the Central Bank could control its implementation and modify certain items. Commercial banks had to present monthly confidential balance sheets, and a body of auditor-inspectors was set up under the Central Bank.

The Central Bank served as the financial agent of the government, which was to place its deposits in the Bank. Seasonal advances to the government could be made provided they did not exceed 10 percent of the government's average cash revenues over the preceeding three years.

The Banco de la Nación had borne the brunt of the banking system's illiquidity, supporting private banks as much as possible in order to protect the depositors.[40] During the early 1930s, when the Banco de la Nación partly fulfilled the role of a government bank, the government's ability to aid banks in difficulty was limited by the lack of a market for government paper, a heavy floating debt, and pressing current government needs for funds. Although the government did not guarantee returns or equity of bank stockholders, it did take measures to safeguard depositors. According to Pinedo, "Because the government had a responsibility, the government had let these banks function knowing—or it ought to have known—that the banks were bankrupt, so that there was reason to say to it: 'And you, carrot-head, how come you let me put my money in these bankrupt banks?'"[41] The government therefore created the Instituto Movilizador de Inversiones Bancarias (I.M.I.B.) to purchase illiquid assets with which the banking system had been burdened through the depression. The I.M.I.B. obtained its resources from the revaluation of gold, a move that was criticized by those who believed that the more than 700 million pesos made available by the revaluation should have been used to finance economic development, rather than to aid private banks.

Pinedo recounted, "A French banker came to me and said, 'I'll put my money in the worst bank, since it will pay the highest interest and it won't be allowed to fail.'" Pinedo further stated that the events predicted by the French banker did not happen, since new banks were founded without liabilities from their predecessors. The I.M.I.B. had no creditors, and therefore could operate freely.[42] It was liquidated in 1943. In addition, the Banco de la Nación obtained resources by floating a bond that gave it the right to obtain funds from the Caja de la Conversión. Pinedo viewed this as different from giving the funds to the Banco, in which case they could then have been withdrawn by its creditors the same day.

At the same time, governments economists discussed the policies which the Central Bank should adopt in order to maintain the value of money. They wanted to return to convertibility under a bullion standard. The return to pegged exchange rates, however, was to be established with a wider gold points difference (the allowed margin of fluctuation being 4 percent), thus to some extent placing the burden of adjustment on exchange rates rather than on internal prices or output.[43] The Central Bank was given the tools needed to regulate the exchange rate in 1935.[44]

The institutional changes described above reflect, inter alia, the government's commitment to orthodox economic principles. Nonetheless, during the thirties, government policy shifted slowly away from measures most of which were consistent with classical analysis and which had been adopted during Pinedo's ministry, to expansionary measures, by the end of the decade. Between 1931 and 1935, for example, public spending was cut, new taxes were created, and the public debt was converted. The most urgent part of the floating debt of the Treasury was paid with a loan which was in part placed with the public and in part with the Caja de Conversión, and which gave rise to an emission of banknotes. The conversion was carried out in a way that reduced government expenditures.[45] An illusion of sound finance was created by the devaluation of the United States dollar, which lightened the burden of payment of foreign debt, and by a change in Argentine budgeting practices, so that receipts were calculated on a fourteen-month basis, and expenditures on a twelve-month basis.[46]

After the Central Bank was created in 1935, the rest of the floating debt, which weighed mainly on the banks, was liquidated with part of the product of the revaluation of gold. As a result of these operations, Argentina was one of the few nations to maintain payment on its domestic and foreign debt during the Depression.[47]

The experience of inflationary expansion from 1935 to mid-1937 led the Banco Central to believe that it needed not only to absorb bank cash, but also to absorb part of the public's purchasing power in order to avoid a very rapid change of economic activity.[48] During the second half of 1937, a decline in domestic economic activity was countered by a credit expansion of the Banco de la Nación, and, in 1938, by government purchases of surplus wheat.

The small budget surpluses of 1935–37 were transformed into a moderately large deficit in 1938. The Central Bank used exchange control to ensure that the expansion would not increase imports, but would stimulate domestic economic activity. This policy continued for the next few years, with the unanticipated result that Argentina was caught without a stockpile of goods during the Second World War (see chapter 8). The Bank also tried to prevent the use of bank loans to purchase stock. Thus, the government recognized that during a depression the stimulation of demand was more important than the availability of loans in maintaining business activity. For this reason, the government needed both to use fiscal policy to stimulate demand, and to use monetary policies and institutional reforms to aid insolvent banks to make loans possible, if economic activity was to be increased.

The importance of maintaining domestic economic activity was underscored when the commercial loan theory was abandoned. The 1938 annual report of the Central Bank, citing the Minister of Finance, states that now, maximum public works are reached

> at the culminating movement of our trade cycle, since the year 1937 may be thus considered. On the contrary, when depression was at its worst, between 1931 and 1933, expenditure on public works dropped to its lowest levels. The State with its programme of public works has therefore followed the same trend as the cyclical movements of our economy, thereby accentuating their fluctuations instead of moderating them. It would have been wiser to accumulate reserves in periods of prosperity and spend them during depression. In this way the State would have helped to alleviate the unemployment which occurs in times of crisis. When the economic situation improves, industry can absorb by itself the greater part of available labour. If state action were to take this direction the periodic crises could be surmounted without such serious effects on the economic life of the country.[49]

At the same time, the Banco Central did not pay much attention to minor credit expansion, since demand deposits were converted to savings deposits more rapidly than loans expanded.[50] The distinction between primary (M1) and secondary (M2) means of payment had begun to be made by Argentine policy makers.

Attempts were made to improve the financial markets. For example, the Central Bank intervened to absorb fluctuations in the bond market, and also converted and redeemed provincial bonds, which was especially important in the Northern provinces, where bonds circulated as money and drove out cash.[51]

Actions were taken by the Securities Commission, which, although it had no compulsory powers, asked the banks not to lend money on bonds issued in spite of its adverse report. It was hoped that this would strengthen the bond market. The short-term Treasury bill market was also aided. The Central Bank stated that previously, bills had a limited circulation because they were made out to order, and consequently could only be transferred by endorsement. In addition, these transactions were subject to income tax and stamp duties, which also hampered the ready negotiation of the bills. Bearer bills were therefore established by decree on February 4, 1938, and they were subsequently exempted from the above-mentioned taxes.

Another technical change, carried out in a less pleasant spirit, was instituted in 1939, when the Bank forced the amalgamation of Jewish banks on the grounds that they were too small, that there were problems of war, and because of "the very distinct manner in which the banks of the aforementioned community operate."[52] (The Argentine historian Scalabrini Ortiz inscribed the volume in the Central Bank library, in which these developments are reported: "I examined it with shame.")

World War II brought with it shifts in policy which, while usually associated with Perón, actually predate his rise to power. To stem the panic caused by the outbreak of the war, the government offered to purchase any amount of national securities offered to it.[53] The Central Bank urged banks in Argentina not to restrict normal business credit, and promised to rediscount.[54] The first steps were taken to use blocked sterling balances to purchase British-owned railroads in Argentina. Promotion of nontraditional exports began, subject to considerations of long-run profitability and possible foreign retaliation.[55] Prebisch stated that in 1940, the government attempted to counter the recession not by increasing its administrative costs, but by increasing expenditures in the private sector, without constant worry about financing. The financial problem would resolve itself easily as the economy recovered, giving the government more tax receipts and the opportunity to impose new taxes. For example, the imposition of an excess profits tax on industry as the economy recovered was considered. "First the economy, one said; later finances."[56] In 1941, the Bank congratulated itself on the maintenance of economic activity, which

> maintains its tempo because the flow of the purchasing power of the community has remained at a high level, as if the country were still exporting its agricultural and pastoral production in normal fashion. This is so because the Government has made intensive use of the resources of the banking system to purchase surplus crops and finance expenditure which cannot be covered by the customary means at the command of the Treasury.[57]

Although there was a good deal of discussion of technical features of government paper and market conditions, there was little public mention of inflation and none of income distribution. In 1942, the Central Bank blamed inflation on the rise in import prices and the need to finance business expansion, and condemned foreign influence in Argentine loan markets. The Central Bank believed that firms operating with guarantees located outside the country had borrowed sums that were too large in proportion to the local solvency of the debtor firms. The Central Bank therefore recommended that within two years, loans of this kind should reach the same ratio, with respect to the solvency of the firms located in Argentina, that was customary in ordinary business, either by gradually reducing the amount of the loans granted or by inducing the debtors to increase their local solvency.[58]

Wholesale prices (reflecting imports) rose more than did the cost of living, which was heavily influenced by the price of domestic food. Despite war shortages, the bank wanted to restructure imports to limit damage to Argentine industry. It also wished to increase currency in circulation, immigration, and the birthrate, in order to facilitate economic growth.[59] Growth was nonetheless limited by the breakdown in foreign trade, especially of capital goods.[60] The effect was all the more severe because of the Bank's refusal to allocate foreign exchange for imports of capital goods (see chapters 6 and 8). Thus, although the Industrial Bank was created in 1943 to make long-term development loans, its operations were necessarily limited by the capital goods shortage. In 1943, the Central Bank proposed the use of foreign exchange, which could not be used to import goods, to buy 500 million pesos of Argentine sterling foreign indebtedness. At the same time, the Bank recognized that depreciation was greater than replacement. The lack of imports also resulted in the excess liquidity of commercial banks. This could not be controlled by the Central Bank since reserve requirements were set by law, and could not be raised. (This power was granted in 1944.)

The political changes brought about by General Farrell, who became President in 1943, are reflected in the 1944 report of the Central Bank. For the first time, the masses are mentioned, as are changes in salaries and the structure of prices.[61] With the departure of Raúl Prebisch from the Central Bank in 1943, the level of its technical analysis fell. The 1944 report indicates that the government thought it could increase all profits, salaries and output despite shortages and inflation. The decline in agriculture, and therefore imports which were needed to maintain and expand Argentine production, led in 1945 to renewed concern over inflation. The Director of the Bank, Sr. Gagneux, was a holdover from the Prebisch years. The obvious strain between the Central Bank and the government was revealed in its 1945 annual report, which stated that

It will be necessary to take action on monetary income. Referring to the development of the inflationary process, we have seen the participation which government expenditures has had in it. It is certain that their reduction would exercise a depressive action on the volume of monetary income, at the same time freeing goods and services which would increase the mass of goods and services at the disposition of the population ... This possibility [of a rise in agricultural prices and output] should not be checked by considerations related to maintaining low prices of articles of prime necessity, for however desirable this would be, and, in effect, it is, the cost of such a policy should not fall exclusively on agricultural producers.[62]

Not surprisingly, the Bank was nationalized in 1946. This move was the most dramatic of those designed to direct Argentine economic performance by changing Argentine economic institutions. Successor governments continued the practice of institutional change to carry out economic policy. Broadly, the Peronists came to believe that control of credit distribution was needed to change the nation's economic structure, and that activities favored by the government would be provided with long-term credit only if the government itself operated the banking system. Thus, the new (1946) bank regime incorporated steps begun in the previous year, when emphasis was placed on gathering data on loans by economic category and geographic region in order to fight inflation and promote economic development. This had been done because many commercial banks were overextended. The Central Bank had changed its computation of reserve requirements rather than enforce the law. Funds had been diverted to speculative uses; the commercial banking system had been poorly adapted for long-term development lending. For these reasons, the Industrial Bank had been created in 1943, and the National Postal Savings System had been allowed to take on banking functions. These steps did not fulfill all of Argentina's development banking needs (see chapter 5); the new Central Bank law was designed to fill the gap and to make the Bank responsive to government policy direction. Moreover, it alleged that prior private influence in the Bank's management did not guarantee coincidence with the needs of general welfare.[63] The Bank's functions were characterized as forming part of national sovereignty.

Under the 1946 bank law—which heavily reflected the views of Miguel Miranda, who headed the Central Bank in that year—the Central Bank was nationalized and its objectives emphasized the promotion of full employment and balanced growth. Commercial banks became agents of the Central Bank, since all deposits received were held for its account. The Central Bank was to continue sectoral allocation of credit, in accordance with the government's development plans, by requiring the banks to rediscount their commercial paper.[64] Note that a precursor of this was sectoral allocation of foreign exchange, although this was said to have been directed to short-term aims.

The Central Bank permitted longer loan terms, and set all interest rates on loans, deposits, and rediscounts. The power to control the money supply and interest rates through open market operations was extended, and the Central Bank was granted supervisory powers over the Stock Exchanges and security dealers. The need to isolate the economy from balance-of-payments fluctuations received further emphasis and the Central Bank was vested with the responsibility of administering a complex system of exchange controls. In a related move, the government created a bank (the Real Estate Investment Institute) that was similar to Mexico's Nacional Financiera: it accepted deposits in its savings accounts for participation in stocks, bonds, and other debt instruments.[65]

Under Miguel Miranda, industrial development loans were emphasized. An examination of the bank credit coefficient for various sectors indicates that the distribution of bank credit among sectors in relation to their share of Argentine gross domestic product differed sharply in 1944-49 from the 1905–29 practices, and that these differences increased after the nationalization of the Central Bank in 1946 (see Tables 4.3 and 4.4). Agricultural output is often produced by small holders outside of the pampas; the bank credit coefficient for agriculture was below the 1925–29 level for 1944–46 and even lower in 1947–49. Agriculture received the least bank credit of any sector in relation to its share of gross domestic product. The bank credit coefficient for cattle declined from its prewar level in 1944–46, but was still above the national average. In 1947–49, its decline continued to the point where the cattle sector, for the first time in Argentine history, received less-than-average treatment by the government. The commerce sector, strongly tied to cattle and agriculture, received similar treatment, while manufacture, newly favored in credit matters by Peron's government, received increasingly better treatment than average: its bank credit coefficient improved sharply in 1947, consistent with the aid promised under the government's plan for 1947–51. Within manufacture, machines, vehicles, and metal production were particularly favored. The details are analyzed in chapter 6.

Table 4.4 Bank Credit Coefficient, 1944–1949

Year	Agriculture	Cattle	Manufacture	Commerce
1944	25.7	112.3	99.2	144.9
1945	39.1	137.6	106.6	118.7
1946	18.9	134.1	115.6	95.2
1947	20.6	96.4	141.8	103.4
1948	23.8	101.4	151.2	92.4
1949	27.9	90.3	131.5	98.3

SOURCES: BCRA, *Memoria Anual,* 1945–1950; República Argentina, Poder Ejecutivo Nacional, *Producto e Ingreso.*
NOTE: Printing and Publishing is included in "other" rather than in "manufacture" because the item is not consistently labeled in the original publication. Relatively small sums of credit appear to be involved. Credit distribution for mixed farming has been allocated half to cattle and half to agriculture.

The table does not include data on the use of funds by IAPI, mortgage loans, or various forms of non-bank credit, etc., but is restricted essentially to rediscounts and advances in current account deposits of the banking system. It is not possible to assemble a complete and consistent series on bank credit coefficients by sector for the years after 1957 on the basis of published data.

Under Miranda and his immediate successors, foreign exchange, which could not be used for other purposes (see chapter 8), was used to purchase existing foreign owned transport and communications firms, and fuel and supplies for public enterprise. The structure of ownership of the Argentine economy changed. As development loans take a long time to mature, and the use of foreign exchange brought few new resources into the economy, the infusions of credit generated an inflation that was combatted by further changes in the bank law in 1949. In that year, government control of banking and finance was increased by making the Central Bank into a dependency of the Ministry of Finance; the presidency and vice presidency of the Bank were held respectively by the secretary and undersecretary of finance. At the same time, provisions governing the maximum amount of government bonds the Bank could hold were liberalized, thus providing means for the inflationary financing of government deficits.[66]

Alfredo Gomez Morales, who became finance minister and Central Bank president in 1949, emphasizes the changes in banking structure and the various measures taken to allocate credit. From 1946 to 1949, the financial role of I.A.P.I.—The Argentine Trade Promotion Institute, created in 1946—had been controversial. It had acted as a financial intermediary in the purchase of foreign-owned transport and communications firms, and in the purchase of fuel and supplies for public enterprises. Moreover, I.A.P.I. received foreign exchange from the Central Bank to finance its foreign trade pacts.[67] In 1949, I.A.P.I. was therefore restricted to financing harvests, and no longer supplied credit needs of the Armed Forces.[68] Banks, which had given loans of 80 percent of the value of stocks pledged as security, thus financing stock market speculation, were no longer allowed to do so; trading in futures was suppressed.[69] Greater aid was given to agriculture in the Pampas in order to produce foreign exchange in the future. The share of bank credit going to agriculture, relative to its needs, increased moderately in 1950, and sharply in 1952 (see Table 4.5). The same is true of the bank credit coefficient for cattle. Nonetheless, agricultural expansion was moderately hampered in 1950 by drought, and very heavily affected by it in 1952. As agricultural and cattle production absorbed increasing shares of credit, and the government wished to avoid inflation, the share of bank credit gains to other sectors in relation to their needs necessarily fell. The bank credit coefficient for commerce and finance fell sharply, and that for manufacture fell moderately, although it continued to be higher than its pre-Perón level. Public works were mildly reduced. The Industrial Bank loans

Table 4.5 Bank Credit Coefficient, 1950–1957

Year	Agriculture	Cattle	Mining, Manu-facturing, and Construction	Commerce
1950	38.2	99.9	166.0	101.4
1951	43.6	108.1	170.9	94.4
1952	141.9[a]	119.8	114.3	65.4
1953	113.0	139.8	118.6	65.5
1954	127.7	151.6	112.4	64.9
1955	127.6	148.9	112.6	70.5
1956	125.5	125.6	118.5	76.2
1957	140.0	147.4	116.0	85.4

SOURCE: Schwartz, *The Argentine Experience with Industrial Credit;* BCRA, *Origen del Producto y Composición del Gasto Nacional,* Suplemento del Boletín Estadistico No. 6, June 1966.

[a]Reflects severe drop in output because of drought.

were limited by requiring that borrowers put up a peso of their own resources for each peso borrowed,[70] while loans were made (see pp. 141ff.) in accordance with national development plan needs.[71]

Argentine foreign exchange was overdrawn by $300 million dollars. Foreign exchange needs were met by requiring the deposit of 20 percent of the proceeds of sales to the United States in the Federal Reserve Bank, to be used to amortize the Argentine banks' foreign debt. This yielded $200 million; this rule was suspended when an Eximbank loan to Argentine private banks, guaranteed by the Central Bank, yielded another $125 million in 1950. This was the only foreign bank loan obtained between 1946 and 1955.[72] Foreign exchange allocation priorities were also followed; existing import permits, which had not been used, were reevaluated.[73]

Moreover, Peronist economists doubted that the structures of the newly created International Monetary Fund (IMF) and International Bank for Reconstruction and Development (IBRD) were compatible with Peronist economic policy. For example, in principle, membership in these organizations required the establishment of a single exchange rate. Argentina had multiple exchange rates designed to encourage imports of industrial goods and funds and to discourage the import of luxuries. Although membership in the IBRD would have given Argentina a quota of $250 million to spend in five years, this would have been at the cost of abandoning the Argentine policy of directing expenditures through multiple rates. Argentina therefore did not become a member of the IMF and the IBRD; similarly, it did not ratify the General Agreement on Tariffs and Trade.[74]

These measures reflect Gomez Morales' competence and Perón's views on economics. Gomez Morales stresses that inflation reflects the coordination of supply and demand, not just an excess quantity of money, a view which reflects his earlier work in the office of price control. Gomez Morales states that

Perón did not understand that it was possible to present an unbalanced budget. Some say 'yes, the Peronist budgets were all balanced or in surplus, but afterwards bank resources were used to finance I.A.P.I.' This is a reflection of . . . bad faith, because I.A.P.I. had . . . profits during its first three or four years, resulting from the difference between the prices [it] paid in the domestic market and the counterparts obtained from exportation, and I would say the last three or four years resulted in deficits, but the profits as much as the losses were in fact the result of the management of the exchange rate. We had worked above all in the last period with an undervalued dollar. Cafiero, who was the Minister of Economy beginning in 1952, correctly insisted in adjusting the exchange rates, with which the deficits of I.A.P.I. would have disappeared, but beginning in 1952 I had the responsibility of managing the entire economic team and I opposed it, because I preferred to have a kind of subsidy to the agricultural sector through the banking system, rather than a devaluation which would affect all the other sectors. The undervaluation was a means confined to a sector of little activity, which then tended to save. Devaluation would have distributed inflation among the dynamic sectors of urban life, whose characteristics were spending before getting.* This way the result was completely different, and permitted us to maintain, beginning with the second half of 1952, a stability of prices and salaries that was never known later. . . .[75]

The anti-inflationary campaign encompassed matters rarely included in macroeconomic text books. Perón personally prepared a series of three radio talks, in which he explained the anti-inflation measures to the nation. The government set an example by freezing or reducing virtually all military expenditures. Conscripts were released three or four months early, arms acquisitions were virtually suspended, self-sufficiency was attempted, renting the fields which they had for [military] exercises. Half of the military attachés returned to the country, some traditional activities were suspended, and so forth.

Coffee serving was suspended in the Civil Service, even though it would seem a puerile thing; 25 percent of imported coffee was drunk by this sector. In the Presidency of the Nation, during the period of Perón, no one took a glass of whiskey. They had no whiskey there, nor coffee; the President offered maté cocido, including to Ambassadors. That is to say, a

*See chapter 3 on this point.

policy of real austerity was implanted, in which for the first time the public sector set the example. In this climate it was possible to overcome the scarcity of grain without importing wheat. We could have imported wheat from the United States without paying for it until the following year: it is more by my initiative—because my father had bakeries—that I maintained we could overcome the situation without importing any wheat. It was enough to increase the percentage of extraction of wheat flour, generally at 70 percent, carrying it to 90 percent. That is to say, if the bread comes out a little more black it is perfectly edible. Thus black bread was eaten here during almost two years, but everyone ate it, from "Anchorena" to the most humble man . . . there wasn't the least protest . . . but at the same time we put into effect a series of steps tending to increase supply . . . The trade balance improved in 53–54."[76]

From 1952 to 1955, the cost of living increased 12 percent. Wages had been frozen in 1952 for two years; and price controls were imposed. In 1954, faced with elections and opposition complaints about austerity policies, Perón raised wages for those earning less than 800 pesos. This led to wage increases throughout the economy, averaging 18 percent.[77]

In contrast to Gomez Morales' views, the Peronist changes in the banking structure have been criticized for destroying existing financial markets and eliminating the interest rate as a guide to allocation of credit.[78] For example, by 1952 the ratio of industrial loans to gross national product was about 7 percent—higher than the total for the United States, which again underscores the greater reliance on bank finance than stock market or bond financing (see note 86 for chapter 6). Yet the bank nationalization was undertaken in part because the government wished to use nonmarket criteria to achieve social aims.[79] From a Peronist point of view, the correct test is whether these aims were achieved. The Argentine economist Carlos Moyano Llerena points out that the new structure was better adapted for open granting of development loans. Bank loans would be for longer time periods as they became responsibilities of the Banco Central de la República Argentina, rather than of private banks.[80] Manufacturing growth under Perón 1950 to 1955 was almost twice as rapid as that under his successors from 1955 to 1960 (see chapter 6). The overall growth rate was also greater under Perón from 1943 to 1955 than under those who succeeded him from 1955 to 1967. Prebisch's test, "First the economy . . . later finances,"[81] was clearly met by Perón from 1943 to 1955.

When the new government took over from Perón, it wished to restore the economy to its previous course. Perón's successors set themselves the task of dismantling economic controls. Denationalization of the banking system was one of the steps recommended by Prebish in 1955. Under legislation instituted in 1956 and 1957, the Central Bank was granted autarchy. It remained wholly owned by the government and its policies had to accord with the Executive's economic policy. The president and vice president were to be appointed by the Executive subject to Senate ratification, and their terms of office ran for seven years (the Executive is elected every six years). Of the remaining members of the Board of Directors eight would, de facto, be nominated by the Executive. They were the presidents of the other government banks, representatives of government departments, and of economic interests.[82]

The Bank retained money and credit power; the National Economic Council and other Ministries were charged with promoting economic activity. I.A.P.I. became part of the Ministry of Economy. The limit on foreign exchange as part of reserves was suspended, as was the gold or foreign exchange cover on note issue.[83]

The commercial banking system was denationalized. The Central Bank kept control over new entries. A new feature, powers of control over financial intermediaries, was adopted, and put into effect in August 1961, when the government authorized the regulation of the capital, interest, and reserves of the finance companies.

Finally, the Central Bank kept powers to determine maximum and minimum interest rates for commercial bank operations, and ceilings for each individual bank's lending, either overall or by type of loan. The Bank was authorized to set and change basic and marginal reserve requirements, to engage in open market operations, and to use the rediscount rate as a policy instrument. Persons to whom the Central Bank objected could not direct banks, as the new government believed that the fundamental problem was not one of systems, but of men.[84]

The question of how to increase development loans through the commercial banking system if the public was unwilling to hold demand deposits decreased in importance, since demand deposits as a share of money supply (for both M1 and M2) increased.[85] In December 1957, the government provided for credit needs best handled outside the commercial banking system by creating three autonomous government banks. These were the National Mortgage Bank, which was once more empowered to raise funds by issuing tax-free mortgage bonds, by accepting savings deposits, and by other forms of borrowing; the Industrial Bank, which was given responsibility for medium- and long-term financing; and the Bank of the Nation, which was to give financial support to agricultural production, and was to take care of the current needs of commerce and industry.

Argentina took several steps in 1956 to obtain and conserve foreign exchange: she joined the International Monetary Fund and the International Bank for Reconstruction and Development, established a ten year debt-funding agreement covering $500 million of Argentine debt with five European creditors and Japan, and established a multilateral payments system with ten European countries.[86]

These acts created the institutions within which Argentina hoped to carry out a new economic policy. At the beginning of this chapter, it was suggested that the objectives of Argentine government monetary policy at the beginning of the twentieth century were sound finance, as indicated by the maintenace of the level of money supply and by the maintenance of a fixed exchange rate; the insulation of the economy from the impact of foreign trade; and the regulation of economic activity by use of monetary policy. These objectives again were adopted by the post-Perón government, while use of the banking system to transform the economy became a secondary objective.

The immediate post-Perón governments failed to meet these objectives, both because of incomplete understanding of the complex situation and because of incomplete control over the economy. For example, in 1956, the governing Junta lifted a number of price controls, and granted wage increases of 30 to 40 percent. Deficits persisted in government enterprises. Inflation increased, exchange depreciated, gold and foreign exchange reserves were lost, and black marketeering flourished. President Frondizi, elected in 1958, adopted a new stabilization program. He obtained $329 million in credits from the International Monetary Fund, the United States, and private banks. He devalued the peso in December 1958. Between then and April 1959, living costs rose 47 percent and wages rose only 37 percent. By December 1959, foreign exchange reserves increased by $220 million, real gross product fell as a result of the domestic credit shortage, the cost of living increased 114 percent, and the rate of exchange fell from between 18 and 70 pesos to the dollar at the end of 1958 to 83 pesos to the dollar at the end of 1959. To prevent a further decline of the peso, President Frondizi obtained another $250 million from the United States, Europe, and the IMF.[87]

In 1960 and 1961, the government increased bank credit; the rate of inflation fell, and real gross domestic product increased, as did imports. The nation rapidly lost foreign exchange reserves; settlement of economic difficulties was complicated by the military coup which removed President Frondizi from office on March 29, 1962. The new military putsch was followed by a striking economic decline, which in part reflected the use of mistaken economic policies (see chapter 8). The peso was devalued in April; the money supply was reduced in 1962 and 1963. As a result of the credit shortage, real gross domestic product fell in both years.

Output fell despite the private sector's attempts to protect itself from the decline in the money supply. When the money supply shrank, and firms were unable to obtain bank loans, they deferred payment of taxes and social security contributions to the government and used these funds in place of those they should have received from the bank in order to pay their bills. This in turn reduced the current income of the government, which turned to the banking system to cover the gap.[88] The rate of inflation more than doubled its 1961 rate. Foreign exchange holdings fell until 1963, and the exchange rate continued its decline.

The Illia (1964-66) and Ongania (1966-69) governments avoided the credit squeeze and fall in gross domestic product that had characterized Argentine policy from 1950 to 1964. The money supply expanded throughout this period; the share of bank credit accorded the public sector fell, although, over the course of Argentine history, there is not a consistent relationship between bank finance of government activities and either growth or inflation rates. The availability of imports and the way in which the government funds are spent determine this relationship. In the mid-sixties, imports were available, and control over various competing groups in the economy great enough that the rate of inflation began to fall under President Illia.

Early in 1967, the Ongania government adopted economic policy measures designed to limit inflation and stimulate production. The details of these policies differed considerably from earlier stabilization efforts. The 1967 devaluation of the peso was accompanied by a tax levied on traditional exports; nontraditional exports were exempt from this tax. The government set norms for acceptable collective-bargaining wage settlements that were to be followed until the end of 1968. Under these norms, wage increases were stipulated at a decreasing rate. At the same time, price-setting policies were established which gave special benefits to firms that maintained prices. Industrial firms participating in the accord had to maintain prices for six months, and then could raise them only because of an increase in import costs. The public sector was to buy only from firms participating in the accord, and was to establish bank credits which would be restricted to firms participating in the plan. By November of that year, 1,971 firms had joined the plan. By 1969, 3,500 firms had joined and the inflation rate fell to one-third of its prior level in 1968 and 1969.

The wage freeze could not be maintained; although the level of real wages increased, the share of wages in gross domestic income fell 5.4 percent from 1967 to 1969. After the Minster of the Economy resigned in June 1969, the plan was abandoned. Nonetheless, while they were in operation, the 1964–69 policies worked better than those of the 1955–63 period, when prices rose from an index of 20.1 to 175.6, while real output rose from 86.3 to 102.8. Under the new policies, prices rose from 229.8 in 1964 to 535.0 in 1969, while physical volume of output rose from 113.5 to 144.4, a much better output/inflation trade-off.

Despite the relative success of monetary policy after 1964, a controversial aspect of the banking structure remained to plague the authorities: foreign banks in Argentina collected deposits from Argentines. The preferred—and perhaps most profitable—customers of those banks were foreign subsidiaries, above all in the chemical and petrochemical, metal products, and transportation material industries. The flow of funds from national to foreign hands was deplored as an additional step in the subordination of Argentine to foreign interests. This, combined with the subsidiaries' easier access to foreign sources of credit, gave them a financial advantage over Argentine competitors. In the early 1970s, laws were passed which enabled expropriation of some foreign banks and restricted the activities of others.

A number of commentators have suggested that monetary authorities in Argentina have had a passive rather than active role in controlling the level of either economic activity or prices. They less frequently discuss the role of monetary authorities in distributing credit. Professor Diaz-Alejandro, for example, believes that cost-push elements such as wage increases and devaluations have played an active role in the inflationary process, with monetary expansion taking a more passive role by validating higher money wages and prices with permissive increases in credit and money.[89] Professor Biggs' presentation of a similar explanation has already been described in chapter 2. An extensive analysis of the relationship between central bank policy and Argentine economic growth was completed in 1964 by the Argentine economist Dagnino Pastore, who estimated that changes in monetary income from 1935 to 1961 could be attributed to a series of differing economic variables. Thus, he believes that changes in monetary income originated eleven or twelve times in money, seven times in investment, five or seven times in liquidity, and once or twice in consumption. Dagnino Pastore presents evidence which indicates that in general, the supply and demand for money was most important in determining changes in monetary income until 1955, and changes in investment were most important in determining those changes until 1960, which confirms the criticism of Argentine economic policy during this period of low real economic growth on the grounds that the policy was inadequate from a Keynesian viewpoint. Dagnino Pastore implies that the Central Bank could not be expected to cope with so varied a series of economic relationships, and states that, in any event, much of the money supply was determined by factors outside of the Central Bank's control. From 1935 to 1961, changes in Argentine money supply were distributed as follows:

> 28 percent by Central Bank credit to the public sector; 28 percent by Central Bank credit to the foreign trade (external) sector; 14 percent by credit to the private sector; 23 percent to the reserve ratio; and 7 percent to the circulation ratio. Thus, only 37 percent of the changes could be attributed to the policy actions of the monetary authority, in the prevailing institutional context.[90]

To summarize the ability of the bank to control the economy (along the lines suggested by Dagnino Pastore), let me note that the most important aspect of Argentine banking history is the mutual dependence of the banks and the government. The breakdown of mutual support under Perón led to a takeover of the banks by the government.

The Central Bank had only limited control over changes in the money supply because it could neither limit its advances to the government nor control the share of the money supply held as cash. Further limits on the Central Banks's ability to control changes in the money supply arose from the fluctuations in foreign trade. This stemmed from the fact that bank credit is part of the money supply, and bank credit for exports depends in part on the size of the harvest and the number of cattle slaughtered, factors only partially influenced by Central Bank policy. Nonetheless, the government bank, the Banco de la Nación, managed to mitigate the effects of gold outflows on domestic money supply from 1913 until the Great Depression.

During the thirties, Central Bank allocation of foreign exchange was an important influence on economic growth. A rough indication of the extent of Central Bank control over the economy from 1935 to 1960 is that credit to the private sector and the reserve ratio determined 37 percent of changes in the money supply. Credit to the private sector was directly allocated to various economic activities under Perón. In some cases, its cost and availability was the single most important determinant of economic growth. (This is examined in detail in chapter 6.)

Thus, although the Central Bank was not independent of the government and did not have complete control over the money supply, it exercised an important influence over the timing, size, and distribution of Argentine economic growth. As analysis of monetary policy alone yields only part of the explanation of Argentine economic history in the twentieth century, the next chapters provide a detailed examination of the policies which, taken together, largely determined the economic history of each sector examined.

Chapter Five: Agriculture

Forms of Exploitation and Overall Policy

AT THE TURN of the century, the most important sources of personal wealth in Argentina were the ownership of land and of related food and fiber processing industries, all of which were controlled by native-born Argentines.[1] The rates of return on investment were higher in these than in other activities both because there was a strong demand for their products and because government policies favored them. The relative attractiveness of agriculture diminished because World War I, the Great Depression, and World War II subsequently limited Argentina's ability to export agricultural produce. Shifts in the composition of government reduced the influence of landholders in the formation of Argentine economic policy, which became progressively less favorable to crop production, and eventually unfavorable to cattle production. As world demand, Argentine purchasing power, and government policy shifted, the level and composition of agricultural output changed in response. This chapter provides a history of the institutional setting within which these changes took place, and a detailed analysis of the policies and technical factors affecting agricultural output.

An estimate of ownership of land and other forms of wealth is available for 1892. Mulhall, an Englishman who lived in Argentina, believed that Argentine wealth equalled 2,407 million gold pesos, of which 646 were in land, 520 in housing, 257 in cattle, 382 in railroads, and 602 in other forms.

Income for that year was thought to be 424.3 million gold pesos, of which 110 came from cattle, 92.4 from agriculture, and 221.9 from other activities.[2]

Argentina, like the United States before it, suffered a scarcity of labor in comparison to its endowment of land. As a consequence of the labor shortage in conjunction with growth in foreign demand for their products, both nations mechanized early: the Argentine census of 1895, for example, reported 35,000 harvesters and alfalfa mowers, 2,800 threshing machines and 5,000 other machines, as well as less sophisticated tools. From this base, Argentina mechanized rapidly: investment in agricultural machines and equipment increased roughly five times between 1900 and 1913;* however, machines and equipment represented less than 3 percent of agricultural wealth before the First World War (see Table 5.1).

Similarly, the rate of investment in agriculture in proportion to its share of gross domestic product was low: 3.4 percent in 1900–4 rising to 8.4 percent in 1924–29. If agricultural equipment was replaced as fast as industrial equipment, which is unlikely, then net investment in agriculture at the turn of the century was negative(!), as it was at the beginning of the Great Depression and during World War II (see Table 5.2). As the use of equipment became more efficient, less additional investment was required to increase output. The low levels of investment in agriculture reflect the relative unattractiveness of agricultural investment, compared to that of other sectors,

---

*The increase in value of equipment is based on my revisions of the statistical appendix to United Nations Economic Commission for Latin America, *El Desarrollo Económico de la Argentina,* 3 vols. (Mexico, 1959). The figures presented in this appendix are based on 1950 price weights. 1950 price weights are distorting when used for much of Argentine economic history. The relative prices between sectors are quite far from world averages, and reflect government intervention, which raised the ratio of industrial to agricultural prices well above their average level in Argentine history. For long series, I have used 1935–39 price weights, which are closer to world prices between industry and agriculture. Incomplete information for earlier periods prevents their use as a base. What does indicate trends, however, is the fact that although 1913 price weights for durable equipment are not available, price weights for metal indicate that 1913 relative prices lie between the 1935–39 and 1950 weights; the ratio of construction to metal prices is: 1913—114.8; 1935–39—100.0; 1950—130.5. The ratio of construction to wholesale price index is: 1913—109.4; 1935–39—100.0; 1950—161.4. There is no durable equipment price index for 1913.

Table 5.1 Argentina: Agricultural Wealth, 1908 and 1914

	Million Gold Pesos		Percent	
	1908	1914	1908	1914
Land	6,495	12,222	74.5	72.4
Cattle	1,479	3,202	16.8	19.0
Fixed installations	630	1,073	7.1	6.2
Machines and equipment	185	405	2.1	2.4
	8,790	16,906	100.0	100.0

SOURCE: Ortiz, *História Económica de la República Argentina*, 2:75.

from the Great Depression onwards, and are consistent with the limited technical progress exhibited by agriculture since that time.

Yet the early attractiveness of Argentine land is witnessed by the fact that its value almost doubled between 1908 and 1914. Part of this increase was due to the rapid increase of the area under cultivation, from 116 million to 152 million hectares, which was in part the result of the rapid extension of the Argentine railroad network. Between these years, the average value of land increased from 56 to 75 pesos per hectare, while machines, equipment, and installations increased from seven

Table 5.2 Rate of Investment in Agriculture, 1900–1904 to 1950–1954

Years	(A) GFDI/GDP 1950 Pesos	(B) GFDI/GDP 1935–39 Pesos	Column (A) Minus Depreciation at Replacement Cost	Column (B) Minus Depreciation at Historic Cost
1900–04	9.9	3.4	−2.1	−1.0
1905–09	18.4	6.5	6.4	2.1
1910–14	18.4	6.4	6.4	2.0
1915–19	13.6	4.8	1.6	.4
1920–24	16.7	6.0	4.7	1.6
1925–29	22.5	8.4	10.5	4.0
1930–34	12.4	3.2	.4	−1.2
1935–39	14.6	5.2	2.6	.8
1940–44	7.5	2.5	−4.5	−1.9
1945–49	13.3	4.6	1.3	.4
1950–54	13.4	4.8	1.4	.4

SOURCES: Ganz, "Problems and Uses of National Wealth Estimates in Latin America," pp. 217–73; Elias, *Estimates of Value Added, Capital and Labor.*
NOTE: Replacement cost in 1950 prices; historic cost in 1935–39 prices.

to nine pesos per hectare. Since the agricultural labor force remained roughly constant at about two million, and wages did not vary much, it is clear that this increase in agricultural land value was a result of the acquisition of means of production and transport facilities, rather than of the effects of any increased exploitation of labor.[3]

When land was a profitable investment, it was so not only for the income it would yield if worked on, but also as real estate whose value would increase whether or not it was used for productive activities. A combination of the attractiveness of Argentine land and government policy led to a very great concentration of land ownership in a very few hands.[4]

United Nations experts believe that in developing economies, the distribution of agricultural property approximates the distribution of wealth, although the size-distribution of property may understate the concentration of wealth, since one family may own more than one farm. In Argentina, there was limited scope for small property holdings. In the richer areas, a smaller amount of land yielded higher incomes than in the poorer areas. Concentration of landholding was lower in the best areas than in the outlying ones, but nonetheless yielded enormous concentration of incomes (see Table 5.3). Argentines owned rich cattle ranches, while foreign-born owners had smaller farms that they used for raising crops.[5] In Buenos Aires in 1914, 59.3 percent of the land was held in properties of more than 1,000 hectares (1 hectare equals 2.471 acres); in all of Argentina, 78.4 percent of the land was held in parcels of over 1,000 hectares by less than 10 percent of the agricultural property owners. In contrast, 59 percent of agricultural properties accounted for only 3.5 percent of the land.[6]

Moreover, when large farms were worked by sharecroppers under tenancy arrangements, the landowners obtained much, but not all, of the income from the land, because there was an almost inexhaustible supply of (im)migrant laborers and sharecroppers to work them. In 1914, 38.4 percent of farms were operated by tenants under arrangements which lasted two or three years; landowners provided land and credit, and gave a stipulated share of the grain harvest to their tenants.

Table 5.3 Size Distribution of Agricultural Properties, 1914–1947

A. Argentina

	Percent of Properties			Percent of Area (est.)		
Size in Hectares	1914	1937	1947	1914	1937	1947
0–20	32.9	34.5	36.4	0.6	n.a.	0.9
21–50	11.3	13.2	13.0	0.8		1.3
51–100	14.8	16.1	16.0	2.1		3.2
101–500	28.3 ⎫		25.4	12.2		14.3
501–1000	4.5 ⎬ 34.9		3.4	5.9		6.4
1001–5000	6.5 ⎭		4.6	29.5		27.7
5001–10,000	1.0 ⎫ 1.3		0.8	15.5		14.7
10,001+	0.7 ⎭		0.7	33.4		31.5

SOURCE: Cortés Conde, "Regimen de la Tierra en Argentina."

B. Buenos Aires (1914–52 and 1960)

	Percent of Area				Size in	% of Area
Size in Hectares	1914	1937	1947	1952	Hectares	1960
<50	2.0	3.3	3.4	3.2	< 25	1.1
51–1000	37.7	58.9	49.9	47.8	25 < 100	6.8
1001–5000	30.4	22.0	32.8	32.3	100 < 1000	43.8
5001+	28.9	15.8	14.7	17.0	1000 < 5000	33.8
					5000+	14.5

SOURCE: H. Giberti, "El Desarrollo Agropecuario"; and Cortés Conde, "Régimen de la Tierra en Argentina."

The sharecropper provided his own house, tools, and labor, and during the last year, planted alfalfa (which enabled the land-owner to raise cattle), and moved to another piece of land. Contracts usually contained a clause which stipulated that improvements were the property of the owner; the tenant had no right to indemnification for them.[7] The system discouraged improvement of the land, and failed to protect the tenant, who was consequently quite poor. Coní estimates that in 1903, a tenant of a 100 hectare farm *lost* 567 pesos a year;[8] tenants could have few animals; they paid rent based on their gross, rather than net, product.[9] On the other hand, large landowners often rented to intermediaries who in turn rented to tenants; the large landowner made profits of up to 80 percent a year. The difficulties of the tenants, and the landlords' refusal to ameliorate their conditions, led to a series of tenant strikes in 1912 and 1913.[10] Most of the tenants were not Argentine citizens; government action to help them was delayed until 1921, when a law allowed tenants to stipulate a minimum four-year contract, and provided some compensation for construction of housing and sheds, while safeguarding the tenant against the seizure of his tools.[11] As a result, 7,932 sharecroppers who raised grain converted to tenants between 1923–24 and 1924–25, while 7,351 new properties were farmed under tenancy arrangements (see Table 5.4 for percentage distribution). In 1931, the minimum lease was extended to five years.[12] By 1937, the average length of residence of farm operators was greater than five years, but tenants moved within farms so that problems of insecurity and short-term tenancy remained. Tenants operated some 44.3 percent of Argentine farms.[13]

New lands were opened up in the form of small farm units far more often than as large ones, and the importance of large farm units fell to 36 percent of the total in 1937, 32 percent in

Table 5.4 Forms of Exploitation of Land Used for Grain and Flax Cultivation, 1906–1926

Years[a]	Percentage			Number of Properties[b]
	Owners	Renters	Sharecroppers	
1906–07	32.4	54.4	13.2	57,056
1907–08	32.2	55.3	12.5	67,040
1908–09	32.5	55.1	12.4	66,049
1909–10	32.0	56.0	12.1	66,896
1910–11	33.1	56.0	10.9	65,111
1911–12	33.1	55.9	11.0	73,461
1912–13	32.6	55.1	12.3	84,076
1913–14	32.4	55.4	12.2	76,212
1914–15	30.6	57.1	12.3	76,955
1915–16	30.2	57.4	12.3	71,297
1916–17	31.1	56.9	12.0	56,506
1923–24[c]	35.7	55.4	8.9	119,999
1924–25[c]	33.2	64.4	2.1	129,794
1925–26[c]	39.1	58.4	2.5	121,905

Source: SRA, *Anuario*, 1928, pp. 126–27.
Note: Excludes maize.
  [a]Data unavailable.
  [b]Includes Buenos Aires, Santa Fe, Córdoba, Entre Ríos, Pampa Central.
  [c]Includes other provinces and territories.

1947, and roughly 26 percent in 1960.[14] Nonetheless, agricultural policies until quite recently reflected the belief that agriculture is typified by oligarchs in the fertile Pampas region. This belief persisted because the largest units control a great deal of land: in 1947, farms of over 5,000 hectares were 1.5 percent of properties and controlled 42.4 percent of the land; 6.1 percent were farms of over 1,000 hectares and controlled 83.9 percent of the land.[15] Moreover, a decreasing share of farms were owner-operated. For example, in 1914, half of Argentine farms were owner-operated; in 1937 this fell to 37.2 percent. The percentage of owner-operators in the Pampas was about 30 percent less than the national average. This reflects the fact that the best lands were located in the Pampas, and they were the first to be distributed, and were held in parcels larger than the national average.[16] As a consequence, new settlers had little land: in 1947, almost two-thirds of the farms on the Pampas were smaller than the minimum size that the Ministry of Agriculture considered necessary to support a farm family.[17]

Alfredo Gomez Morales summarizes rural conditions in the 1930s:

> The conditions in which the Argentine rural areas developed impressed me tremendously. When I had access to the rental contracts and the conditions of development of the system of renting where, generally, the farms were rented to an intermediary and he in his turn created the colonies. And I have seen something very curious: that where the renter was the proprietor himself, in general the conditions were more benevolent for the agriculturalist. In the large farms where an intermediary acted, whether by power of attorney or as direct renter to subrent later, there the conditions were truly draconian, since these intermediaries required the colonist to sell to given firms, to take insurance with others, and very often, in order to renew the contracts, they took a "commission." We came to the conclusion that sometimes these intermediaries had more money than the land owner. It was a wretched system of exploitation. Except for a few cases, where the personal intervention of the owner, and his sense of things gave it a different character.

I had also encountered a situation in which the large farms based in Buenos Aires . . . had contracts which were the most extortionate of all. Thus, they established clauses by means of which was set . . . rent, which generally was paid in kind, for example, in healthy, dry and clean grain, delivered in season. They required this percentage to vary according to productivity per hectare. That is to say, if productivity increased, the rental price did also. The agriculturalist did not even have the chance of a good year. These readjustment clauses absorbed this possibility. Contracts which limited the number of cattle that could be had, let them have a cow, and some of them did not let them have more than a certain number of domestic animals. Really these conditions were tremendously odious. The contracts were supposedly filed with the Justice of the Peace, but when the agriculturalist needed them, they frequently were not found.[18]

The national share of owner-operators was stable until 1947, but by 1960 it had increased to 50 percent, both within the Pampas and nationally, reflecting a shift in government agricultural policy. From 1946 to 1954, 522,700 hectares of land were bought from existing owners and distributed to 3,218 families, in contrast with the 55,000 hectares distributed from 1941 to 1946.[19] The reasons for the reform were economic as well as political: land owners obtained higher maize yields than renters; it was believed that land reform would result in more intensive use of the land.[20] Thus, land colonization laws required residence and personal exploitation of property. At the same time, conditions of and access to tenancy changed. Agricultural rents for tenants and sharecroppers were frozen in September 1942, and reduced 20 percent in December 1943. This reduction was maintained until 1949–50; rents were increased 15 percent in 1952. A 1948 law extended bank credit for the purchase of land for up to 100 percent of the purchase price. As a result, tenant farms dropped from 44 to 33 percent of total farms by 1952.[21] Although over two million hectares had been expropriated for colonization, between 1946 and 1959 massive land reform was avoided because large amounts of land were in the hands of third persons who had bought it in good faith.[22]

While wheat profits were limited during the war, and rose sharply for the next four years, landlords did not share in this rise because of the government regulation of tenancy and sharecropping contracts. By 1950, the landlords' share of profits on contracts with tenants had fallen to one-quarter of its prewar level, and to three-quarters of its prewar level on sharecroppers' contracts. During this period, tenants' share of profits rose 17 percent, and sharecroppers', 20 percent.[23]

An alternative evaluation is provided by Jarvis, who maintains that Peron's antiagriculture policies were borne by rural labor, whose income fell more than that of owners. Tenants who acquired temporary free control of land benefited in the short run, but later they lost as well.[24]

In order to defend themselves against tenants and sharecroppers, landlords bought out tenants' contracts when they could, and shifted to cattle production. As tenants and farm laborers left for the more attractive cities, the landlords also called for immigration as a new source of cheap labor. Although Perón agreed to sponsor immigration, the newly arrived immigrants tended to stay in the cities, instead of working on farms.

The farm labor shortage resulted in less intensive care of the land, weed control declined, abandonment of 20–30 percent of corn and small grain was common in the postwar years, and corn yields were below the levels that had been obtained in the 1920s.[25]

Those least benefited by the Peronist laws were the farm workers in the far north, many of whom had immigrated from Paraguay and Bolivia. But at least some nominal legal changes favoring the establishment of unions, the spread of schools, and the improvement of hygiene, were obtained under Perón.[26] After his overthrow, legal changes prevented the further distribution of land.

In 1955, a law was enacted which provided that unless land purchase and sale were agreed on, tenancy contracts were automatically extended. In 1958, tenants who refused to buy land when offered the option were evicted, and so did not benefit from a frozen rent. 1959 witnessed the largest number of new rent contracts in fifteen years. The policy of extending contracts was reinstated in 1963, while government financial assistance in land purchase was again granted in 1967, but failed to make adequate provision for reimbursement for investments made by the tenant. This was an important omission, because even if price controls or minimum contract terms do not exist, the presence of total indemnification at replacement cost for improvements made by the tenant makes tenancy a stable institution. This is simply because if the contract is terminated, the indemnification of the tenant for improvements represents an important outlay to the owner.[27] Similarly, if the tenant leaves the land, the owner has not only to replace the management and labor provided by the tenant, but the agricultural implements as well.[28]

As landlords, like other men, respond to profit opportunities, the question is often raised, why do they act to inhibit improvement of the land by tenants? Indeed, why don't they themselves modernize? The most frequent response is that landowners are so rich that they do not care to. More to the point, greater profit was made on resale of land as its real estate value rose than on farming operations. Adoption of modern techniques often required the presence of the educated landowner, who had more profitable and pleasant ways of spending his time.[29] Moreover, the attractiveness of investment in agriculture compared to other alternatives in Argentina declined throughout the century as a result of government policy. For example, agriculture, which accounted for 29.3 percent of gross domestic product, provided up to 15.7 percent of national and provincial tax revenue in 1910; by 1925, agriculture accounted for 27 percent of gross domestic product and provided up to 24.8 percent of taxes.[30]

Thus, government agricultural policy extended into areas additional to landholding and tenancy policies. Government policy towards each region and group took the form of price fixing and taxation of each crop and livestock. As the Argentine economist Lucio Reca has pointed out, these policies strongly influenced the profits earned on various agricultural activities, and therefore have had an important role in determining shifts in agricultural production. The regional incidence of these policies can be inferred from the fact that the

Pampas are mainly devoted to wheat and livestock, and the rest of the country to other agricultural and industrial crops. More than half of Argentina's traditional crops—wheat, corn, and flax—were exported. Their production reached its peak in the early thirties, maintained this level, and then collapsed. Production of nontraditional crops in the Pampas, grown for the domestic market, tripled between the mid-twenties and the early sixties.[31] During this same period, beef cattle production in the Pampas increased by 50 percent, while other livestock production doubled. The overall increase in Pampean agricultural output was 27 percent. In contrast, total output outside the Pampas doubled along with a threefold increase in crop output, while the export oriented grain crops declined almost continually until the early sixties. The typical, non-Pampean crops, which were used mainly for domestic consumption, increased by more than 300 percent.[32]

In judging the difference between Perón's policies affecting beef production and those affecting grain production, Jarvis asserts that Perón discriminated more strongly against grain producers, who were both politically weaker and produced products with less potential export value, than he did against the cattle barons.[33]

These production trends reflect government policies which were designed to mitigate the effect of world conditions on Argentine agriculture by shifting production from exports to crops for the domestic market, maintaining a minimum agricultural income, and improving the technical efficiency of the export sector.[34] These policies were part of an overall strategy of economic autonomy and income maintenance.[35]

Policy by Product, 1930–69

Grain. The timing of government action depended on shocks and pressure groups, as well as on the ability to pay.[36] The government established minimum crop prices to maintain income when tenants, who had entered into agricultural leasing contracts covering several years when grain prices were high, were obligated to continue paying high rents after prices fell. The fall in prices resulted, in part, from an overvalued exchange rate of 3.88 pesos to the dollar, so that the government's exchange rate policy was to some extent responsible for agricultural difficulties.[37] Land rental prices eventually fell, but by less than the fall in grain prices. Grain profits fell more rapidly than average from 1925–29 to 1930–34, and wheat production fell 8.2 percent. Tenants therefore advocated minimum prices for grain, which were established in 1933 at 10 percent above market prices for wheat and flax, and 20 percent above market prices for corn.[38] The price supports were financed by granting exporters an exchange rate lower than the market rate, a difference which was used as a subsidy for selected crops. The government supported the price of export crops whenever agricultural income was deemed insufficient during the 1930s and pre-Perón 1940s.

Price support was buttressed by regulation and provision of technical services similar to those established by the various Agricultural Adjustment Acts in the New Deal of the United States. Regulating Boards were established for each major agricultural commodity group; grading standards were established in 1935–36.[39] Although membership of these boards included representatives of government and of producers from the interior provinces, they were dominated by large producers, often from the Pampas.[40] Although the Justo government stated that destruction of surplus stocks to maintain prices was limited, later Peronist critics pointed out that in a majority of cases production was constrained by regulating boards.[41] The boards could not afford to set support prices above market prices because there were not enough grain elevators in which to store the grain which would have been produced in response to a high support price policy; there were, in fact, only 23 elevators with a capacity of 400,000 tons in 1930.[42] The lack of grain elevators also led to high production costs through added expense for bags and the loss of crops which were inadequately protected from the weather.[43] This problem was largely solved by the early 1950s, when 95 percent of the grain was shipped in bulk.

The profitability of grain depended on world prices, Argentine producers' prices, and the cost and availability of factors of production. The government did not attempt to influence world grain prices during the thirties, but instead increased the share of world price that the farmer received by building a badly needed highway network. As late as 1923, there were only 1,273 kilometers of all-weather roads; in rainy years, it cost an estimated 10 percent of Santa Fe farmers' income to transport crops from farms to railway stations.[44] By 1938, Argentina had 17,000 kilometers of all-weather roads.[45] The cost of transport fell in the areas with roads; however, only an estimated 22 percent of Argentine roads were all-weather roads in the 1960s.[46]

Perón's attempts to increase world grain prices in the 1940s failed (see chapter 8, p. 232).

Argentines claim that wheat export sales fell because of the United States' refusal to let Marshall Plan Funds be used for the purchase of Argentine wheat, since United States surplus wheat was available. From April 3, 1948 to June 30, 1951, $1,105.7 million dollars of wheat and wheat flour (13,494 metric tons) were procured from the U.S. commercial and government stocks by the Economic Cooperation Administration. It is not certain that Argentina would have been able to sell as much wheat as she wished in the absence of either Marshall Plan funds or United States wheat surpluses, since the Argentine wheat export price was above the United States subsidized ("dumping") price, while the low prices paid to Argentine producers led them to shift production away from wheat to beef, and to nontraditional grains and livestock.[47]

It is worth noting that the 1930s grain price paid by the government to producers was above the world price. Under Perón, it was below the world price, with wheat prices less than half the world price. The government intended to invest in industrial development the funds that resulted from the difference between the price it paid Argentine wheat producers and the price it received for wheat on the world market. Moreover, uncertainty about prices made production unattractive. The government-set prices were announced just before the harvest, rather than at planting time. In later years, under Perón, prices were announced at planting time but had to be abandoned and revised upward because of inflation.

Perón's policy towards agriculture changed as Argentina began to run out of foreign exchange in 1948. In April, 1950, the government asked farmers to increase the areas planted with wheat by 50 percent and with corn by 25 percent, while announcing that the prices for the 1950–51 crops were increased by 20 percent for wheat and 30 percent for corn. All prices included a bonus for grain produced by owner-operators and tenants. These prices were announced well in advance of the planting season. Unfortunately, they became meaningless in the presence of steady inflation; therefore, grain prices were increased by 10 percent at the beginning of 1951.[48] Despite inflation, the Argentine wheat producers' position improved; they had received only 47 percent of the world wheat price in 1947–49, but had increased their share to 68 percent by 1950–52.[49]

In another move to aid agriculture, the government doubled the credit allocated to agriculture in 1950, and lowered the interest rate to 5 percent—two percentage points below the rate applied since 1946. Selected seed was sold to producers at prices below cost, and foreign exchange was allocated for the import of farm machinery.[50] More agricultural machinery was imported under Perón than during the thirties. This was an important step because imports of agricultural machinery had been severely limited from 1931 to 1936 and from 1939 to 1946.[51]

The Sociedad Rural Argentina complained in its 1949 Annual Report that Argentine tractor importations were defective in quantity as well as in quality. A large share of the imported tractors were not adapted to the country's basic needs. Many of the machines had small power and gasoline motors and could therefore not be used for heavy tasks, which required more powerful units fired by cheap fuels.[52]

Grain production increased by at least one-third, and perhaps as much as one-half, in 1950–51,[53] but it was severely cut the following year because of one of the worst droughts suffered by Argentina during the twentieth century.[54] Grain production fell by about half, but recovered to its former level during the remaining Perón years.[55] Although the difference between Argentine and world prices for agricultural products declined sharply following the overthrow of Perón, grain output did not exceed that of the best Peronist year until 1964.

Wheat yields were 10 percent higher than in Australia, and only 13 percent below those of the United States.[56] This relatively efficient performance reflected government policies which lowered the cost of some aspects of wheat production while raising others. Improved seed has been available since 1935, and it is used on virtually all Argentine wheat land. Investment in fertilizer, even at artificially high Argentine prices, would have yielded a 50 percent return.[57] Argentine farmers almost uniformly refused to apply fertilizer to wheat production. Similarly, there was little use of pesticides and herbicides (see Table 5.5). Mechanization was widely adopted, but was limited by the high cost of Argentine tractors. In 1947, Argentina had 29,150 tractors; in 1950, despite a 40 percent increase in the number of tractors, only 8 percent of the area under cultivation was operated by tractor power. The majority of tractors were used on farms of between 250 and 1,000 acres; on the basis of one tractor per 500 acres Argentina had 41 percent of the tractors it needed in 1956.[58] Expansion of the use of tractors was limited in part by the fact that until 1961 Argentine tractor manufacturers were required to use 55 percent local parts, which were roughly three times as expensive as imports. A 1964 study indicates that a 50 horsepower tractor cost $6,579 dollars in Argentina, $4,925 dollars in Chile and $2,338 dollars in England. Production of harvesters and equipment, on the other hand, was priced competitively.[59] Shortages of agricultural labor and increasing agricultural wages led to increasing mechanization under Perón (see chapter 3).

Government policies influenced the marketing as well as the production of grain. Successive grain regulating boards provided loans for seeds, granted advances on grain that they would buy, established grading of grain in Argentina (rather than abroad), and constructed grain elevators (which avoided importing bags).[60] All grain storage bins and elevators were placed under government control in 1944. Weil, who was an adviser of Federico Pinedo, states that this may have been the result of anti-Semitism rather than agricultural policy, since the largest facilities were owned by Jews.[61] Moreover, grain

Table 5.5 Argentina: Employment of Technology and the Technology Gap for Selected Crops, 1965 (percentages of the area affected)

Indicator	Corn	Wheat	Malt Barley	Linseed	Sunflower	Grain Sorghum	Cotton	Tobacco	Sugar Cane	Wine Grapes
Improved seed	70	100	80	85	55	50	45	—[a]	15	No data
Fertilizer	0	0.5	0	0	0	0	0	17[b]	60	0
Insecticides	1	5	0	85	90	5	90	—[b]	0	98
Herbicides	90	10	2	40	0	25	5	—[c]	1	0.1
Mechanization	—[d]	—[d]	—[d]	—[d]	—[d]	—[d]	50	50	—[e]	0
Irrigation	—[f]	0	0	0	0	0	—[f]	—[f]	—[g]	90
Cultural practices[h]	50	55	7	40	60	75	15	60	20	70
Technology Gap I	High[i]	None	No data	Medium[j]	Medium	No data	High	Medium	Negative	Negative
Technology Gap II	Medium	No data	No data	None	None	No data	None	No data	No data	No data
Technology Gap III	High	High	High	Medium	High	No data	High	Medium[k]	High	High

SOURCE: Fienup, Brannon, and Fender, *Agricultural Development of Argentina*, pp. 122–23.

Technology Gap I—between Maximum Research Station Yield and Maximum Yield of Best Farmers.

Technology Gap II—between Maximum Yield of Best Farmers and Field Trials of Farm Conditions Supervised by Station Personnel.

Technology Gap III—between Maximum Yield of Best Farmers and Average Yield in Major Production Area.

[a] Burley tobacco 90 percent, Virginia 60–70 percent, Criollo 25 percent.

[b] Almost 100 percent of the producers use insecticides in the seedbed, and about 60 percent employ them in the field.

[c] About 30 percent of the producers use herbicides in the seedbed but none in the field.

[d] Mechanized in most production aspects. This is somewhat misleading, however, because although most of the activities are mechanized, in many cases the machinery is not the best adapted to the task and is in short supply, thus leading to inefficient production practices.

[e] Many harvesting operations still require a large amount of hand labor. Mills are not properly equipped to handle mechanically harvested cane.

[f] Some irrigated production, but considered to be practically insignificant.

[g] Almost 100 percent irrigated in Salta and Jujuy and about 35 percent in Tucumán.

[h] "Cultural practices" refer to time of planting, seedbed preparation, plant population, etc.

[i] 50 percent or more.   [j] 25–50 percent.   [k] For Criollo Salteño, Technology Gap III is high.

elevator capacity tripled from 164 thousand toneladas in 1946 to 500 thousand toneladas in 1951.[62]

Nonetheless, a shortage of grain elevators and transport remained. In the 1960s, for example, half the corn harvest moved in bags rather than in bulk, as did some of the wheat harvest.[63] Until the early 1960s, any increase in storage capacity resulted from new government-constructed, public elevators. But by the mid-1960s, storage facilities on the farm had become important, stimulated by bonus prices paid for bulk delivery of grains, credit availability, and the financial losses resulting from lack of usable facilities in the 1964 bumper harvest.[64] Remaining grain storage difficulties persist in a number of areas. Not all facilities at the port of Rosario can be used, because silting of the Paraná River makes it difficult for ships to reach the city. Terminal grain elevator charges are set by the National Grain Board: as a result, no new terminal elevators have been constructed by private firms, while those previously existing were nationalized by Perón.[65]

One reason for the lack of increased output was limited access to new technical production information during the war and early 1950s.[66] Even when information became available, it was not efficiently disseminated. The experimental stations' research and information services are consciously designed for the largest farmers, allowing each agent to affect the largest amount of production; yet the smallest yields are obtained by smaller farmers, who are in greater need of technical assistance. Large farmers, on the other hand, sometimes obtain better yields than the research stations. Further, the research stations are oriented to technical rather than cost considerations. To increase yields in practice, the research stations need to adapt their recommendations to conditions facing small farmers, and to take profitability into account.

The level of cereal and flax output is influenced by government policy. A regression system for analyzing agricultural output is presented in Table A.2. As cereals and flax is a category which includes all grains, factors such as changes in the prior year's real unit cattle profits (see Table B.2), which mainly influence wheat output, are not statistically significant at the 10 percent level for the larger group. Instead, the changes in the prior year's real unit profits of wheat, forrage crops, vegetables and legumes, fruits and flowers, oilseeds and wool are those variables subject to government policy whose variation is most significantly associated with wheat output.

Beef. The primary objects of Government policy towards the beef cattle industry were to guarantee existing levels of exports (of chilled beef) during the Depression, to promote beef sales, to prevent the spread of *aftosa* ("hoof-and-mouth disease"), and to intervene against the highly profitable foreign controlled *frigoríficos* ("beef-packing plants") on behalf of Argentine producers,[67] who were barely breaking even. Exports were promoted by trade treaties, and aftosa limited by regulating internal cattle shipments. Argentine beef producers were helped when their government attempted to end the frigoríficos' practice of setting the price they would pay for cattle after they had been slaughtered. The government decreed that cattle could only be killed after having been paid for at a price agreed upon before slaughtering. In an effort to break the foreign packing pool, the government obtained a guarantee from Great Britain, as part of the Roca-Runciman Treaty, that 15 percent of the chilled beef purchased from Argentina by Britain was to come from Argentine frigoríficos. A national frigorífico was set up, but leased in part to foreign packers, who purchased cattle from the largest Argentine producers. The government set minimum prices for chilled beef, but not for other livestock products.[68] Beef profits fell faster than average from 1925–29 to 1930–34, and the number of cattle slaughtered fell 14.7 percent. Although the form of government intervention on behalf of cattle producers was different from that on behalf of grain producers in the Pampas, the results were roughly similar: there occurred a moderate shift of resources in the pre-Perón period from traditional livestock such as beef to milk and pork.[69]

World War II heightened Argentina's difficulties in marketing traditional exports. The uncertain access to foreign markets, combined with the apparent association of large Argentine stockraisers with foreign packers at the expense of small Argentine producers and consumers, made continued support of traditional agriculture seem both uneconomic and impolitic. The reserve crisis of 1948 led Perón to ease taxation of cattle exports; moreover, Perón's increase of agricultural wages had a smaller impact on cattle production than on labor-intensive crop production. After 1948, beef output in the Pampas increased, while that of crops and other livestock fell.

In the case of beef cattle, livestock production methods in Argentina differ substantially from those in the United States. The high cost of grain, compared to meat prices, precluded feeding grain to cattle and sheep in Argentina. Cows and calves are fed almost entirely by the direct grazing of grass and forage crops on the natural unimproved pastures, which occupy approximately half of the Pampas, although steers are fattened on improved pasture.[70] This, combined with the lack of supplemental feeding, causes seasonal animal nutrition problems. Any prolonged drought that seriously reduces pasture production results in herd liquidation and high production losses. Thus weather has an important effect on the cattle cycle, tending to interrupt it or to accentuate the extremes more than would be the case if supplemental feeding or improved pastures were available. To the extent that their development requires attractive grain prices and cheap fertilizer, government policy has hindered their growth. This is reflected in the low growth of productivity in the beef cattle industry from 1935 to 1963.

A basic indication of productivity in the livestock industry can be obtained by dividing livestock units by the land area devoted to livestock; this ratio is called the carrying capacity of the land. Between 1935–39 and 1960–63, carrying capacity in the Pampas increased only 4 percent. Fienup indicates that the remarkably small increase in carrying capacity, despite a large increase in the area of seeded improved pastures, during this period, implies a decrease in the productivity of natural pastures. This is attributed to overgrazing, especially during dry periods, and the resulting erosion and invasion by weeds. It seems likely that with a lower cattle population, fewer nutrients would be required to maintain the herd, and more would be available for actual fattening. This is also true of sheep herds.[71] Similarly, use of improved pasture would more than double carrying capacity per hectare.[72]

Cattle production is influenced by government policy. A regression analysis examining variables subject to government influence indicates that cattle slaughter depends upon last year's herd size and changes in last year's real unit profits of forrage crops, industrial crops (such as cotton and vegetable oil, for example), fruit and flowers, milk, wheat, corn, and nonagricultural activities. Herd increase is significantly associated with the prior year's herd size, and with changes in all real unit profits of agricultural and nonagricultural activities, with the exception of fruit and flowers. Herd size in turn depends upon the prior year's herd size and last year's changes in all real unit profits.

The results of the regression analysis confirm my belief that an increase in this year's cattle profits leads to an increase in this year's natural increase of cattle. Similarly, an increase in cattle profits this year yields a decrease in slaughter. As changes in real alternate profits and past level of herd are significant, the system reported here estimates the characteristics of cattle herds better than do regressions including cattle profits alone. The implication of this analysis is that the government, by manipulation of profits between sectors, can achieve a fairly prompt change in cattle herd size, increase, and slaughter, if it desires to do so.

Crops Other Than Beef or Wheat. The Argentine government extended tariff protection to crops grown outside of the Pampas from the late nineteenth century on; the wine, sugar, and yerba maté industries were those best-known for their early reliance on tariff protection; while tobacco, vegetable oil, and cotton production also benefited from *ad valorem* tariffs of more than 25 percent. Although urban interests occasionally obtained exceptions to such duties, politicians from the northern and western regions were able to maintain the aid their constituents needed to continue their farming operations.

The government's policy favoring the production of crops other than beef and wheat expanded during the Depression, and lasted through 1941. It included the establishment of National Boards to develop and regulate the wine, milk, cotton, yerba maté, quebracho, oil, fruit, and nationally produced food products industries. (The change in unit profits for the production of agricultural products other than beef or wheat are presented in Table B.2.) To protect existing producers, the National Wine Board in 1935 bought surplus wine, made loans to grape growers, agreed with the Mendozan Provincial Government to distill inferior grade wines and sediment, established time periods during which grapes were to be harvested, established tax-free alcohol zones in Mendoza, and paid for the uprooting of grape arbors. Wines were publicized, sales regulated through buffer stocks, and statistics gathered. Although the government continued its program of quality controls under Perón, it did not set prices for nontraditional crops.[73] Marketing obtained more aid than production techniques: by the early 1960s, grape yields in Argentina were about 55 percent of those in California, and the best Argentine farmers obtained yields 10 percent higher than those of experimental stations.[74]

The production and marketing of yerba maté, which was grown in Corrientes and Misiones, was complicated by the fact that Brazil bought Argentine wheat and meat, and, in exchange, sold Brazilian yerba maté to Argentina.[75] To maintain trade with Brazil, new Argentine yerba plantations were taxed for five years. The government suppressed a 10 percent tax on the importation of Brazilian yerba; however, to maintain revenue, it imposed a tax on all processed yerba, regardless of its origin. The receipts from this tax were used to subsidize national yerba producers.

A board established quality and sanitary controls for the processing of yerba, established a minimum price, entered into yerba loan and marketing agreements with the producers, and undertook the construction of warehouses.

The National Cotton Board established grading standards and regulated technical and health aspects of cotton ginning. The Board's main concern was to increase the production of cotton seed adapted to each production zone. It established experimental stations, bought desired seeds at a premium, and sold them at a discount to cotton farmers. In the early 1960s, experimental station yields were 50 percent higher than those of the best farmers.[76]

For the country to achieve self-sufficiency in tobacco, studies were undertaken to determine which varieties were best suited to each production zone. Yields obtained by research stations are close to 40 percent higher than those obtained by the best farmers.[77]

In order to promote the export of fruit, grading standards were adopted, and reduced railroad rates were granted on fruit transport. The government aided fruit distribution in the capital, and provided aid to fruit growers in time of national disaster.

The regression equations for products other than grain or cattle indicate that the variables influenced by government policy which are significantly associated with output are changes in real unit profits. For products that are produced by family farms, the population size is also significantly associated with output. The changes in real unit profits that are significantly associated with changes in output vary from this year's changes, for fruit and vegetables, to changes four years ago, for wool, depending upon the technical characteristics of the products. (Details for each product are provided in Table A.2.)

General Technical Considerations

Argentine agriculture is faced with technical problems ranging from the inadequate education of farmers to insufficient credit and marketing facilities. For example, formal education in rural areas was limited: in 1961, fewer than 40 percent of students entering the first grade completed primary school, with completions ranging from 64.5 percent in the Federal District to 13.6 percent in Corrientes.[78] Argentine rural workers fourteen or older are generally very poorly educated: 20 percent are illiterate and 50 percent have only a first grade education. About one-quarter of primary school graduates go to secondary school. This, combined with limited agricultural training facilities, limits the number of skilled personnel in agricultural and stock-raising specialties. A case in point is that if Argentina were to employ one veterinarian per 8,000 animals (the F.A.O. guide), it would take more than thirty years for Argentina to produce the 5,300 veterinarians required for its livestock industry.[79]

Agricultural research and extension services are the result of an attempt to overcome these technical problems. In 1956 these services were substantially improved by the newly created Instituto Nacional de Tecnología Agropecuaria (INTA), which in 1958 took over the research stations of the Secretariat of Agriculture. In the past, research had been centered on plant sciences. INTA's devotion to production-oriented research and extension services was reinforced by the fact that INTA is supported by a 1½ percent tax on all agricultural exports.[80]

Overall agricultural research support is only one-quarter that of Australia and New Zealand, coming to no more than .06 percent of gross domestic product over 1956–65.[81] Some of the achievements of INTA have been: increased beef yield per hectare by selective breeding; a reduction by half of the time needed to market a steer through improved feeding and management practices; the doubling of butterfat yield per hectare; renewed efforts at disease control; improved sheep raising practices (reduced stocking rates); improvement of varieties of poultry, peach trees, wine grapes, oil seeds, tobacco, wheat, and corn.[82]

Nonetheless, a very limited supply of educational and research facilities still exists; but this can only explain part of the shortage of skilled agricultural personnel. Within agriculture, as elsewhere, salary differentials were insufficient to attract workers into moderately skilled occupations.[83] Between 1949 and 1966, salaries ranged from 10 to 30 percent above an unskilled laborer's salary for a foreman, from 3 to 30 percent for a tractor mechanic, and from 2 to 30 percent for a tractor operator. As all wages rose more rapidly than product prices, and the increasing power of unions was disliked by employers, machines were substituted for labor wherever possible.[84]

In addition to bottlenecks in research and education, Argentine agriculture has been plagued by transport, marketing, and credit difficulties. The poor conditions of railroads led producers to ship 70 percent of their grain by truck. Unfortunately, 78 percent of the roads are unpaved and often impassable when wet, a condition that takes a particularly heavy toll on perishable plants and animals.[85] And even worse, improvements in transport are insufficiently rewarded, as there is little quality control. According to United States agricultural economists, it is not unusual for buyers to be forced to purchase lower-quality fruit in order to be allowed to purchase some of the higher quality. Inadequate cold storage at the shipping points or at destinations, as well as inadequate refrigerated trucks, contribute to the loss of quality during the marketing process. For example, eggs may be left in the sun for hours, until transport becomes available. Other losses occur because fresh fruits are handled roughly in the packing sheds and are bruised when transported over rough roads to the markets. Further deterioration occurs because stocks of groceries in the retail stores are not rotated systematically, and a buyer might be sold a year-old package of flour, or one packed the same week.[86]

Argentine farmers also faced difficulties in financing production. To some extent, agricultural credit is supplied on the provision of a warehouse receipt for produce. If storage facilities are inadequate, so necessarily is credit. Thus the American historian Tulchin has laid the problem of credit availability before Perón to foreigners who controlled railroads and storage facilities. Although ownership of these facilities has changed, they remain inadequate. Feinup, however, stresses the general scarcity of credit in the postwar period, when a lack of credit from normal credit agencies led the intermediate marketing agencies to obtain credit from others by delaying payment to their suppliers, who, in turn, delayed payment for their supplies. This resulted in the producers receiving payment in installments over a long period of time—a year or more in some cases. In periods of sharp inflation, this means that the producer receives substantially less for his product. The chronic problem of an inadequate credit supply for farmers is, therefore, basically a problem of inadequate credit at other levels of the market. Production decisions are vitally influenced by the delayed receipts for sales and the subsequent credit implications.[87]

A number of technologically backward practices have continued to be used in Argentina as a result of government actions affecting the rate of return on investment in modernization. Perón's industrialization program resulted in high-cost fertilizers, herbicides, pesticides, and machinery. As a result, cattle instead of chemicals fertilized the soil: unprofitable beef cattle operations are carried out in corn-producing areas in order to maintain soil fertility.[88] At the same time, farmers could earn more by better techniques of grain farming, but they do not because the new techniques would yield less stubble for cattle.

If fertilizer were available at world prices, the introduction of new varieties of crops which respond well to the application of fertilizer would result in a further increase in yields.[89]

As a result of the limited adoption of modern techniques (see Table 5.5), actual yields remain below potential, and crops, according to a recent UNFAO study, are grown on only one-third of the land that might be used.[90]

In conclusion, a large share of agricultural output can be explained by factors largely subject to government control. The information presented in this chapter, and in Appendices A and B, provides data that can let the government know both the pricing pattern needed to increase several categories of agricultural output (if the government wishes to do so), and the trade-off in changed levels of output of other sectors that such a pricing pattern would entail.

Chapter Six: Manufacture

THE ARGENTINE MANUFACTURING sector has grown steadily throughout the twentieth century: it increased from 11 percent of gross domestic product in 1900 to 33.7 percent in 1969. This growth took place for a variety of reasons: an increased population with purchasing power led to an increase in the demand for mass consumer goods, only some of which could be economically imported. As the economy developed, there was an increasing need for capital equipment, although the low share of investment in gross domestic product necessarily limited the development of a heavy equipment industry in a moderate-sized nation. I believe that after World War I, an increased desire for economic autarchy led to the stimulation of manufacturing growth by government protection. This took the form of tariffs and other trade policy instruments, as well as preferential credit arrangements, which gave the protected sectors high domestic prices and profits.

The Argentine pattern of industrial growth differed from that of the United Kingdom. Unlike Britain, which was a heavily populated country filled with artisans and entrepreneurs whose craft shops grew into factories, and drove out inefficient competitors as a byproduct of growth, Argentina was labor short. Moreover, since the most attractive investment opportunities at the turn of the century were in agriculture, investment in manufacture was often left to foreigners in default of Argentine interest.

In addition, the technical knowledge necessary to manufacture was, for the most part, more readily available to foreign immigrants and entrepreneurs than to Argentines, so that the new foreign firms were concentrated in industries that grew at above average rates, and which were characterized by the use of new, capital-intensive technology and by an oligopolistic market structure.[1] Small firms often were founded to service new, large-scale industries.

Argentine policy makers responded more to native-born constituents than to immigrants. As a result, when protection was granted to manufacturing, it was given to coalitions of Argentine-born entrepreneurs who wished to maintain income outside of Buenos Aires and to increase the use of raw material byproducts and of some manufactures. Workers and consumers were less often the beneficiaries of government intervention. The immediate effect of protection was that the protected industries grew faster than the average of all manufacturing industries, and reliance on imports declined for the economy as a whole. (see Table 6.1).

This pattern of protection, which was maintained until the early 1920s,[2] reflected Argentine conditions at the turn of the century. In 1895, Argentina was partly industrial: it had 2,204 industrial establishments, which were capitalized at 284 million pesos, and which employed approximately 146,000 workers in a labor force estimated at almost 2 million. Foreign-born Argentines made up 84.2 percent of the owners and 63.3 percent of the employees. Capital invested was largely in raw materials processing and consumer oriented industries: 23.6 percent in food, 16.3 percent in construction, 16 percent in clothing, 9.3 percent in metal and metal products, 8.7 percent in furniture, and less than 5 percent in chemical products, printing, and others. The location of the firms was highly concentrated: over half were in Buenos Aires and the Federal District, and 83.8 percent were in the littoral region (Buenos Aires, Federal District, Sante Fe, Entre Rios, and Corrientes). More than two-thirds of the workers were located in Buenos Aires and the Federal District, with 85 percent in the littoral region. This concentration resulted from both the natural advantages of Buenos Aires and the littoral region, and from government policies aiding these areas.

Table 6.1 Merchandise Imports as Percentage of Aggregate Supply, 1900–1904 to 1969

	1900–04	1925–29	1937–39	1946–49	1950–54	1960–61	1969
Manufacturing (a)	59	51	37	20			n.a.
(b)		34	22	15	10	11	n.a.
Foodstuffs	6	5	5	2	2	2	2
Textiles and apparel	55	45	44	15	5	4	5
Wood products	39	37	32	18	16	17	40
Paper and cardboard	25	31	40	30	17	18	27
Chemicals	45	38	40	19	14	15	19
Petroleum refining	100	53	16	22	14	10	16
Rubber products	100	93	12	22	14	18	5
Stone, glass, and ceramics	15	27	18	9	3	3	9
Metals	87	65	46	37	21	22	16
Machinery, vehicles, and equipment, excluding electrical	92	79	49	43	23	25	27
Electric machinery and appliances	100	98	56	22	8	9	26
Other	—	49	41	31	18	20	—

SOURCE: (a) Jorge, *Industria y Concentración Económica*; (b) Díaz Alejandro, *Essays on the Economic History of Argentina*; UN, *Yearbook of International Trade Statistics*; BCRA, *Origen del Producto y Distribución del Ingreso*.

During much of Argentine history, the government protected Buenos Aires at the expense of the northern and western provinces. Thus, the economic dominance of Buenos Aires at the beginning of the century was not only the result of location and resources favorable to production for the foreign market; government aid in obtaining foreign loans was not always available to other provinces at comparable stages of development.[3] For example, as part of the agreement with foreign creditors reached in 1893 (the Arreglo Romero), Argentina took over the debts of the provinces. The government's assumption of those debts signified the end of independent provincial action, since the level of local sales taxes was determined by the federal government, taxes by the provinces on exports were prohibited, and foreign borrowing was not immediately feasible. As a result, the provinces relied mainly on funds from the federal government, whose finances were chaotic but showed a distinct regional bias in the pattern of receipts and expenditures. In 1895, for example, the federal government's tax system was regressive; 75 percent of their funds came from foreign trade, 15 percent from the use of public services, 12 percent from excise taxes, and the remainder from other sources. This implies that the poorest provinces fared worst in the government's revenue system. An indication of the provinces' wealth is given by the per-capita level of their provincial and municipal budgets. In 1899, this level in the East-Center was three and a half times the national average.[4]

In 1895, federal government expenditures in the East-Center region were 31 percent above national average, which could be expected to increase the region's advantage. In 1914, the federal government gave priority to investment in the South, while the East-Center ranked second on a per-capita basis.[5] The provinces complained about inadequate funding, but with little effect. For example, Ezequiel Ramos Mexia, Minister of Agriculture and Public Works from 1905 to 1913, stated that it was unjust to accuse him of being "'the enemy of the provinces' . . . . desiring to take all the money of the Country to the desert territories which are uninhabited even by birds."[6] (In 1914, the territories [in the South], with 1.4 percent of the nation's population, and millions of birds, received 16.8

percent of federal expenditure in capital account.)[7] He argued that the provinces could only obtain increased funds if the federal finances were placed in order. The funds would be well used if public investments in the provinces were instituted as part of an overall plan. He suggested that investment in public works be financed by a Consolidated Public Works Fund, which would float moderate-sized loans abroad at invervals of at least two years.[8]

His program missed the point that government aid to the East-Center region had little spillover effect on the rest of the nation, since the East-Center's trade links to the other regions within Argentina were weak so that "within Argentina the multiplier effects on income of the growing exports were not transmitted to other regions by increasing import from them since most of this stimulus was channeled to the rest of the world."[9] Regional economic concentration decreased with the growth of manufactures. In 1913, about 70 percent of the firms and workers were located in the littoral. At the same time, the share of foreign entrepreneurs (64.6 percent) and workers (51.2 percent) decreased. Their distribution, according to industry and province, sheds light on the pattern of protection followed.

In 1913, two-thirds of the industrial owners in Argentina were foreign born. They outnumbered Argentine owners in all sectors of the economy but textiles (fiber, thread, and cloth), a sector which accounted for 5 percent of the entrepreneurs, but only 2 percent of the capital invested and 3.8 percent of workers. Argentine ownership in the remaining sectors was greatest in the most profitable sectors of the economy: food, construction, clothing, and furniture. The initially less profitable modern sectors—metallurgy and chemical products—were left to the foreign born. Similarly, although there were more foreign-born than Argentine owners in the littoral region, Argentine owners outnumbered foreign-born entrepreneurs in the interior.[10]

Foreign-born Argentines frequently did not become citizens in order to avoid military service. Foreign-born workers therefore lacked both the vote and political influence, although large foreign firms were highly important. Further, although each province's representation in the Chamber of Deputies was proportionate to its population, representation in the Senate was two seats for each province and the Federal District, which favored the provinces at the expense of cities in which immigrants were concentrated.

The government protected the part of manufacture that had the largest share of Argentine ownership, and was most closely linked to the traditional agricultural export sector. Many capital goods, especially those for agriculture, and equipment for the transportation sector, entered duty-free and provided more than 90 percent of the total supply. Processed food and clothing received greater than average tariff protection; 12 percent of clothing and little food was imported. Although chemical products were protected, the level was just below the average rate of protection given (excluding duty-free items), while some of the inputs in the metal and graphic arts (printing) sectors were taxed. Sectors with strong elements of Argentine ownership received tariff protection, while foreign-dominated sectors in some cases received "negative tariff protection." Where tariff protection existed, it was not much greater than the 20 to 25 percent which the U.S. economist F. Taussig considered unlikely to provide a strong stimulus to the protected activity, and considerably below the levels granted to traditional activities. Argentine nominal tariff protection was strikingly below that of the United States (see Table 6.2).

It is not surprising that the greatest participation in value added of manufacturing output from the turn of the century to 1925–29 took place in the food and beverages industries—estimated at between 27.5 and 34.3 percent—the lowest in heavy industry. The distribution of growth between sectors was not the result of comparative advantage alone, but also reflected government policy which protected light but hindered heavy manufacture.[11]

The level of government protection shifted during the twentieth century. Tariffs were levied on *aforos* ("assessments") i.e., on the official values of items, rather than on market prices. But while market prices rose, official values, set in 1906, did not, and by 1919 official values were only 35 percent of their invoiced value, and the level of protection had declined[12] (see Table 6.3). Argentine manufactures, however,

Table 6.2 Argentine and United States' Nominal Tariff Protection 1902–1962

	1902[a]	1913[a]	1913	1918	1922	1925[a]	1928	1932	1934	1962[a]
U.S.	73	44	40	24	38	37	39	59	46	112
Argentina	28	28	25	10	16	29	26	37	31	141

SOURCES: (a) Little, Scitovsky, and Scott, *Industry and Trade in Some Developing Countries*, p. 163. All others, Vernon Phelps, *International Economic Position*, pp. 202–5.

Table 6.3 Percentage Difference Between Official and Real Tariff Values, 1906–1940

Year	Percent	Year	Percent	Year	Percent	Year	Percent
1906	—	1917	106.1	1925	32.1	1933	−7.7
1910	7.8	1918	201.8	1926	19.1	1934	8.3
1911	10.4	1919	185.4	1927	16.7	1935	4.8
1912	16.1	1920	186.4	1928	−1.3	1936	−4.4
1913	17.7	1921	122.4	1929	−2.2	1937	2.8
1914	18.6	1922	84.8	1930	−2.0	1938	2.9
1915	34.6	1923	87.7	1931	−2.8	1939	7.2
1916	68.4	1924	40.0	1932	−3.9	1940	38.9

SOURCE: Jorge, *Industria y Concentración Económica*, pp. 62–63.

had been protected during the First World War by the unavailability of foreign goods. And since foreign exchange was scarce until 1924, it developed that Argentine manufactures were protected from foreign competition for eleven years.

The isolation imposed by World War I led two groups to seek increased protection. The government needed new tax receipts to replace the shortfall in customs revenues, and traditional export groups wanted to develop domestic markets to replace European customers.[13] In 1917, Congress placed a surcharge of 2 to 7 percent on all existing tariff duties in order to increase revenue; in 1918, it approved an export tax, but refused to impose an income tax. In order to provide markets for hides, a doubling in the tariff on shoes was proposed in 1918. In this instance, the littoral and interior provinces outvoted Buenos Aires, which defended consumer interests, and the bill passed. Domestic producers also fought other attempts to reduce the cost of living by liberalizing imports; the best known example of this is the fight over sugar.

During the war years, frosts reduced the sugar production to between one-quarter and one-third of the 1914 level, and its price rose rapidly. Urban groups protested, while producers fought the importation of sugar. The producers were in a stronger position than many other manufacturers. The sugar industry was owned by native-born Argentines who were financed by powerful Buenos Aires banks. Moreover, the sugar industry provided over half of the jobs of the 550,000 inhabitants of Argentina's three northwestern provinces (Jujuy, Salta, and Tucumán).[14] Although the work conditions were wretched, the alternative—unemployment—was worse; nonetheless, in 1917, the President purchased foreign sugar and sold it at local police stations. In 1919, the weather and sugar production improved, and the government stopped permitting imports,[15] but refused to permit exports of Argentine sugar. The government alternately favored consumers and producers, in the successful expectation of increasing its seats in Congress.

In 1919–20, tariff duties were increased by 20 percent as a result of pressure from Argentine manufacturers and the government's need for more revenue.[16] The relative position of the interior provinces improved during the war years, due in part to tariff protection and in part to the fact that Buenos Aires relied on domestic rather than foreign supplies. Moreover, average provincial budget expenditures per capita had risen from 64.1 percent of the Buenos Aires level in 1899 to 83.3 percent in 1920.[17]

In 1922, the President of the Sociedad Rural Argentina advocated protection of shoes and leather products, edible oils, wool, textiles, and tobacco goods, in the face of increased tariffs for Argentine products in the United States and Europe.[18] In his inaugural message in 1923, President Alvear stated that the protection of industries using Argentine raw materials should not hinder the stimulation of industries which, although they used imported raw materials, would be beneficial for the country.[19] In November 1923, all aforos were increased by 60 percent, and specific duties by 25 percent. Nonetheless, sugar duties were reduced, as were those on yerba maté, which was also produced in the North. At the same time that northern industries were harmed by tariff cuts and a regressive national tax system, those located in Buenos Aires were favored by freight rates which discriminated in their favor, so that the East-Center region contained the vast majority of industrial plants and employment,[20] and attracted highly skilled immigrants whose concentration in the East-Center region was significantly greater than that of native-born Argentines. As immigrants often brought new technology and trade contacts with them, their distribution further benefited the East-Center region.[21]

President Alvear's 1924 policy of permitting unrestricted export of scrap iron and steel hampered the growth of Argentina's metal industry, as European producers bought Argentine scrap and sold finished products to Argentina at a lower price than that of Argentine manufacturers.

Support for tariffs to protect Argetnine manufacturers was strikingly weakened by British threats to reduce imports from Argentina. The threat was well taken, because half of Argentina's rural produce was exported (most of its meat was included in this amount); and 25 to 30 percent of its total exports were sold to Great Britain. Further, during the twenties the Argentines sold more to Great Britain than they bought from it.[22] Alternative markets were limited by increased tariffs in France, Spain, and Italy, and by the United States' prohibition of imports of fresh and refrigerated Argentine meat. The British attempted to recoup their trade losses by threatening to place tariffs on all goods coming from outside the Empire unless imports of British goods increased. Rural producers, in an attempt to maintain export sales, switched their support from protection of local industry to free trade; the Sociedad Rural Argentina adopted "Buy from those who buy from us!" as its slogan in 1927.[23] A British economic mission arrived in Argentina in 1929, and threatened to close British markets to Argentine goods unless President Yrigoyen promised trading concessions. The resulting agreement, which did not go into effect since President Yrigoyen was soon after overthrown, committed Argentina to buy nine million pounds of British goods in return for equivalent British purchases of traditional Argentine exports. Furthermore, Yrigoyen granted a 50 percent tariff reduction on yarn and cotton containing artificial silk imported from the United Kingdom. The British Ambassador said:

> In point of fact, we obtained nine million pounds of orders from the Argentine government which otherwise we had not the slightest chance of obtaining as our prices are too high. . . . In return we undertook to buy only a very small fraction of what we inevitably take. *In fact, we obtained something for nothing.* People in this country have not realized the extreme friendliness of the Argentine government in this matter. Again and again did the President say to Lord D'Abernon and me in the course of the negotiations, "I do not care at all about the details. I want this to be a great moral gesture towards your country."[24]

The tariff protection granted to manufacture from 1900 to 1929 was reinforced by exchange rate and exchange control policy. The exchange rate was roughly stable from 1900 to 1916.[25] The peso increased in value from 1917 to 1920, then depreciated until 1926. The high cost of foreign exchange from

1920 to 1926 combined with its scarcity in the early twenties to protect Argentine manufacturers from foreign competition. As British and United States prices rose faster than Argentine prices, protection of Argentine industry was greater than an examination of tariffs or exchange rate alone indicates.

Although Argentine industry was more exposed to foreign competition in 1920–21, than it was in 1914, tariff increases led to 1914 levels of protection in 1922. Protection continued to increase above the 1922 levels: the combined effect of Argentine tariffs and devaluation rose by 41 percent for imports from the United States and by 35 percent for imports from the United Kingdom by 1929.[26] Tariff protection, combined with an expanding Argentine market, led to a tripling of the rate at which new Argentine industrial firms were founded, and a sextupling of the rate at which foreign industrial firms entered Argentina during the twenties, compared to the rate that obtained during the prior two decades.[27] As a consequence, the importance of foreign firms in Argentine industry increased; new investment in Argentine industry (defined here to include mining and construction as well as manufacture), reached a high point of 18.9 percent of industrial product in 1925–29 (see Table 6.4). The productivity of investment in industry increased. As a result, the share of industry in gross domestic product increased from 11.7 percent in 1920 to 14.6 percent in 1930.[28]

Conditions in the twenties were more favorable for industrial growth than those in the thirties: the share of industry in gross domestic product grew more slowly in the latter decade, reaching 15.8 percent in 1940. The very slight increase in capital needed to obtain additional industrial output during the thirties indicates that growth during this decade largely reflected the use of excess capacity that must have existed during the twenties. This, in combination with the decline in industrial growth rate, casts doubt on the assertion that Argentine industrial growth "took off" during the thirties, stimulated by the shock of the Great Depression.[29]

The Great Depression increased the shift in emphasis of protective legislation from the level of protection to discrimination among trading partners in ways that would permit the

Table 6.4 Gross Fixed Domestic Investment in Industry as a Share of Gross Domestic Product Originating in Industry, 1900–1904 to 1950–1954

Years	(A) Based on 1950 Price Weights	(B) Based on 1935–39 Price Weights	(C) Column (A) Minus Depreciation at Replacement Cost, 1950 Price Weights	(D) Column (B) Minus Depreciation at Historic Cost, 1935–39 Price Weights
1900–04	24.7	14.2	12.7	9.8
1905–09	24.8	14.8	12.8	10.4
1910–14	25.8	15.0	13.8	10.6
1915–19	11.4	6.1	−.6	1.7
1920–24	19.5	10.7	7.5	6.3
1925–29	23.0	18.9	11.0	14.5
1930–34	15.0	8.0	3.0	3.6
1935–39	15.7	8.8	3.7	4.4
1940–44	10.8	5.9	−1.2	1.5
1945–49	18.5	12.1	6.5	7.7
1950–54	15.3	8.4	3.3	4.0

SOURCE: Ganz, "Problems and Uses of National Wealth Estimates," pp. 217–73; Elias, *Estimates of Value Added, Capital and Labor.*
NOTE: Industry includes manufacturing, mining, and construction. For a discussion of 1960 and 1935–39 price weights, see p. 90.

maintenance of international trade, and, with it, government customs receipts. Government attempts to maintain domestic output and employment relied on traditional methods from 1931 to 1935. Government expenditures were reduced and taxes increased in hopes of balancing the budget; the money supply was also reduced. The number of goods subject to duties were increased in 1931; Argentine tariffs were increased in 1931 and 1932, and began to approach the level of American tariffs (see Table 6.2).

Reductions in tariff rates were made when they were favorable to industry; for example, duties on crude fuel and diesel oil, and on natural silk intended for manufacture, were lowered.[30] The Argentine economist Aldo Ferrer notes that "devaluation of the peso and differential rates of exchange tended to create a gap between the prices of domestic goods and imported goods which stimulated the establishment of local manufactures, and quantitative restrictions also helped to do this."[31]

Villaneuva points out that many of the industrial firms benefited were foreign owned; foreigners were divided into those who owned local manufacturing plants and those who wished to export competing manufactures to Argentina. Thus, foreign governments would not necessarily oppose Argentine tariff structure in trade negotiations.

Argentines distinguished between the United States, which bought little from Argentina, and Great Britain, which was a more important customer. The difference in the tariff and devaluation policies on goods from the United States and those from Britain, begun during the twenties, continued during the thirties. An early example is that of reducing imports from the United States by placing sanitary regulations on the imports of apples (1931) and imposing a high duty.[32] Further difficulties arose in 1932, when American firms in Argentina feared that they would have to close because they could not obtain foreign exchange to pay for imports from the United States.[33]

Trade with Great Britain was favored in 1933, when Argentina reinforced its tariff policies with a series of preferential foreign exchange agreements, the best known of which is the Roca-Runciman Treaty of 1933. This treaty guaranteed Argentine sales of chilled beef to Britain at mid-1932 levels in exchange for assurances that funds arising from such sales be substantially spent in Great Britain. Specifically:

> Whenever any system of exchange control is in operation in Argentina, the conditions under which foreign currency shall be made available in any year shall be such as to secure that there shall be available, for the purpose of meeting applications for current remittances from Argentina to the United Kingdom, the full amount of the sterling exchange arising from the sale of Argentine products in the United Kingdom after deduction of a reasonable sum annually towards the payment of the service of the Argentine public external debts (national, provincial, and municipal) payable in countries other than the United Kingdom.[34]

A protocol to the treaty provided that no new or increased levies, or additional quantitative limitations, would be established on major grain and meat exports.

The treaty was buttressed by exchange controls, tariff, and loan policies favoring Great Britain. Tariff rates on British goods were either reduced by close to one-half the 1930 level,[35] or bound by a supplementary agreement signed later in 1933. Argentine industrialists, however, had time to lobby to ensure that vital Argentine manufactures were excluded from the list, as the Argentine government, in a protocol to the Roca-Runciman Treaty, bound itself to reduce duties only "so far as fiscal considerations and the interests of national industries permit." Finally, a loan was to be raised, the proceeds of which were to be used for repatriation of British funds blocked in Argentina.[36]

Exchange allocation agreements similar to the Roca-Runciman Treaty were signed with an additional thirteen nations by April 1937. Although these agreements made possible continued sales of Argentine agricultural exports, prices of these products fell by half. This is not surprising, since the prices of products sold in world markets are always sharply influenced by world income and price levels. Meanwhile, the prices of products sold in Argentine markets, and not exported, were either constant or fell less than export prices. Industry benefited more than agriculture from higher prices, and also from preferential allocation of foreign exchange for raw materials needed for national industries and for fuel.[37] Thus, although the physical output of agriculture increased during the thirties, the share of manufacture in gross domestic product nevertheless continued to increase, rising from 14.2 percent in 1929 to 16.2 percent in 1939. During these years, the share of agriculture fell from 26.2 to 24.7 percent.

During the thirties the Argentine government's policies continued to aid light rather than heavy industry, as foreign exchange was allocated for intermediate goods needed for existing industry; but exchange requests for the import of capital equipment were often postponed. Imports of industrial machinery and equipment fell from 13.1 percent of imports during the twenties to 10.6 percent of imports during the thirties, while imports of intermediate goods rose from 26.9 to 36.5 percent.[38]

These policies indicate the government's short-term outlook, which was brought about by day-to-day needs for domestic funds and foreign exchange. The policies also reflected both government ideology and the fact that much of Argentine industry was in the hands of foreigners. For example, the Roca-Runciman Treaty specified that 85 percent of the meat-packing business, the largest industry in 1939, be reserved to six British and American firms. As existing Argentine meat packers accounted for only 4 percent of the industry, the Treaty both sheltered and set a limit to future Argentine frigoríficos' growth. It was implied that the meat would be carried in British ships.[39]

The meat-packing firms used their market power to earn remarkably high profits during the early depression years: they averaged 12.6 percent annually between 1929 and 1934. During these years, the profits of (Argentine) estancieros, from whom they purchased meat, averaged 3.8 percent. Favored large suppliers of packing houses fared much better. Minister of Agriculture Duhau received an alleged 30 pesos per steer above average market prices; his average profits were 37 percent.[40]

The implication was that Duhau used his influence to aid the frigoríficos, which were shown, in 1935, to have falsified records to avoid tax payments and foreign exchange regulations. Moreover, the government permitted the foreign packers to keep as much as 25 percent of their foreign exchange earnings for their own use, a privilege granted no other exporters, including the Argentine meat packer.[41] The frigoríficos paid more for inferior Australian than for Argentine beef. Further development of meat packing would depend on the government's ability to separate the issue of foreign dominance from economic growth.

The second largest industry was construction: it needed little protection, and was largely in Argentine hands. The third largest industry was electric power. The Compañia Argentina de Electricidad (CADE), which served Buenos Aires and provided 50 percent of Argentina's and most of the city's power, was European-owned. A Swiss firm provided another 15 percent of the country's electrical power, and most of the rest was in foreign hands as well.

Under CADE's initial contract, its concession was to expire in 1957, and its installations to pass gratis to the Municipal Government. In 1936, the Buenos Aires City Council voted two (probably unconstitutional) ordinances: the first extended the concession until 1971; the second obligated the city to purchase the company's buildings, properties, and installations.[42]

The fourth largest industry was petroleum refining. Oil was first discovered in 1907 at Comodoro Rivadavia in Patagonia. This was exploited until 1915 as a government monopoly. Shortages of coal during the First World War, in addition to rapidly changing technology, made more rapid development of oil essential. Private firms were therefore admitted into the industry. In 1923, the government created Yacimientos Petrolíferos Fiscales (Y.P.F.) to carry out all phases of oil production. Y.P.F. increased its share of the market from 1929 to 1943, tripling production from 1930 to 1945. However, petroleum growth did not keep pace with Argentina's increased fuel requirements; the share of fuel and lubricant imports increased from 4.8 percent of total imports during the twenties to 6.2 percent during the thirties.[43]

The fifth largest industry, flour milling, was in private Argentine hands. Flour milling and cereal exporting was dominated by four firms which controlled 85 percent of the market. The firms also had international connections, which gave rise to allegations that world price maintenance, rather than expanded Argentine exports, was the main goal of these firms. One implication of this allegation is that since warehouse receipts, which they controlled and which were the basis of credit and money supply in rural areas, were restricted, Argentine credit and money supply was restricted because domestic credit needs were subordinated to international exporting interests. This allegation would follow whether or not the exporters were aware of the monetary implications of their export policy.[44]

The sixth largest industry, textiles, was also dominated by private Argentine owners. It contained many small and medium-sized firms, and was the industry where the largest fortunes were made.[45] Of the one hundred largest incomes in Argentina in 1941, seventeen were made by textile manufacturers and three by stocking manufacturers.[46]

This pattern of industrial structure, treaty obligations, ownership, and influence, partly explains the pattern of manufacturing growth from 1925–29 to 1937–39. Foodstuffs and beverages slightly increased their share of manufacturing from 36.6 percent to 37.3 percent, equal to 9.8 percent of gross domestic product. (These figures are BCRA; they show similar trends, but a different level from CONADE); electricity generated by public utilities increased at an annual rate of 6.7 percent from 1928–29 to 1938–39; petroleum refining grew from 1.6 to 4.9 percent of manufacturing (1925–29 to 1937–39); textiles production grew from 2.9 to 7.4 percent. More modest growth occurred in industries that benefited from protection incidential to exchange control, rather than from a policy of developing heavy industry. Production of metals increased from 4.5 to 6.4 percent, and vehicles and machinery from 2.9 to 5.6 percent, of manufacturing. Rubber products production began, *pari passu*, with the development of automobiles, and electric machinery and appliances with the growth of the electric power industry. On the other hand, chemicals, wood, paper and printing, leather products, stone, glass, and ceramics, as well as other manufacturing handicrafts, declined.[47]

To the extent that growth was concentrated in foreign-owned industry, it was politically suspect by Argentine nationalists and populists, who were also angered by the losses suffered by Argentine owned industry: 3,420 industrial firms and 13,031 jobs were lost in the northern provinces of Santiago del Estero, La Rioja, Tucumán, and Salta between 1914 and 1935.[48] These losses were as much the result of government policy as were the gains recorded by other sectors: the government taxed products produced in the North, but spent the tax receipts elsewhere. It permitted the importation of products competing with those of the North, but prohibited the export of a variety of crops which the North could have produced in order to maintain a low cost of living in the cities, and to maintain international trade.[49] Further, the policy of saving what was strongest, in industry as in the rest of the economy, without consulting small entrepreneurs or labor leaders, alienated a majority of Argentines.[50] Although saving the strongest appears reasonable to administrators, Argentines refer to the period when this policy was in effect as the infamous decade. Living conditions were not as bad as those of any period before the mid-twenties, but they deteriorated sharply in the early thirties.[51] Furthermore, estimates regarding real wages, living conditions, and investment patterns throw the argument into relief and support those who criticize the policies.

President Uriburu denounced the minimum wage law and other pro-labor legislation on December 14, 1930.[52] The government's attempts to balance its budget led to the firing of some 20,000 people from jobs in various ministries by October 1931, while total expenditure on public works was reduced.[53] From 1930 to 1934, in contrast to 1925–29, partial and full unemployment in the labor force led to a 34.9 percent increase in the share of strikes motivated by demands for higher wages, as compared to those for organization, a shorter work day, better working conditions, or other reasons. The strongest groups within labor concentrated on maintaining their own position, rather than on extending the benefits of unionization to less fortunate workers. The real salary of strikers was 19.9 percent above their 1925–29 level in 1930–34, but 9.3 percent below it in 1935–39.[54] Towards 1935, employment began to increase,[55] but the share of strikes for higher pay rose a further 23.1 percent in 1935–39, compared to the preceding five years. The loss of real labor income due to strikes more than doubled between 1925–29 and 1930–34, and rose a further 26.7 percent between 1930–34 and 1935–39. An examination of data for Buenos Aires, where unions were strongest, provides a minimum estimate of labor difficulties. It indicates a 2.9 percent increase in real wages and a 3.7 percent reduction of the work week from 1925–29 to 1930–34; and a 0.7 percent fall in real wages with a 4.6 percent fall in the work week from 1930–34 to 1935–39. Meanwhile, the population continued to grow. Take-home pay per capita fell 9.3 percent from 1925–29 to 1930–34, and recovered two-thirds of this loss by 1935–39, while take-home pay per capita as a share of per capita gross domestic product remained roughly constant (see Table 6.5).

The difficulties of the early thirties are underscored by the progressive worsening of social indicators when compared to

Table 6.5 Real Take-Home Pay Per Capita, 1925–29 to 1935–39

	1925–29	1930–34	1935–39
(1) Real wage rate	100.0	99.1	93.9
(2) Occupation	100.0	107.1	126.8
(3) Real take-home pay—(1) × (2)	100.0	106.1	119.1
(4) Population	100.0	117.0	123.0
(5) Real take-home pay per capita (3)/(4)	100.0	90.7	96.8
(6) Real GDP per capita (1950 weights)	100.0	90.5	96.8
(7) Real GDP per capita (1935–39 weights)	100.0	89.1	98.8

Sources: *Revista Económica Argentina* (March–June 1943) p. 218; Murmis and Portantiero, *Estudios Sobre Orígines del Peronismo,* p. 85; Randall, *Comparative Economic History of Latin America,* ch. 7.

the late twenties: the death rate, for example, increased 2.5 percent, infant mortality 7 percent, and the marriage rate fell 4.3 percent. Many Argentines judge their well-being by the amount of beef they eat: beef consumption per capita fell 11.8 percent, despite a fall in its real price of 6.4 percent. Since the decline in average labor income in Buenos Aires was not greater than the decline in income for the economy as a whole, the distribution of income among different categories of workers must have been unequal: few agricultural workers were organized, workers in the North and East of Argentina "were at the mercy of empresarios who at the same time were political chiefs, especially in the sugar mills, factories, yerba plantations and the mines."[56] On the other hand, trolley and train workers, municipal and commercial employees were heavily enrolled in unions.[57]

The abrupt reversal of the trend of improving conditions for workers during the twentieth century raises the question of whether oppression of the weakest groups of workers was actually of any benefit to the economy. It is sometimes argued that income should be shifted from the poor to the rich, as the rich save at a higher rate than the poor, and savings are needed for investment. But in Argentina, workers and entrepreneurs save at the same rate (see chapter 3).

Moreover, more than half of Argentine investment goods were imported during the thirties; under the 1930s exchange control, investment depended more on the ability to import capital goods than on domestic savings. The ability to earn exchange depended on the export of beef and wheat. However, increased profitability of agriculture would not have increased export sales and foreign exchange receipts because the fall in exports was due to marketing rather than supply problems. Thus, investment and industrial growth could only be increased either by aid to the Argentine capital goods industry, or, given the high levels of unemployment, by deficit spending by the government. Increased agricultural demand could come only through additional domestic sales.

It seems likely that if the anti-labor policy of the government had been softened, domestic demand for food would have increased, and it is possible that food prices would have increased enough to make it profitable to maintain production. This is plausible because a larger share of increased income given to the poor is spent on food compared to the share of extra income spent on food by the rich. A higher labor cost in the production of beef, which is not labor intensive, could have been more than offset by increased demand from all Argentine workers. Wheat production, which is labor intensive compared to that of beef, would not have benefited as strongly by such a policy.

The evidence indicates that the anti-labor policies of the early thirties were unnecessary to increase savings or investment, or to increase imports, and may have actually reduced agricultural profits and production. The policies, adopted through a combination of social prejudice and conservative economic theory, reduced popular welfare; reduced the growth rate of the share of manufacture in gross domestic product; and resulted in a real growth rate virtually identical to that of Great Britain, and below that of Japan, Germany, and Australia, although above that of the United States, France, and Canada. Moreover, during the late thirties, insufficient attention was given to stockpiling products unavailable in Argentina, which left Argentina once again vulnerable to reductions in international trade when war broke out. For example, the government refused to permit the import of machinery to distill alcohol from corn. During the Second World War, Argentina was not able to distill fuel from grain, which forced a wasteful burning of corn in cakes for heat and electricity.[58]

In 1937, 225 million pesos of bonds held in the United States were repatriated. During 1939, restrictions on imports from the United States were increased. Argentina built up its gold reserves, but lacked vehicles, steel, machinery, and replacements for existing equipment. The importation of these capital goods was made more difficult by Argentina's bilateral trade treaties. Because England was at war, it could not supply machinery and industrial raw materials, while existing agreements bound Argentina to purchase from England rather than the United States. England insisted that the agreements be enforced, and that sterling earned from Argentine exports to Britain not be spent elsewhere, although Britain could not provide the goods. Blocked balances reached 55 million pesos in 1940, and soared afterwards.[59] The Argentine government gave double permission to import: first from the United Kingdom, to fulfill treaty obligations; and then from the United States, to get goods.[60]

It is likely that the restrictions on U.S. imports were increased in 1939 as a bargaining point. An Argentine economic mission, headed by Raúl Prebisch, went to the United States in 1940. The mission failed in its attempts to get United States assistance to buy British owned railroads in Argentina, but succeeded in using its restrictions on United States goods to obtain tariff concessions on Argentine goods.[61] Two agreements were concluded: the first provided a loan of 60 million dollars to finance increased trade; the second created a 50 million dollar fund for currency stabilization. Argentina, however, postponed legislative action on these agreements.[62]

In October 1941, the first commercial agreement with the United States since 1853 was negotiated. The United States agreed to cut tariffs on items comprising 93 percent of Argentine exports to the United States; tariffs on linseed and canned meat were cut by 50 percent. Argentines agreed to cut tariffs on 30 percent of United States exports to Argentina. The United States agreed that the Argentine reductions would not take effect until Argentine customs rose to the average of the receipts of the past ten years.[63]

Argentina attempted to use trade regulations to promote nontraditional exports, although the practical effect of the policies was limited by wartime deterioration of trade. For example, in 1941, Argentina's trade regulating corporation told automobile importers that in order to get permission to import autos from the United States, they would have to use some of the proceeds they would earn for the export of nontraditional items. In order to avoid disastrous competition among themselves, they were told they had to form a corporation for this purpose, and to share the profits and import permissions in proportion to their share in the trade. The corporation was to receive funds by selling exchange for imports of automotive products at a higher rate than it received for the export of nontraditional goods. The funds were to be used to study the United States market or the market for various products, for the payment of subsidies, or for industrial studies in Argentina. Because of storage difficulties, the "plan waited for better times."[64]

Further attempts in this direction were limited by the breakdown of U.S.–Argentine relations, which shifted to hostility because Argentina remained neutral at the outset of the war. Latin American nations which were allied with the United States obtained money and equipment under lend-lease; Argentina did not.[65] Furthermore, in 1943, when Argentina was the only American nation in which Axis agents operated "with impunity," the United States Board of Economic Warfare utilized export controls to limit shipments of consumer goods, machine equipment, and transportation replacements to Argentina. Only materials essential to operate meat-packing plants, and to operate beryllium and tungsten mines, the outputs of which were sold to the United States, were exempt from controls.[66] United States attempts to persuade Britain to embargo Argentine goods failed. The British depended upon Argentine meat supplies, and the United States would not reduce its own meat consumption by the 10 percent that would be required to provide meat to Britain if Argentine supplies were cut off.[67]

The focus of Argentine domestic economic policy shifted following the coup by General Ramirez on June 4, 1943: shifts in political power and alignment were internal. The Junta reduced food prices and rent, raised public employees' salaries, aided Argentine "colectivo" owners (see the section on transport in chapter 7), and discharged much of the government bureaucracy. The relations between Argentina and the Allies remained strained; the war-engendered shortages of supplies reinforced military preoccupation with self-sufficiency. A policy of deliberate industrialization, combined with increased government control of the economy, began to emerge. The overall government economic policy was to improve the conditions obtained by Argentina in foreign trade by creating a state trading agency; to reduce foreign control of the Argentine economy by buying out some existing owners and limiting the action of others; and to improve workers' living conditions while assuring an adequate labor supply.

Although the program of self-sufficiency predates Perón's presidency, its sharpest expression is contained in his speeches, one of which is quoted in the *Plan de Gobierno, 1947–51,* published in Buenos Aires in 1946.

> We are not in any way enemies of capital, and it will be seen in the future that we have been its true defenders. It is necessary to discriminate clearly between that which is international capitalism of large consortiums of foreign exploitation and that which is national industrial and commercial capitalism. We have defended the latter and attacked the former without respite or quarter. International capitalism is cold and inhuman; national industrial and commercial capitalism represents, in our feelings, the worktools of businessmen. International capitalism is an instrument of exploitation and national capital is one of welfare. The former represents—for that reason—misery, while the second is prosperity.
>
> We are not enemies of capital—even foreign—which sticks to its business, but yes, we are of capitalism, even Argentine, which establishes itself in oligarchy to dispute with the nation the right to govern itself, and with the Government the privilege of defending the country against ignominy and treason.
>
> In 1810 we were liberated politically. Today we long to be economically independent. Vassallage for vassallage, I do not know which would be worse.[68]

The key to understanding the government's program was contained in its definition of national interest. The nation was to be self-sufficient militarily, and, as far as possible, economically. The government therefore established four entities to supply essential goods—Fabricaciones Militares, DINFIA, AFNE, and DINIE. This system included both special legislation and the creation of an Industrial Bank.[69]

At the outbreak of World War II, the Argentine government itself produced some strategic supplies: oil, electrical parts, and airplanes. Its range of production was extended when the government created Fabricaciones Militares in 1941, to produce war supplies and develop related industries. In practice, this became a broad program of production to replace imports. By the early 1960s, 20 percent of Fabricaciones Militares' production was for military purposes, and 80 percent for civilian use. The major industrial activity controlled by Fabricaciones Militares was a pig iron factory, Altos Hornos de Zapla. During the 1950s, this was the only plant of its kind in Argentina. When SOMISA, a mixed government and private steel firm, was founded and began production, the share of the Zapla plant fell to 10 percent of Argentine production. Fabricaciones Militares also produced arms and explosives, chemical products for manufacture of explosives and for industrial use, and electrical parts used by the state oil and electrical parts firms (Y.P.F. and ENTEL).[70]

An existing military airplane factory, which began operations in 1927, was brought under the control of DINFIA (Dirección Nacional de Fabricaciones e Investigaciones Aeronáuticas, formerly known as Industrias Aeronáuticas y Metalúrgicas del Estado), in 1952. DINFIA enforced industrial and air transport policy, taking charge of aeronautic research and manufacture, broadly defined to include related industries. Five kinds of aircraft were produced; in the early sixties, eighty airplanes were manufactured yearly. In 1952, DINFIA extended its operations to the automobile industry, first alone, and then in conjunction with foreign capital (Kaiser, Fiat and Goliat Hausa).

Military self-sufficiency was also promoted by the state shipbuilding industry, Astilleros y Fábricas Navales del

Estado (AFNE), which built ships and manufactured explosives.[71]

In 1947 DINIE (Dirección Nacional de Industrias del Estado) was created to run thirty-eight German firms, which the government had taken over as enemy property at the end of World War II. These firms produced metallurgical, textile, drug, chemical, and other products. DINIE later entered into the development of industrial policy, and was to adjust its acts to the aims of the second five-year plan. It was hoped that the state's experience in running these firms would provide it with an understanding of the conditions that industry faced, in the same way in which the Tennessee Valley Authority provided information about the electric industry in the United States.[72] DINIE was hampered in its execution of policy by squabbles over whether the firms should be returned to former owners, sold to private owners, or remain in the hands of the state. Investment was limited to key sectors, such as petrochemicals, distillation of anhydride alcohol, cement production, and production of alkalies (in areas outside of Buenos Aires). These firms began to be transferred to private ownership in 1957.[73]

In addition to directly owned firms, the government established mixed firms, joining government and private resources. The best known of these is SOMISA (Sociedad Mixta Siderurgia Argentina), which was created in 1947. The rules governing SOMISA demonstrate the preoccupation with steel as a military necessity. Although foreign supplies could be used and foreign credit was counted on to finance them,[74] enough Argentine raw materials had to be purchased to maintain Argentine mining production. Argentine prices were intended to roughly match international steel prices. Planning was placed under the direction of Fabricaciones Militares, which was the government's representative in SOMISA. The other partners were the other Argentine steel firms (Siderurgica). Capital was set at 100 million pesos, with 80 percent subscribed by the government, and the remainder by private capital. The private shareholders had to be Argentine. Each government share had ten votes; a private share had one. Private shareholders were guaranteed a minimum return of 4 percent. Sums in excess of this were to be paid into a reserve fund. The state was responsible both for paying the 4 percent dividend, and for covering any deficits.[75]

But the hoped-for foreign credits for steel were not immediately forthcoming, according to Gomez Morales,

> because the philosophy which existed in the prewar and immediate postwar period was that a country without a substantial resource base of iron and coal that could be turned into coke was not an appropriate one in which to develop an iron and steel industry. Today, the concept has changed because technology, means of communication and transport, etc., have resulted in countries lacking iron, such as Japan and Italy, achieving an efficient iron and steel industry. . . . More for political reasons than for anything else, right after the visit of Milton Eisenhower in 1953, the EXIMBANK gave us a credit for blast furnaces at the beginning of 1955.[76]

Coking plants were bought, and electric powerhouses constructed. The steel laminating plant of SOMISA was bought for cash, under optimal conditions. It was a plant ordered by the Czechoslovaks, which the United States had not allowed to be exported, and which was crated in the port of New York.[77]

The second best-known mixed society was ANATOR, created in 1946 under Fabricaciones Militares, which manufactures chemical products.[78]

The state also entered into production in the course of administration. For example, the Dirección General de Industrias de Madera manufactures furniture for public administration; the government also carries out auto repair and maintenance operations; the Sanitation Department laboratory produces coagulants and other chemical products for water purification; and government documents are printed by official printers.[79]

In 1960, just before SOMISA's production became important, state-owned and mixed enterprises produced 1 percent of Argentine industrial output. Most of this was concentrated in "metals" and "vehicles and machinery," accounting for 5 percent of the output and 9 percent of the salaries of these two groups. Industry as a whole, in 1960, produced 580,000 pesos per worker; metallurgy produced 411,000 pesos per worker.

The public enterprises, however, produced startingly less per worker: AFNE, 150,000 pesos; DINFIA, 210,000; Fabricaciones Militares, 220,000; and DINIE, 290,000. If workers in state and other enterprises had similar equipment, then the figures per worker indicate inefficient, less profitable operations of state enterprise.

The system of promoting industrial development through special laws and the creation of an industrial bank was more effective than direct state manufacturing production. The promotion of industries of "national interest" was established in 1944, and the legislation was in effect until 1957. Under its provisions, an industry could be designated as in the national interest if: (1) it employed 100 percent of Argentine raw material and its production was for the domestic market;[80] (2) it produced articles of basic necessity; (3) it produced goods needed for national defense.

Under the law governing industries of national interest, benefits were given to between thirty-four and forty industries, for periods typically of three or five years' duration, between the years 1945 and 1957.[81] In general, import substitution industries were designated as in the national interest and were protected by tariff surcharges of up to 50 percent; defense industries could obtain greater than 50 percent surcharges. National interest industries could be granted quotas on competing imports, to guarantee a market; and defense industries could receive subsidies. In some cases, special "facilities to get *permisos de cambio*" ("access to foreign exchange") were granted.[82] In some cases, tax benefits were granted. In others, special laws were passed governing, for example, such industries as automobiles (1944), steel (1947), tractors (1952), petrochemicals (1951), cellulose (1957), and internal combustion engines (1960). (An estimate of the effect of protection on growth is given in Table 6.7.)

The capstone of the system of protecting industries of national interest was the creation in 1943 of the Industrial Bank as a decentralized government body to finance industry and mining. The bank at first provided rising shares of finance going to industry in the late 1940s, increasing from 22.1 percent in 1946 to 78.3 percent in 1949; averaging about half in the early 1950s; and falling to just under 15 percent following the shift in banking structure enacted after the overthrow of Perón.

The bank was operated under conflicting guidelines. One was to encourage investment, while concentrating its loans among small- and medium-sized firms located outside of Buenos Aires. Since these firms were hard-pressed for funds for conventional business transactions, the Industrial Bank was increasingly pressured into becoming an ordinary commercial bank. Short-term loans rose from one-half to three-quarters of the total from 1946 to 1953.[83] The shift in composition of those loans indicates the difficulties that the Industrial Bank had in reaching its objectives. Credits granted to individual firms constituted 15 percent of the total in 1946, fell to 10 percent in 1949–50, and rose to 12 percent in 1952–54. Corporations received 42 percent in 1946–54. Regional decentralization of credit was successful: the share of Gran Buenos Aires fell from 76 percent in 1947 to 48 percent in 1954. While this share increased briefly following the overthrow of Perón, it again fell to 55 percent in 1959–63. Similarly, the Industrial Bank was an important source of funds for industries designated as "in the national interest."[84]

The Industrial Bank had been criticized for making loans for a wide variety of purposes, rather than concentrating its loans in ways that would result in greater economic development. Loans to finance investment fell from 34 percent in 1946 to 12 to 25 percent in 1952–57. Moreover, from 1944 to 1955, the food, beverage, tobacco, textile, and clothing industries received the greatest share of funds, although machines and vehicles also received "fully justified differential aid."

This policy shifted following Perón's ouster: metals received most Industrial Bank loans in 1958, and loans to the electric parts industry increased sharply. Credit allocation to each sector was uneven thereafter, although chemicals, paper, and print continued to receive less than average credit in proportion to their share of gross domestic product.

Industrial Bank policy is often evaluated using criteria suggested by theories of economic development. Under Perón, Industrial Bank loans were justified by an appeal to import substitution theory; after Perón, they were justified by their usefulness in increasing industrial capacity. Argentine analysts note that the impact of the shift in composition of Industrial Bank loans was lessened by the decline in the Industrial Bank's share of total Argentine credit.[85] However, the pattern of loan extension by the banking system as a whole coincided with that of the Industrial Bank in seven out of nine cases (see Table 6.6).

Since Argentine banks were nationalized, their overall loan policy also reflected government priorities. The level of loans to industry increased slightly from 1943 until the end of 1945, then grew rapidly until 1952, when the ratio of industrial loans to gross national product was about 7 percent, higher than the total for the United States (which again underscores the greater reliance on bank finance than on stock market or bond financing).[86]

An insight into government financial policy can be obtained by comparing bank finance as a share of value added by each manufacturing group (called the bank credit coefficient) to the average for all manufactures (see Table 6.6). According to this analysis, food and beverages were most favored before Perón's fall, but received average treatment thereafter. Metals excluding machinery received below-average treatment under Perón, above average thereafter. Electric parts, machinery and vehicles, and petroleum derivatives had consistently below average bank credit coefficients, although favorable treatment was promised by the Industrial Bank to foreign manufacturers of tractors and automobiles.[87] The latter industries were characterized by greater than average foreign investment. In general, these industries were favored by other techniques; Argentine finance, before the sixties, was directed to firms of Argentine ownership.

The main thrust of Perón's manufacturing policy was to change the structure of Argentine industry by giving industrialists incentives to produce goods that the government desired. A survey of 1,000 firms participating in the five-year plan indicates that 828 of them made profits of over 20 percent; the remaining firms broke even or showed losses.[88] National-interest industries fall into twenty-five categories. In thirteen cases, national-interest industries grew three times faster than the manufacturing industry as a whole from 1950 to 1955; in eight

Table 6.6 Bank Credit Coefficients for Eleven Industrial Groups 1950–1955 and 1956–1961

	1950–55	1956–61	Change
Food and beverages			
Overall	134.1	102.1	−32.0
Industrial Bank	92.6	92.0	−.6
Textiles			
Overall	99.1	114.8	15.7
Industrial Bank	168.9	165.3	−3.6
Leather			
Overall	77.4	71.3	−6.1
Industrial Bank	86.8	115.0	28.2
Woodworking			
Overall	86.9	98.2	11.3
Industrial Bank	114.9	130.7	15.8
Paper			
Overall	54.6	80.1	25.5
Industrial Bank	46.2	98.8	52.6
Manufacturing, excluding machinery			
Overall	88.4	115.8	27.4
Industrial Bank	121.8	128.8	7.0
Machines and vehicles			
Overall	93.8	79.6	−14.2
Industrial Bank	195.7	122.1	−73.6
Electrical appliances			
Overall	28.1	53.0	24.9
Industrial Bank		101.7	
Building materials			
Overall	73.8	81.9	8.1
Industrial Bank	103.8	96.1	−7.7
Petroleum and chemical products			
Overall	40.0	58.8	18.8
Industrial Bank	57.2	63.0	5.8
Various manufactures			
Overall	29.7	26.9	−2.8
Industrial Bank	6.4	13.9	7.5

Source: Altimir, Santamaria, and Sourrouille, "Los Instrumentos de Promoción Industrial," pp. 718–21, 898–900.

cases the declaration of an industry as one of "national interest" was made too late in the period to include the industry for comparison. In only four cases did the industry grow at below-average rates.[89]

Although Perón fell from power in 1955, the effects of the national interest industry program continued to be felt. Seventeen of the industries which Perón had encouraged grew faster than the manufacturing average from 1955 to 1969; national-interest industries' physical volume of production grew at more than twice the average industrial rate. Motors, vehicles, and machines, which had received preferential credit from the Industrial Bank, grew especially rapidly (see Table 6.7). Chemicals, plastics, and drugs, which grew faster than manufacture as a whole, received less than average access to Industrial Bank credit; their growth reflects the benefit of import quotas and tariffs levied on competing goods.[90]

Was Perón's success in changing the structure of manufacture achieved at too great a cost? The choice of industries protected, the level of protection, and the structure of protection have all been criticized.

Protection was granted to industries without regard to comparative advantage (see Table 6.8), whether on a current or long-term basis. When uncompetitive industries were pro-

Table 6.7 Protected Industries: Physical Volume of Output (1950–1969)

Year	Cellulose	Siderurgy	Motors	Agricultural Machines and Equipment	Automobiles	All Manufactures
1950	68.4	31.1	12.1	15.7	23.8	66.8
1951	77.3	35.2	12.1	15.9	24.5	68.6
1952	67.7	33.2	11.6	15.2	25.7	67.3
1953	61.5	34.2	10.6	15.0	26.2	66.9
1954	80.6	56.9	23.5	26.0	27.0	72.2
1955	95.8	72.0	27.9	44.4	31.7	81.1
1956	96.3	68.7	30.3	61.4	28.5	86.7
1957	102.9	76.9	55.5	73.3	36.8	93.5
1958	118.6	100.3	82.0	82.1	43.8	101.3
1959	118.5	89.2	61.3	77.7	42.8	90.9
1960	100.0	100.0	100.0	100.0	100.0	100.0
1961	126.3	124.2	146.0	88.8	141.5	110.0
1962	121.5	115.2	191.1	72.0	146.5	103.9
1963	120.7	123.5	244.6	75.2	119.4	99.7
1964	144.4	179.3	477.6	85.4	169.0	118.4
1965	184.0	199.9	469.6	88.8	200.8	134.8
1966	188.3	178.3	675.3	78.7	192.2	136.0
1967	165.2	191.5	572.5	72.6	198.3	137.9
1968	186.4	237.1	544.6	76.0	205.3	147.4
1969	205.1	255.9	750.7	79.8	251.7	163.7

SOURCE: BCRA, *Origen del Producto y Distribución del Ingreso.*

Table 6.8 Industries Singled Out for Differential Protection, 1945–1955

	Industries Receiving Differential Protection through Specific Enactments	Industries Receiving Differential Protection or Mentioned in the First Five-Year Plan
Advantageous costs or clearly favorable position with respect to foreign products	21	29
Satisfactory position	6	7
Varied position (some low and some high cost within category favored)	14	16
Somewhat high costs or unfavorable position	3	4
High costs; clearly unfavorable position	14	19

SOURCE: Schwartz, *Argentine Experience with Industrial Credit,* 1:119; based on 91 industries.

tected, Perón's policy was questioned on the grounds that greater output could have been obtained if investment had been made, instead, in industries that had a comparative advantage. This argument loses some of its force when one realizes that agriculture is often cited as Argentina's field of comparative advantage, and that sale of agricultural products depends more on foreign markets than other Argentine products do. As the sale of agricultural products was limited by other nations' various tariff and nontariff restrictions, it would have been difficult to expand the export sales of agricultural products, and to follow comparative advantage: production would have had to be either for the domestic or the foreign markets. Exports would have grown, in the view of Argentine businessmen, if there had been excess capacity,[91] and few foreign restrictions on such sales. The cost of protecting industries that do not have a comparative advantage is far less than commonly estimated, since, if protection were removed and the protected industry failed, the economic resources released in the process could not be employed elsewhere. This is because industries which had a comparative advantage were faced with a roughly saturated domestic market, and produced goods whose export could not be expanded.

The cost of removing protection is estimated by comparing real growth rates in the last five years of Perón's regime with the five years immediately following. The dismantling of Perón's trade and credit policies[92] led to a fall of 8 percent in the nonmanufacturing real growth rate and a 50 percent fall in the manufacturing real growth rate (see Table 6.9). (Indirect evidence which indicates that the fall in growth may well have resulted from reduced protection rather than from other factors is provided by the fact that Mexico, which had the least protection in Latin America, had unemployment rates estimated at 21 percent in 1970; while Argentina, with the highest protection, had unemployment of at most 10 percent in the 1960s. In Argentina, the loss of protection was accompanied by a fall in production that was not adequately compensated by the increased efficiency of production among the remaining activities.)

The level of protection placed on Argentine goods has been criticized, but that level is difficult to measure. *Ad valorem* nominal protection is protection on the price paid for an import. In practice, however, prices fluctuate, and nominal *ad valorem* tariffs are levied based on a price the government sets as typical of the product imported. As mentioned earlier in the chapter, the official appraisal price on which the tariff is levied is called an aforo.

The nominal level of protection increased from 1943 to 1948, but the use of an aforo system, which could not keep up with price increases, lessened its effectiveness. As Argentina

Table 6.9 Real Manufacturing Growth Rate, 1943–1955, 1950–1955, and 1955–1960; Six Estimates

Years	Central Bank	CONADE	ECLA	Elías	Schwartz[a] A	B
1943–55	47	79	65	80	133	137
1950–55	21.4	21.7	n.a.	15.6	39.9	42.2
1955–60	23.3	19.0	n.a.	14.3	20.7	25.2

SOURCE: Randall, "Lies, Damn Lies, and Argentine Gross Domestic Product," Appendix.

[a]Estimate A based on data for Argentina; B on data for province of Buenos Aires.

ran out of exchange reserves, restrictions on imports were increased, beginning in September, 1948. A shift in which industries were protected followed Perón's ouster, but the level of protection remained high. An American economist, Hugh Schwartz, argues that

> some notion of the level of protection that prevailed is suggested by an international comparison of import duties for the period after 1958, when most of Argentina's remaining direct controls were replaced by higher tariffs and surcharges. Argentine import duties exceeded those in all Latin America, and were far greater than in a reputed protectionist European nation such as France. . . . They were higher not only for durable goods and current consumer manufactures, but also for unprocessed foodstuffs, non-industrial raw materials, intermediate products and capital goods.[93]

The fact that tariffs were levied on imports of goods used in production is important because the earlier in the production process that protection is granted, the greater the cost of protection to a nation. Each industry using a protected input pays more than world price for the protected item. As a result, if it is not to suffer from low profits, it passes on the cost increase, and charges higher than world average price for its product. Consequently, protection against imports is also required for an industry using protected inputs. Thus, the high cost of protected inputs weakens the protection given to manufacture. The level of tariff protection, adjusted for the tariffs on inputs, is called effective protection.

It is usually said that the higher the level of effective protection, the greater the loss of a product to a nation due to protection. In cases where imports are limited and the protected product sells for less than the "aforo price plus tariff," the amount of effective protection is overstated. This appears to be the case of the most detailed estimates of effective protection in Argentina.[94] These estimates were prepared by an Argentine economist, Claudio Loser, and are presented in Table 6.10. They indicate that the effective protection given to Argentine industry rose from 46 percent in 1939 (113 percent if food and beverages are excluded) to 364 percent (or 538 percent) in 1950;

Table 6.10 Effective Protection in Manufacturing, Cost of Protection and Real Exchange Rate: 1939–1968

| | Effective Protection | | Cost of Protection | | |
| | All Industrials | Relative to Internal Value Added in | | Real |
Year	All Industrials	Except Food	Industrial Sector	Relative to GNP	Exchange Rate
1939	.46	1.13	.14	.017	1.02
1940	—	—	—	—	1.09
1941	2.02	3.00	.38	.045	1.15
1942	—	—	—	—	1.01
1943	1.87	3.19	.30	.044	.96
1944	1.84	3.28	.33	.045	.90
1945	1.82	3.00	.29	.041	.84
1946	1.69	3.06	.27	.040	.82
1947	2.94	4.69	.66	.124	.98
1948	2.85	4.34	.58	.110	.91
1949	2.98	4.63	.60	.106	1.01
1950	3.64	5.38	.51	.092	1.09
1951	2.84	4.16	.46	.082	.81
1952	2.49	3.39	.51	.097	.60
1953	1.86	2.50	.45	.082	.53
1954	2.46	3.22	.50	.095	.52
1955	2.39	3.13	.47	.094	.14
1956	1.51	1.93	.46	.092	.91
1957	1.37	1.88	.41	.087	.76
1958	1.42	1.87	.40	.088	.59
1959	.60	.78	.34	.072	1.16
1960	.72	.86	.36	.082	1.00
1961	.97	1.17	.40	.095	.92
1962	.78	1.03	.39	.088	1.15
1963	.72	.93	.35	.077	.88
1964	.74	.67	.28	.070	.79
1965	.79	.89	.39	.102	.82
1966	1.28	1.61	.48	.122	.93
1967	1.55	1.93	.41	.102	1.04
1968	1.27	1.54	.44	.113	.97

SOURCE: Loser, *The Intensity of Trade Restrictions in Argentina*, p. 51.

declined until 1953; rose through 1955; and declined to 60 percent (or 78 percent) in 1959; increasing to 155 percent (or 193 percent) in 1967. Loser calculates the cost of protection to Argentina as the percentage of protection applied to the total value produced within the nation. In Table 6.10 column 3 multiplied by 100 shows the percentage value added in protected sectors (excluding food and beverages) that is wasted; column 4 multiplied by 100 indicates the percentage of gross national product that is wasted because of protection, when no substitution in production is possible, and when it is also assumed that there are constant returns to scale, a constant range of products, and constant technology and skills.[95]

The estimates made on the basis of these assumptions are startling. Loser indicates that protection cost Argentina 1.7 percent of its gross product in 1939, 4.4 percent during the war years, 9.8 percent under Perón, and 9.1 percent thereafter, as the declining level of industrial protection was offset by the increasing share of industry in gross product. Loser's estimates should be reduced by about 4 percent for an undervalued exchange rate, and about 25 percent to allow for substitution in production. Further reductions should be made to reflect the fact that "the imposition of tariffs makes it possible to maintain the balance of payments equilibrium at a lower exchange rate ... than that existing under free trade." The lower the exchange rate, the lower the price of imports, and *pari passu,* the protection given by a tariff.[96]

It is unlikely that the cost of effective protection in Argentina was greater than 5 percent of gross domestic product. The estimates of effective protection in Argentina, before reduction, places them below those (possibly overstated) for Brazil and Chile in the early 1960s, when Argentine protection was below its postwar average. At this time, Argentine protection was triple that of protectionist Japan, and seven times that of lightly protected Sweden (see Tables 6.11 and 6.12).

The adjusted estimate of the cost of effective protection of 5 percent of gross domestic product is high, compared to that arrived at by an alternate approach. An American economist, Harvey Leibenstein, compiled estimates indicating that foregone production due to misallocation of resources ranges from .01 percent of gross domestic product because of monopoly, to 1 percent resulting from tariffs. On the other hand, a recent estimate of wastage due to monopoly in the United States reaches 6 percent of the gross national product, in part because it includes the cost of excess capacity in monopolistic industry.

Protection of industry is often associated with excess capacity in the protected industry. In Argentina in the early

Table 6.11 Average of Nominal And Effective Rates of Duties For Four Commodity Categories, 1962

	U.S.		U.K.		Common Market		Sweden		Japan		Brazil (1966)		Chile (1961)		Mexico (1960)	
	N	E	N	E	N	E	N	E	N	E	N	E	N	E	N	E
Intermediate products I	8.8	17.6	11.1	23.1	7.6	12.0	3.0	5.3	11.4	23.8	68	115	60	105	14	25
Intermediate products II	15.2	28.6	17.2	34.3	13.3	28.3	8.5	20.8	16.6	34.5	121	187	113	195	33	56
Consumer goods	17.5	25.9	23.8	40.4	17.8	30.9	12.4	23.9	27.5	50.5	—	—	—	—	—	—
Investment goods	10.3	13.9	17.0	23.0	11.7	15.0	8.5	12.1	17.1	22.0	—	—	—	—	—	—
All commodities	11.6	20.0	15.5	27.8	11.9	18.6	6.8	12.5	16.2	29.5	86	127	89	158	20	32
Net Protection[a]											47	79	13	54	10	21

SOURCES: Bela Balassa, "Tariff Protection in Industrial Countries," pp. 588, 591; Balassa, "Effective Protection in Developing Countries," pp. 307 and 315; Brazil, Chile, and Mexico; Macario, "Protectionism and Industrialization in Latin America."

Balassa's computations are based on the assumption that input coefficients are fixed in the relevant rate ($\sigma = 0$ for quantity). The same production functions were used for all countries, which Balassa justifies on the grounds that if the elasticity of substitution is equal to unity ($\sigma = 1$ for value), then a difference in relative prices does not affect the coefficients.

Basevi argues that effective protection should be measured by share of value added by labor rather than by total share of value added, as capital is mobile between nations while labor is not. In the mid-fifties, effective protection for the United States was one and a half times as high as nominal rates, and effective rates of protection on value added by labor were four to five times as high as nominal tariff rates. See Giorgio Basevi, "The United States Tariff Structure," p. 159.

NOTE: Tariff averages have been obtained by weighting with the combined imports of the five areas.

N Nominal

E Effective

[a]Balassa's estimates were constructed by adjusting for overvaluation of exchange rate compared to that which would have prevailed in a free trade situation.

Table 6.12 Over-all Tariff Averages and Standard Deviations, 1962

	Nominal Tariffs			Effective Tariffs			Uniform Tariff Equivalents
	Weighted Average	Standard Deviation	Coefficient of Variation	Weighted Average	Standard Deviation	Coefficient of Variation	
United States	11.6	6.9	.59	20.0	16.6	.83	16.7
United Kingdom	15.5	6.2	.40	27.8	12.1	.44	23.8
Common Market	11.9	3.6	.30	18.6	11.5	.62	17.3
Sweden	6.8	4.6	.67	12.5	10.6	.85	12.2
Japan	16.2	7.6	.47	29.5	15.6	.53	26.4

Source and Notes: See Table 6.11.

1960s, protected industries had greater idle capacity than the nonprotected ones.[97] Therefore, the efficiency of investment in protected industries has been challenged. When an investment is made, the investor has to choose between a large- and a small-scale plant. When economies of scale exist, the choice may be between a plant with excess capacity now, that will have a lower cost per unit when demand expands in the future; and a small plant which could be fully utilized now, but with higher costs than those of a large plant operated at full capacity. If the large plant is built, the unused portion ties up capital with no immediate return. If the small plant is built, it may be a high-cost operation in the long run. Finally, if new technology becomes available, existing plants may have to be scrapped, and a new plant built, if lowest costs are to be obtained.

Another aspect of the cost of protection is explored by Alain de Janvry, an American econometrician who analyzes the cost of protecting obsolete plant against competition in the case of an Argentine fertilizer factory. Writing in 1971, de Janvry estimated that if the government were to close the small fertilizer factory and compensate the owners, and then invest additional sums in bulk fertilizer storage facilities, the internal rate of return in one year would be 93 percent. Over ten years, as farmers responded to the availability of cheap fertilizer, the rate of return would be 622 percent.[98]

Impressive as these estimates are, the dominance of costs resulting from monopoly and tariff protection have been challenged. Leibenstein states that they are much less important than motivation in accounting for variations in output. He cites International Labor Organization (ILO) studies indicating that with existing capital, changes in labor productivity range from 5 to 250 percent in the firms studied.[99] Even when the manufacturing sector is only 10 percent of gross national product (which is below the Argentine level), an increase of labor productivity of 50 percent would increase gross national product by 5 percent, which is equal to the estimate of the greatest possible gain from removing protection. The gain from removing protection would, of course, have to be lowered by transitional costs involved in abandoning equipment in industries that fail under the impact of increased competition.

The cost of protection may have been harder to bear in Argentina than in the United States, because Argentina had a lower per capita income. Paradoxically, the heavy protection bill was directly attributable to Argentine development efforts. Newly protected industries had high import requirements, and accounted for 80 to 90 percent of the increase in Argentine imports between 1953 and 1960.[100] Even more oddly, duties on imports of products that competed with national interest industries were often below the average tariff, while duties on food and beverages were considerably above it.

The pattern of effective protection is not entirely consistent with earlier descriptions of credit allocation policy (see Table 6.13). The food and beverages, and agricultural industries show the same policy movements: although they had larger than average shares of bank credit as a share of their gross domestic product (bank credit coefficient), they received negative tariff protection under Perón. After Perón, their bank credit coefficient was slightly above average and they were accorded light effective protection (see Tables 6.6 and 6.13). These industries grew more slowly than the manufacturing average under Perón, reflecting both low income elasticities of demand and the probability that protection was more important to them than bank credit.

Textiles, paper, and building materials form another group. Under Perón, these industries demonstrated a below-average bank credit coefficient, combined with increasing effective protection. After Perón, their bank credit coefficient increased, while the effective protection granted them decreased. Their growth rate was below the manufacturing average under Perón, despite high income elasticities of demand for paper and building materials, implying that bank credit was more important than protection, and that both were more important than income elasticity of demand in explaining the growth rate. In the case of textiles, the slow growth rate is in part attributable to a low income elasticity of demand.

Wood, metals, machinery, and electric products were protected in the late forties, protection for wood and metal fell after the ouster of Perón, and protection of vehicles and machinery and electrical products increased from 1955 to 1958, falling thereafter. The bank credit coefficient of wood and metals rose from less to more than average levels between 1950 and 1961; that of electrical products rose but did not reach average levels. However, production of these products grew more rapidly than the manufacturing average under Perón, but declined to a level below manufacturing average thereafter, which implies that protection was more important to them than bank credit. This point is reinforced by the high income elasticity of demand for metals, machinery, and electrical products. It is weakened for wood, which exhibited a low income elasticity of demand.

The fall in protection of chemicals in the early forties, and of metals, vehicles and machinery, and electrical products in the late forties, is attributed by Loser to the fact that economies of scale, and the acquisition of industrial experience, reduced the amount of protection needed for these industries. Petroleum, with a high income elasticity of demand, however, was "disprotected": a low tariff on its inputs and a subsidized exchange rate, which made possible the import of competing products, resulted in negative protection. This is also true for rubber and related products. Petroleum maintained a consistently lower than average bank credit coefficient, but grew at faster than average rates from 1943 to 1955. Clothing, construction, and services were also disprotected, as there were high tariffs on their inputs and no protection on their products[101] (see Table 6.7).

The general pattern that emerges is that protection was more important than bank credit as a determinant of economic growth, and that income elasticity of demand did not, by itself, explain the growth rate by sector. Although the demand for mass-consumption goods other than food has been shown by Diaz-Alejandro to be significantly dependent on the wage share of gross domestic income,[102] these industries grew more slowly than heavy industry, which suggests that protection and credit allocation explain a larger share of growth than does income redistribution during the Peronist period. A detailed examination of the relationship of the wage share of gross domestic income to consumption is provided in chapter 3.

In general, effective protection determines the profitability

Table 6.13 Nominal and Effective Protection of Industry, 1939–1968

Year	Food and Beverages			Tobacco Products			Textile Products		
	N	$E\sigma=0$	$E\sigma=1$	N	$E\sigma=0$	$E\sigma=1$	N	$E\sigma=0$	$E\sigma=1$
1939	-0.01	-0.33	-0.12	—	—	—	0.27	0.87	0.57
1940–46	-0.13	-0.28	-0.24	—	—	—	0.29	0.71	0.66
1947–55	-0.13	-0.35	-0.15	—	—	—	0.78	4.07	2.33
1956–68	0.02	0.10	0.08	-0.05	-0.07	-0.07	0.50	2.05	1.26

	Apparel[a]			Wood and Products			Paper & Paper Board[a]		
	N	$E\sigma=0$	$E\sigma=1$	N	$E\sigma=0$	$E\sigma=1$	N	$E\sigma=0$	$E\sigma=1$
1939	-0.30	-1.00	-0.80	0.89	2.82	1.93	0.29	4.43	0.81
1940–46	-0.37	-1.00	-0.93	0.50	0.76	0.44	0.55	7.83	1.89
1947–55	0.17	-0.55	-0.17	0.35	0.53	0.38	0.65	7.61	2.66
1956–68	0.16	0.01	0.09	0.06	0.02	-0.05	0.36	1.58	1.15

	Chemical Products			Petroleum Products[a]			Rubber and Products		
	N	$E\sigma=0$	$E\sigma=1$	N	$E\sigma=0$	$E\sigma=1$	N	$E\sigma=0$	$E\sigma=1$
1938	0.30	0.73	0.91	0.14	0.10	0.09	-0.23	-0.25	-0.24
1940–46	0.49	1.43	1.72	0.02	-0.06	-0.06	0.04	-0.64	-0.30
1947–55	0.30	1.30	0.89	-0.10	-0.22	-0.20	0.23	3.21	1.26
1956–68	0.30	1.85	0.91	-0.09	-0.06	-0.06	0.21	1.37	0.75

	Leather Products			Building Materials			Metals		
	N	E	σ	N	E	σ	N	E	σ
1939	−0.04	−0.16	−0.13	0.38	4.92	1.44	0.12	0.00	0.06
1940–46	0.04	0.10	0.12	0.48	6.17	1.84	1.32	9.49	3.94
1947–55	0.06	0.22	0.24	1.02	12.89	4.32	0.76	4.45	1.70
1956–68	0.01	0.23	0.00	0.55	5.64	1.88	0.25	0.59	0.51

	Vehicles and Machinery			Electrical Machinery			Agricultural Products		
	N	E	σ	N	E	σ	N	E	σ
1939	—	—	—	—	—	—	0.02	0.04	0.03
1940–46	—	—	—	—	—	—	−0.33	−0.44	−0.42
1947–55	1.04	9.27	2.56	1.88	6.39	22.27	−0.25	−0.38	−0.35
1956–68	0.41	1.41	1.03	0.26	0.99	0.86	0.01	0.02	0.02

	Construction			Services			All Industries
	N	E	σ	N	E	σ	
1939	0.00	−0.23	−0.31	0.00	−0.03	−0.07	0.46
1940–46	0.00	−0.40	−0.45	0.00	−0.03	−0.06	1.84
1947–55	0.00	−0.24	−0.46	0.00	−0.03	−0.04	2.72
1956–68	0.00	−0.16	−0.27	0.00	−0.01	−0.02	1.06

SOURCE: Loser, *The Intensity of Trade Restrictions in Argentina.*

N   Nominal protection
E   Effective protection
σ   Elasticity of substitution
 [a]No data for 1940 and 1942.

of an industry, while bank credit tends to be allocated based on profitability. Where credit was available, but profits were limited, above average growth was unlikely.[103]

To a great extent, Perón achieved the economic results he desired. His enemies, who succeeded him, had other aims. Although their goals were clear, they underestimated the costs of transition from a statist to a free-enterprise economy. Thus, the best known criticism of Perón's economic policies was doctrinaire rather than technical. For example, on July 27, 1954, the conservative spokesman Federico Pinedo evaluated Perón's program, opposing it, arguing that "to me it is evident that if one wishes the Argentine economy to revive," the Argentine economy should be freed from regulation, more attention paid to the creation than to the distribution of income, and taxes on excess profits repealed in order to spur reinvestment of profits. Further, money should not be created in order to stimulate production; instead, financial instruments designed to attract funds to savings and away from current consumption should be introduced. Production should take place guided by the profit motive, not by the arbitrary decisions of government planners.[104]

Although Pinedo did not join the government until 1962, his attitudes were probably shared by much of the business community and by some of the military. Conservative Argentines sometimes say, in Pinedo's favor, that his actions during the thirties deviated from the above policy by reason of necessity; and they abjured government intervention in normal times. This attitude hindered the succeeding governments' ability to enforce economic policy decisions.

In 1955, the generals who overthrew Perón began to dismantle his economic controls. They invited Dr. Raúl Prebisch to analyze Argentina's economic situation. Although only some of his proposals were adopted, and he reputedly said in 1971 that they were formed without detailed observation of all the political sectors of the country,[105] his views are well worth studying. Dr. Prebisch's view of the performance of the economy as a whole was that "Argentina sought to increase consumption without sufficiently increasing production. National produce per capita increased only 3.5 percent during 1946–

1955, with the result that Argentina, in the effort to increase consumption, resorted to borrowing abroad and letting its industrial plant run down."

This inadequate production was in turn the result of the insufficiency of foreign exchange to pay for imports of fuels, raw materials, machinery, and equipment. Even if machinery were imported, it could not be utilized owing to lack of electric power; meanwhile, goods that were produced by the machines could not be transported because of the deterioration of the transport system.

The weakness of Argentina's foreign exchange position was attributed by Prebisch to insufficient investment in farm production for export, and to the insufficient development of import-substitutes, most notably oil.

Additional mistaken policies included the government's purchase of foreign firms (instead of encouraging the participation of foreign capital), the development of an excessive government bureaucracy, the exchange permit system, and deliberate inflation. Inflation was the result both of wage and salary increases in excess of increases in productivity in a number of sectors of the economy, and of the expansion of bank credit to cover deficits arising from surplus crop disposal, the transportation system, and mortgage credit operations.

Dr. Prebisch urged that Argentina's traditional exports (grain and livestock products) be encouraged by a substantial rise in the prices paid for them, which could be effected by a reduction of the overvalued exchange rates. New exports, especially manufactured goods, were to be encouraged, and imports to be limited to essential production goods by a system of import taxes on foreign cars and import priorities for transport and production goods. Argentina was to renounce its nationalist aversion to foreign capital, and to obtain funds from abroad to finance the needed imports, especially for the oil industry. It was to consider joining both the IMF and IBRD, and to avoid deferred-payment arrangements so as to reduce future pressures on the balance of payments.

Dr. Prebisch underscored the need for fiscal improvements, noting that taxes on consumption had increased from 39 percent of total revenue in 1946 to 46 percent in 1955. He wanted to reduce the regressiveness of the tax system and to introduce effective methods of collecting taxes. He also hoped to reduce the number of government workers by attrition, rather than by wholesale firing. Intractable problems, such as the mounting deficit of the increasingly inefficient government transport system, were to await technical studies. With the new military junta in power, Dr. Prebisch apparently did not think it wise to say what was obvious to foreign observers— that the size and cost of the armed forces should be drastically reduced.

Dr. Prebisch also recommended that the Argentine Central Bank be freed from direct control by the Ministry of Finance. It was to have full power to issue general directives and to supervise the operations of the banking system. Commercial bank deposits, which had been "nationalized" and taken over by the Central Bank under Perón, were to be returned to the depository banks. The Industrial Bank, which was under government control, was to become an autonomous development bank. Short-term debts were to be funded on a long-term basis, and the use of the Cédula Hipotecario (mortgage bond), which Perón had suspended in 1946, was to be allowed.

Within the framework outlined above, Dr. Prebisch had a number of specific analyses and recommendations for industry. These included vigorously initiating practices which would increase productivity, and encouraging new activities which would offer more solid bases for industrial development, permit the better use of resources and of market capacity, and which would bring with them, moreover, appreciable savings of foreign exchange.

The iron and steel, and allied metallurgical and mechanical industries were singled out for development. The products to be developed included special steels, Diesel engines, railroad wagons, tractors, small automobiles, and products of other mechanical and metallurgical industries. Other import substitution industries, which would permit an inexpensive reduction in the use of foreign exchange, were to be developed. They included the paper and cellulose industry (appropriate trees were to be planted); basic chemicals industries; and the petrochemical industry, which was to use gas byproducts of oil production to produce pesticides, plastics, solvents, and antiknock products. Productivity was to be increased by immediate improvement in methods, by education in the more efficient use of existing machinery, and by the import and manufacture of more productive machines. Mining output was to be promoted by selling exchange from the export of mining products in the free market, and by technical and credit aid from the government.[106]

The Prebisch proposals were criticized both on political grounds and because they neither established priorities among the various recommendations nor contained an estimate of the cost of implementing them, both of which would be needed for a detailed national development plan.

The post-Perón government incorporated at least some of Dr. Prebisch's recommendations in its measures to promote industrial development. The law governing national interest industries was replaced in 1958 by a law of industrial promotion, which the executive was to implement by issuing decrees. The government stated that it wished to create and maintain conditions needed to give security to an integrated development of industrial production. The government was to keep the following objectives in view: balance of payments equilibrium; use of actual and potential resources; industrial decentralization; the improvement, widening, and diversification of industrial production; improved techniques of productive processes; and the maintenance of national defense, health, and security. The government was empowered to lift import duties on equipment that Argentine industry could not provide, levy taxes or impose quotas on imports competing with Argentine goods, assign preferential exchange rates to exports of industrial products, allow preferential credit treatment for industrial development, grant preferential supply of raw material, energy, fuel, and transport facilities, accord preferential treatment in the purchases of government firms, and grant exemption or lowering of taxes for stipulated periods. After 1958, tax benefits replaced bank credit as the major promotional technique, which weakened the program because tax evasion is widespread. A national industrial promotion council (CON-

API) was also to have been established, but the Executive instead relied on two alternate methods of implementing the Industrial Promotion Law: special decrees for each industry, and special decrees for regions.

The decrees which supplemented the 1958 law favored the petrochemical, cellulose, automotive, and siderurgical industries, and the following areas: the Rio Chubut, Rio Colorado, Patagonia, the Northwest, and Corrientes. Beginning in 1955, contracts were signed with foreign petrochemical firms. In 1958, Y.P.F. decided not to manufacture petrochemicals, and sold its natural gas and other oil products to industry. In 1961, a general regime for petrochemicals was established. If its plans had been realized, there would have been excess capacity.[107]

The cellulose industry was helped by exchange reform. During the postwar period, cellulose imports were granted a preferential exchange rate, with the result that the price of cellulose in Argentina was reduced to roughly half that paid in the international market. Cellulose was declared of national interest in 1957, and in 1958, the preferential exchange rate was abolished. Production increased from sixty thousand tons per year in 1954–57, to more than one hundred thousand tons in the early sixties.[108]

The automobile industry was subjected to a special regimen in 1959. At this time, Argentine auto firms assembled cars using Argentine and foreign parts; they were to carry out some manufacturing processes within the limits set by the decree. Imported components were to be decreased from between 20 and 45 percent of vehicles, according to type, in 1960, to between 5 and 20 percent in 1964. No more than 60 percent of the final value of the automobile was allowed to be imported, and parts dealers could not import when Argentine components were available. Firms were permitted to increase production to 50 percent above authorized limits if more than 75 percent of the parts incorporated were Argentine; when the percentage exceeded 90, production plans would be approved automatically. In 1961, there were twenty-two firms (one for each one million Argentines), of which eighteen had filed production plans. Despite the backlog of demand for autos, this resulted in underutilization of capacity, high unit costs of production, and sales based on credit terms offered to buyers, rather than on diminishing costs of production. This led to an increase in finance charges, and a diversion of funds from capital markets to the financing of consumers' durables. During these years, tractor and engine production was encouraged. Auto production, and that of other national interest industries, is shown in Table 6.7.[109]

The steel industry was granted duty-free imports for plants operating under the 1961 law. In 1962, new firms (steel, cellulose, and petrochemicals) were granted import facilities (unless Argentine supplies were available) and tax benefits, including the use of rapid depreciation in computing taxes, and the reduction of the profits tax. The industries were also granted preferential allocation of supplies, and given preference in credit; cellulose was given a lower price on gas. Although automobiles, cellulose, and siderurgical production grew faster than average manufacturing production in the 1960s, the rate of growth was below that of the 1950s (see Table 6.7). An explanation of these events is provided in a study of businessmen's response to the 1958 industrial promotion measures, which indicated that according to a 1962 survey of 223 firms, only 32 percent of the decisions to invest were influenced by industrial promotion schemes. Within this group, 14 percent were based on financial aid, 12 percent on exchange benefits for the import of capital goods, and only 6 percent on tax benefits. In response to another question, the firms stated that the measures that induced them to increase investment were larger credit volume (21 percent), exchange and tariff benefits (17 percent), tax benefits (17 percent), and protection of industry (13 percent). Of the factors outside industrial promotion regimens, monetary stability was most important (18 percent).[110] The 1958 plan was modified in 1963 and 1964 by a general decree regulating industrial promotion.[111]

The poor growth record of industry as a whole in the post-Perón period cast doubt on the wisdom of the government's policies, despite the fact that the government succeeded in obtaining better than average performance from favored industries. Both the level and composition of post-Perón industrial performance have been criticized: manufacturing output increased 39.9 percent from 1950 to 1955, but only 20.7 percent from 1955 to 1960 (see Table 6.9). Moreover, recent manufacturing growth has been criticized on the grounds that there was too little regional diversification and too much unemployment. This was associated with heavy representation of foreign-owned firms, which applied capital-intensive technology, in rapidly growing activities.[112]

An additional criticism of direct foreign investment in Argentina is presented by an Argentine economist, Delfina Linck: direct foreign investment carries with it the obligation to repay the foreign investor in his own currency. Assuming that there are no changes in foreign exchange availability, and that the goods produced as a result of direct foreign investment are made from local materials, if sales of goods resulting from direct foreign investment are entirely directed to the local market, receipts will be in local currency. When repayment of investment is made, the demand for foreign exchange will increase, and, in the absence of a new supply of foreign exchange, the price of local currency will fall. On the other hand, if the goods produced as a result of direct foreign investment are exported, they provide the foreign exchange needed for repayment, and there will be few balance-of-payments problems. In Argentina, 87 percent of the sales of multinational corporations were to the local market in 1966.[113]

On the other hand, defenders of foreign investment point out that in the absence of direct foreign investment, balance-of-payments problems might arise if the goods which foreign investors would have produced were instead imported into Argentina, or if local firms manufactured the same goods at as high a foreign exchange cost for imported physical inputs and technology as that involved in foreign investment. Although no foreign exchange would be needed to pay local owners (as opposed to foreign owners) a local firm would probably have more difficulty than a foreign one in establishing foreign exchange export markets for its product.

For example, between 1938 and 1963, the most rapid rate of growth of nontraditional exports occurred in the metal industry, which had heavy foreign participation. Similarly, petroleum and gas, which had been developed with foreign participation, expanded their absolute value of exports considerably. On the other hand, sugar cane, chocolate, and tobacco exports also increased substantially in volume, although at lower rates. In general, the most rapid increase in nontraditional exports was associated with the presence of foreign manufacture of the product in question.[114]

Similarly, if foreign investment were made in an activity in which local capital would not invest, the presence of foreign investment would increase local income, and, with it, the demand for imports. On balance, many Latin American economists believe that over the long run, the foreign exchange costs involved in direct foreign investment, given the limited level of exports, are probably higher than those that the local manufacture of the same goods would have entailed.

The rhythm of economic activity is influenced by the willingness of banks to lend funds to industry. Foreign banks increased their share of Argentine bank loans from 16 percent in 1966 to 22.3 percent in 1970, a move which was viewed as a denationalization of investment decision making. The foreign banks' share of bank deposits rose from 31.6 to 40.5 percent during this period.[115] Foreign banks' lending patterns differed from the average pattern of all banks in Argentina. In 1970, foreign banks lent 3.4 percent more than average to highly concentrated industries, 11 percent more than average to moderately concentrated industries, and 26.4 percent less than average to lightly concentrated industries. As foreign firms were found largely in the concentrated industries, foreign banks apparently lent mainly to foreign firms. As deposits were made from the local market, this was viewed as diversion of local resources to foreign firms that would transfer profits abroad, rather than return them to the local market. The fact that lenders often found large loans to be more profitable than small ones did not reduce the force of this argument, especially as the share of profits remitted abroad increased from 40.5 percent of the declared profits of U.S. investment in Argentine manufactures in 1966 to 74.7 percent in 1970.[116] This implicitly limited reinvestment: foreign firms' share of output of the 100 largest firms in Argentina fell from 78.5 percent in 1966 to 76.4

percent in 1969, a share that was still substantially above the foreign firms' 60.1 percent of output of the 100 largest firms in 1956.[117] Moreover, overall concentration of production increased after Perón: the 100 largest firms controlled 18.0 percent of manufacturing output in 1956, 24.0 percent in 1966, and 26.2 percent in 1969.[118] Their concentration was greatest in the most rapidly growing industries. Foreign firms, which entered Argentina following authorizations granted during 1959–63, were more heavily concentrated in these areas than domestic firms, because of their easy access to capital and their control of new technology. As a result, both the number of foreign firms in the top 100 Argentine firms, and their share of manufacturing output, increased; the latter from about 11 percent of the total in 1956 to about 20 percent in 1969.[119]

Industrial concentration increased most rapidly during periods of credit contraction, when smaller firms could not obtain credit. Some foreign observers believed that the credit contraction was a necessary retrenchment following the adoption of a development program with foreign exchange costs that could not be met.[120] (Many Argentines noted that some of the contraction was associated with the advice of the International Monetary Fund, whose financial advisers were accused of giving advice based on the needs of their own nations' firms rather than on the welfare of Argentina.) Despite charges and countercharges, the developing concentration of foreign ownership stemmed from Argentine development strategy. Once a policy of import substitution was set, it was necessary to obtain the technology with which to produce goods previously imported. Either licensing agreements or direct investment were possible. Where the latter takes place, foreign penetration of the market is inevitable. Export promotion may have the same effect, if the government believes that only subsidiaries of foreign firms that export to the home country can obtain sales to the home country on favorable terms; for example, by lobbying for low tariffs.

The concentration of foreign firms in rapidly growing, capital-intensive sectors of industry gave rise to increasing political tensions. For example, between 1953 and 1963, real wages increased most rapidly in highly concentrated industries. Output per worker rose at an even faster rate, so that the real wages as a share of value added fell most rapidly in this sector.[121] The presumably efficient use of machinery therefore gave rise, on occasion, to fears for employment, and charges of exploitation. (Argentine economists noted that if United States industrial techniques were introduced to Argentina, there would be 40 percent unemployment, and Argentine industry was more efficient than any other sector.)[122]

As a result of mounting sentiment against foreigners, the government nationalized foreign-owned overseas telecommunications firms in 1969, reduced protective tariffs on automobiles and petrochemicals (foreigners dominated their production), and restricted foreign bank activities.[123] Yet hostility to foreigners continued. For example, in 1971, Buenos Aires' walls were plastered with posters saying: "I work, you work, for whom do we work?" followed by a list of foreign firms, and exhortations to vote for those who would do something about foreign domination.[124]

The National Development Council therefore recommended in May 1971 that the following steps be taken: the creation of a public body to sustain and expand the participation of national capital in manufacturing production; a "Buy Argentine" Law; a program for the scientific development and incorporation of new technologies in the productive process; a program of industrial reconversion; the creation of a National Development Bank; a program for the modernization of agriculture; the reform and decentralization of the educational system; a plan of public investment to develop economic infrastructure; the creation of a national foreign trade body; programs to reduce salary differences between activities and regions; tax and administrative reform; establishment of the basic foundations of national development and security. The Latin American Free Trade Association (LAFTA) was not mentioned in these recommendations; presumably, Argentine–Latin American trade was to be studied by the recommended national foreign trade body.[125]

The most important part of this program was the attempt to reduce differences of salaries between activities and regions: regional income inequality did not increase between 1946 and 1953, but increased 5 percent from 1953 to 1959, and a further 16 percent by 1961.[126]

Although both educational and investment policies helped, regional difficulties were intensified by the fact that money given to the outlying regions would tend to be spent on goods made in the East-Center region. A study of the location of expenditures indicates that

> Buenos Aires, Córdoba, and Sante Fe are almost self-sufficient: i.e. they are able to supply themselves with most of their own regional total demand. These provinces constituted some 80 percent of the entire country's interregional trade in 1959, and, if we add Mendoza, Entre Ríos, and Tucumán, we find that 87 percent of their total domestic sales take place within themselves. This situation clearly shows the high degree of interconnection existing between very few provinces, while the remaining ones are almost isolated from any trade-contact with the growing regions.[127]

The situation was exacerbated by protection of industries in or near Buenos Aires, which led to the high costs of industrial inputs for agricultural producers in the North and the West. For obvious political reasons, the government could not solve its regional problems by dismantling its protective system; instead, it could shift the impact of protection by locating protected industries in areas outside of Buenos Aires and promoting the export of products manufactured in the interior. The timing of the adoption of such policies reflected the fact that whenever unemployment in Córdoba and Rosario increased in the sixties, political violence rose sharply. Amelioration of provincial conditions tended to follow stepped up guerrilla activities. For example, from 1968 to 1971, per capita investment in Patagonia (Chubut, Santa Cruz, and Tierra del Fuego) was almost five times, and in Comahue (Rio Negro, Neuquén, and La Pampa) three and one-third times greater than the national average; while investment in East-Center (except for the capital) was about one-third below it.[128]

Employment and welfare, as well as narrower definitions of profitability, were included in government investment decisions. Although Argentine protection of industry is often criticized because it results in high-cost goods, if the higher prices paid for industrial inputs is taken into account, we can see that

Argentine industrialists are efficient,[129] and that they made adequate provision for growth from 1900 to 1914, 1925 to 1929, and from 1945 to 1949: net domestic capital formation was positive throughout the twentieth century, except for World War I and World War II, when it was extremely small, or negative, because imported supplies were unavailable. From 1950 to 1954, capital formation was limited by the extraordinary rise in the cost of investment goods; in 1950 the ratio of investment prices to average prices was almost three times the 1935–39 ratio.

It is likely that Argentine industrial policy in the seventies will reflect the profitability of industrial firms, the effect of industrial policies on other economic and regional sectors, and the changing views of appropriate balance between domestic and foreign ownership. The government is likely to focus on changes in the structure of protection, to include employment and regional considerations in reaching its decisions, and to change conditions governing foreign investment.

Chapter Seven: Railroads and Oil

We do not need to go to England to find railway directors
as one would go in search of a pure-blooded Durham bull.
Buenos Aires legislator.

GOVERNMENT POLICY GOVERNING the railroad and the
petroleum industries has been sharply debated throughout the
twentieth century, both because these businesses were characterized by the presence of foreign capital in a semi-monopoly
position, and because limits on the provision of services of
either sector could seriously hamper the rest of the economy. In
the case of railroads, this was because little road transport
existed before 1930, and in the case of petroleum, because there
existed only limited alternative sources of power.

In the nineteenth century, economic nationalism focused
on increasing Argentine economic power, in part by using
foreign factors of production. Favorable treatment of railroads
was part of a policy of creating a favorable investment climate
for all Argentine projects. Railroads were especially important;
they accounted for about 10 percent of Argentine wealth in
1916; from 1915 to 1919 railroad income was greater than that
of the national government.[1] The very size of the railroads, as
well as their poor performance, led to a shift in Argentine
attitudes: twentieth-century economic nationalism increasingly centered on establishing Argentine control over the
economy.

If Argentina had been a colony, railroads might have been
provided by the metropolitan government, without requiring

payment in foreign exchange for investment. The transfer of railroad technology, and of technicians from the home country, would have been a normal event. In the mid-nineteenth century, however, although Argentina could not provide railroads without foreign help, Argentine railways were considered an essential element of the Argentine nation. For example, Juan Bautista Alberdi, whose book strongly influenced the Constitution of 1853, wrote "Railways will bring about the unity of the Argentine Republic better than any number of Congresses. Congress will be able to declare that it is one and indivisible; but without railways, which will draw the remote extremes close together, it will always remain divisible and divided despite all legislative decrees."[2] The Constitution of 1853 consequently gave Congress the power to promote the construction of railroads.[3] As Argentine private investors were uninterested in railroad investment, the first Argentine railroad was financed by the Province of Buenos Aires, which paid one-third of the cost and provided a free right of way.[4] It built the line with the aid of 160 British workmen, and, as expected, imported the locomotive, rolling stock, and tracks from England.[5]

During the 1860s, British capital accounted for the building of two of Argentina's railways, the Central Argentine and the Great Southern, although disagreements between United States and British interests led to a delay in railroad construction. The foreign investors agreed to build lines where the state wished, while the government guaranteed minimum profits.[6] By 1870, more than half of Argentine railway mileage was owned by foreigners (see Table 7.1). A general law governing railroads was passed in 1872. It provided that railroads construct and maintain electric telegraphs along the entire road; transport mail without charge, and soldiers at half the lowest rate; give precedence to the transport of daily provisions for towns linked by the railroad, to passengers' packages not exceeding fifty kilograms, and to objects that the national or provincial government declared urgent. Rates charged were to be equal for all customers, including reductions for all bulk shipments or longer delivery time. All materials needed for the construction and operation of railroads were free of import

Table 7.1 Argentine and Foreign Railroad Lengths, and Percent Distribution, 1857–1960

Year	Government and Private Argentine Railroads (in km)	Percent of Total	Foreign Railroads (in km)	Percent of Total	Total
1857	10	100.0	—	0	10
1860	40	100.0	—	0	40
1865	249	100.0	—	0	249
1870	287	64.5	445	35.5	732
1880	436	17.3	2,080	82.7	2,516
1890	922	9.8	8,510	90.2	9,432
1900	2,016	12.2	14,547	87.8	16,563
1910	3,490	12.5	24,503	87.5	27,993
1920	4,916	14.5	28,968	85.5	33,884
1930	7,853	20.6	30,269	79.4	38,122
1940	12,685	30.7	28,598	69.3	41,283
1946	41,600	100.0	—	0	41,600
1949	42,838	100.0	—	0	42,838
1950	42,865	100.0	—	0	42,865
1955	43,952	100.0	—	0	43,952
1960	43,956	100.0	—	0	43,956

SOURCE: Defilipe, *Geografía Económica Argentina*, p. 257.

duties, and railroad constructions needed to maintain operations were exempt from tax, while provincial governments would not tax railroads constructed or guaranteed by the national government.[7]

Argentine experience under this law provides the background for understanding twentieth-century railroad legislation: in practice, the railroads did not provide the services agreed to, and as a result, Argentines resented guarantee payments. The government of Buenos Aires–owned Oeste railroad made profits, so many Argentines believed that government ownership would assure better operation of the railways at lower costs. In the late 1870s, President Avelleneda refused to continue paying guarantees to companies that did not check their expenditures.

Although the railroads operating in Buenos Aires were self-liquidating, they were resented because they did not provide sufficient rolling stock to move grain quickly at harvest, and there were no adequate bulk storage or harbor facilities to ease shipment to domestic and foreign markets. All privately owned railroads were attacked: those that were profitable because they apparently made excessive profits from high freight rates, and the others because they relied on guarantees paid by the government but deliberately failed to provide proper service.[8] In a famous case, the Central Argentine railroad refused to pay sums it owed the government under its concession, which guaranteed it an annual profit of 7 percent on an estimated value of 6,400 pounds sterling per mile. But it also stipulated that whenever profits exceeded that amount the railway would reimburse the government for the guarantees paid to it in the past. When that contingency occurred, the directors of the Central Argentine simply refused to pay. When the government insisted, the directors stopped the flow of freight. They also refused to put further capital investment into the important arterial routes across the northern Pampas. Frank Parish, then chairman of both the Central Argentine and the Great Southern, demanded that the government cancel the debt. At the same time, he asked to have the guarantee terms dropped from the company's concession. Then, through clever book work, the Central Argentine eliminated its past obligation to the government by raising its capital value by the amount of the debt.[9]

Despite calls for expropriation, advocates of laissez faire were were in power. Argentine economic development still required massive funds; it was easy to play on fears that reduced handouts to railroad investors would scare away all foreign investment. Further, new construction in thinly settled areas could pay for itself only after many years. As had also happened in the United States in similar circumstances, the government provided funds, land, and exemption from import duties to a private railroad to extend its lines. In contrast to the United States, however, the railroad owners were foreign.[10]

Moves towards a unified railroad system took place in fits and starts. The Province of Buenos Aires sold the Oeste to British interests in 1889, avoiding competition with the Southern, giving the British a railroad monopoly in Buenos Aires, and reducing the government-owned railroad mileage to roughly 10 percent of the total.[11] On the other hand, the government maintained its ownership of the less profitable

Andean line until 1909. This fit a pattern of ownership that prevailed between 1890 and the First World War, when several sales and transfers of railroad ownership established a unified railroad network. The government purchased railroads in the North, and extended the tracks of its lines, especially in the southern Territories. It also sold State railroad lines serving the same areas as the British companies.[12] The effect of these transfers of ownership was first a decline in the government share of railroad mileage in the 1880s, and then a gradual increase through the twentieth century, culminating in the purchase of all foreign-owned railroads after World War II (see Table 7.1).

Although the railroads owned by the government were built through the least settled areas, they increased government revenues, providing about 1 percent of general revenues in 1889, a figure that had risen to 4.6 percent by 1908. In addition, the increase in economic activity associated with the development of railroads led to an increase in tax receipts.[13] Private firms, which obtained the most profitable railroads, were increasingly held accountable for their performance. Guarantee payments to the East Argentine Railroad Co. were suspended in 1889 until the line complied with the law. The status quo was reinforced in other respects in 1891 by new railroad legislation, which largely restated existing laws and concessions, and did not place private railroads under uniform legislation. The law permitted reduced rates for large shipments, and followed a familiar pattern of protecting large Argentine producers against foreign operators, but ignoring the needs of smaller farmers (see chapter 5).

The guarantee problem was settled in two stages. In 1895, the size of guarantee payments was reduced when railroads lowered their fixed costs. In 1907, the Ley Mitre (Mitre Law) established a uniform code for Argentine railroads. The law abolished guarantee payments, and replaced them with a forty-year exemption from duty on all equipment and materials imported by the railroad companies. The railroads, in turn, were to pay an annual tax of 3 percent of their profits, for the purpose of constructing and maintaining feeder roads to railway stations and ports. The government was given the right to interfere in rate fixing whenever a company earned profits greater than 17 percent for three consecutive years, providing that the company's operating expenses did not exceed 60 percent of gross income. Salera states:

> given the 60 percent maximum operating expenditure provision, the 17 percent gross return reduces to 10.2 percent as costs, leaving 6.8 percent as the maximum annual net income which might be earned for any three consecutive years without penalty of rate reductions. . . . In those cases in which it was considered that a three-year average annual net return on capital would exceed 6.8 percent, the railways would invariably undertake various types of construction activity by incurring service and equipment costs bestowing sizeable net benefits upon concerns having direct and indirect holdings in the railroads themselves.[14]

The railroad owners believed that the law gave them the right to raise rates without government permission whenever profits fell below 6.8 percent for three consecutive years.

The Mitre Law sparked new railroad construction at a rate of 1,100 miles per year from 1907 to 1914. The terms were agreeable to foreign capital: the companies had the option of accepting or rejecting the terms of the Ley Mitre until their original concessions ran out. All of the British-owned firms opted for the new law. The profits made were declared at 4 to 5 percent of capital from 1908 to 1913, falling to 2.44 percent by 1917. The profit rates would have been somewhat higher had the government lines been excluded from the calculations.

Despite the real difficulties of the war years, the estimates reflect transfer pricing and other accounting practices used to keep profit estimates low enough to avoid government intervention in freight rates.[15] As scandals in accounting and other practices of both government and private railroads were uncovered at various points in their history, it is difficult to pass judgment on their comparative efficiency (or their other merits), although Scalabrini Ortiz presents evidence for 1939–40 that shows lower unit costs, and higher profits in 1941–42 for the government than for the private railroads.[16] The debate over railroad policy was carried out on political grounds, since much of what was criticized would occur under any "natural monopoly."

The Argentine economic historian Ricardo M. Ortíz attempted to evaluate the economics of the Ley Mitre. He argued that from 1908 to 1945, goods imported duty-free under its provisions amounted to 838 million gold pesos (equal to 463 million paper pesos) in revenue. The railroads, however, paid tax on only 3 percent of their income, which yielded 120 million paper pesos. If the railroads had paid duty on imports and no income tax, the increased government tax receipts would have financed 6,000 kilometers of six-meter-wide concrete roads. Similarly, exemption from other taxes brought the total foregone government income to 15 million paper pesos per year. The tax payments made by the railroads, mentioned above, came to about 3 million pesos per year.[17]

The Argentine railroad network was extended under the Ley Mitre. However, the construction was criticized on the grounds that some of it was an unnecessary duplication of track constructed as competition between different lines. Other construction was criticized on the grounds that it created feeder lines through territory already served by the railroad, rather than trunk lines through territory that did not yet have railroads. Ortíz also criticized the Ley Mitre because the private railroads were consolidated into four large blocks under its provisions.[18]

Finally, Ortíz criticized the rate pattern set by the railroads. In one case, the Ferrocarril Provincial railroad in the Province of Buenos Aires lowered the freight rate on corn because of low prices during the worst part of the economic crisis of the thirties. The other private railroads appealed for a rate increase on the grounds that the lowered rates would increase the Ferrocarril Provincial's zone of influence at the expense of their own. Regarding ship and railroad competition, freight rates from river ports to the port of Buenos Aires were lower than shipping rates to the port, but higher between areas linked by land (not river) or ports without steamship facilities to Buenos Aires.[19] Argentine railroad practices were thus as unpopular as those of North American railroads at the same stage of economic development.

Although the Argentines did not succeed in forming a lobby as powerful as the Granger movement in the United States, the government's railroad policy nonetheless was carried out against a counterpoint of opposition. One nationalist charged that the [British-owned] railroads, instead of strengthening Argentina, would turn it into another Ireland. A member of the Chamber of Deputies from Sante Fe stated that Argentine protests against the sale of the Andino were in vain, because "greater than the voice of the deputies: greater than the stock exchange: greater than the counsel of the administrators of this railway: greater than the advice of the Minister and of the Congress of the nation, has been the omnipotent, preponderant, authoritarian will of the English."[20]

The U.S. historian Winthrop Wright argues that "the climate of opinion became increasingly anti-foreign after 1910 . . . [and advocated] nationalization of the railways. . . . But the nationalistic expression of politicians, workers and the press lacked direction. They contained as much anti-monopolistic content as anti-British feelings."[21]

The relations between the British railroad owners and the Argentines worsened during World War I; a disruption of the world economy coincided with the presidency of Hipólito Yrigoyen, an opponent of the traditional ruling class. The railroads had appointed members of the Argentine elite to their Board of Directors; these were personae non gratae with Yrigoyen. The firms made major decisions in London, and the Argentines felt snubbed. At the same time, the railroads wanted economic help from the Argentines. The world war had led to a reduction of railroad traffic, and to difficulty in obtaining funds and equipment from Great Britain. In addition, strikes resulted in reduced hours and a larger labor force.

The railroad management requested an increase in freight rates, which had lagged behind prices,[22] and cited annual profits averaging 3.5 percent from 1915 to 1919. Under the Ley Mitre, they claimed, they had theright to raise rates. The government countered that the low profit estimates were based on calculations that included watered stock. The government therefore refused to recognize large quantities of common stock, thereby reducing the capital value of the railroad, which was the base on which profits were calculated. As a result, profit estimates increased, which limited the companies' ability to change freight rates without government interference. The increase in freight rates was granted in 1922, just before Yrigoyen left office: at any earlier date, it would have been impolitic to antagonize Argentine voters for the mere benefit of foreign owners.[23]

Controversy between the British and Argentine governments over the railroads next took the form of a contest over the control of decision making. Shortly after President Alvear took office, he learned that a proposed British loan stipulated that if it were used for Argentine-owned railroad construction, the railroad lines could not be placed where they could compete with established British companies. The president stated that Argentina was not a British colony, and took steps to seek a loan from other sources. The British dropped the stipulation.[24] Nonetheless, Alvear believed that Argentina was dependent on world markets: "Like it or not, we are dependent upon England, we perpetuate France, we are able to trade with the U.S., and it is not worth the consequences to change the prosperity of the country through lyrical words . . . that do not have any juridical effect, and that would only earn us the bad will of the countries that have been victorious in a tremendous war."[25]

As the world economy began to recover during the postwar period, so did the railroads. Annual profits averaged 5 percent between 1921 and 1928. The railroad companies completed feeder routes to trunk lines, but did not undertake major expansion, which was concentrated in the government railroad system. Because railroad profits depended on the nation's economic growth, rather than on guarantee payments, the railroad companies worried increasingly about the decline in grain production. They estimated that "for every pound sterling they received for carrying grain to a port, they received another in return freight on a great number of articles needed to sustain the large grain-producing populations. It took few men to raise cattle, and the men who tended the *estancias* had few wants and little capital, therefore cutting down the amount of important return trade."[26] Presumably, the remainder of the foreign exchange earned was spent in Buenos Aires or abroad.

The railroads and the national government cooperated in encouraging agricultural development by establishing educational and agricultural extension services, and by establishing a land colonization consortium. Nothing appears to have been done to provide grain elevators.

The economic impact of the agrarian programs was small; the psychological impact reduced Argentine hostility to the railroads, while corruption in the [government-owned] lines left the public with few palatable alternatives to foreign capital.[27]

Britain's unfavorable balance of trade with Argentina influenced the management of Argentine railroads. While U.S. manufacturers had been the largest suppliers of railroad equipment to the state-owned railroads since the turn of the century, the British-owned lines relied exclusively on British supplies. In 1929, in order to maintain the British market for Argentine meat and cereal, Argentina signed the D'Abernon Trade Pact, which included a "reciprocity credits system," by which the state-owned railways could purchase equipment from British manufacturers without calling for open bids on the contracts, as stipulated by law, despite the fact that British equipment was more expensive than that of their Belgian, United States, and German competitors.[28]

British gains were smaller than the agreement indicated. As the depression worsened, Argentina restricted the transfer of funds abroad and set unfavorable exchange rates, bringing complaints from British investors in Argentine rails. They received no dividends; in fact, the value of their stocks fell.[29] The 1933 Roca-Runciman agreement contained two provisions which affected the British-owned railroads: the first maintained the duty-free import of coal, while the second declared:

the Argentine Government, fully appreciating the benefits rendered by the collaboration of British capital in public utility and other undertakings, whether State, municipal, or private, carrying on business in Argentina, and following their traditional policy of friendship, hereby declare their intention to accord to those undertakings, as far as lies within their constitutional sphere of action, such benevolent treatment as may conduce to the further economic development of the country, and to the due and legitimate protection of the interests concerned in their operation.[30]

Salera wrote that this provision appeared to have been insisted upon by Mr. Runciman:

principally with a view to (1) providing a basis for obtaining the most favorable remittance terms for British railways in the event of further peso depreciation and/or currency manipulations; (2) softening the impact of labor legislation upon the cost position of the railways by linking such action directly with the expected functioning of the Roca pact, and (3) providing a precedent for use in a future in which the relative importance of trade and capital aspects of Anglo-Argentine commercial bargaining may have shifted markedly to the latter.[31]

The British received less benevolent treatment than they had hoped for, but more than many observers thought they deserved. Under the exchange control measures announced on November 28, 1933, the government established a profitable spread between its buying and selling rate. The railways were permitted to buy pounds at 16 pesos per pound sterling, compared to the average rate of 17. The peso cost of pounds sterling had risen by 25 percent during 1933; the railroads complained that the difference between the old parity rate and the new government selling rate was an unjust tax which caused them an exchange loss.[32] This loss was used in calculating profits under the Ley Mitre by revaluing downward all—not just current—assets. Exchange profits had not been calculated during earlier periods when the peso had appreciated. Their inclusion was severely criticized, as were earlier episodes of juggling books.

The railroads asked for a rate of 15 pesos per pound sterling. In 1936 they obtained a rate of 15.75 pesos in exchange for a 10 percent reduction in the freight rate on corn. The government stipulated that remittances at the new rate could not exceed the sum transferred on the same account in 1935. A current estimate was that the four largest railroads would lose 3,500,000 pesos because of reduced freight rates, and gain 13,000,000 from the change in exchange rates.[33] In exchange, the companies were to represent the views of the Argentine government in the forthcoming negotiations to renew the Roca-Runciman Treaty. The railroads were told they could expect reprisals if the treaty negotiations failed.[34]

In a related development, the Argentine government purchased the financially weak, British-owned Córdoba Central Railway, for 10 million pounds sterling,[35] a sum equal to 53 percent of its nominal value. However, although the value of the railroad's stocks and bonds had risen due to the expected sale of the line, ordinary shares traded at 2 percent of nominal value, and debentures at 30 percent of par. In addition, Congress granted a wage subsidy of 1,500,000 pesos for the road, and absorbed its deficit of 5,000,000 pesos before the government purchased it. Odd accounting practices further helped the British investors to arrive at a high estimate of nominal value. The acquisition of the Córdoba Central more than doubled the length of the government railways,[36] and gave the government-owned railroads a direct link to Buenos Aires. This avoided transshipment costs between government and British railroads; it also increased shipments from Buenos Aires at the expense of those from Rosario and Sante Fe.

Despite the signing of the Roca-Runciman agreement, and the favorable rulings mentioned above, many other Argentine government actions proved disadvantageous to the British railroads. The Argentine government wished to increase production, and it therefore competed with the British railroads in order to reduce the cost of transporting agricultural produce and cattle by using the state-owned railways. They did so both by opening new areas to railroad transport, as well as competing with existing lines; and by building federal highways, which were to be increased from 2,700 miles of paved roads in 1932 to 55,000 miles of all-weather roads by 1947.[37]

The government's transportation program reflected the weak record of the British-owned railroads in technological innovation, whose directors had spoken of modernization, but failed to make widespread use of "piggy back" transport or to substitute electric for steam locomotives. Although such improvements would have been profitable in the long run, they entailed high initial costs and would have damaged the British coal and shipping industries. A spokesman for the British-owned railroads complained that any losses of the railroads owned by the government were absorbed by the taxpayers, and that they thus could afford "intensified and illogical" rate cutting, which offered unfair and ruinous competition to his company.[38]

The British government, whose own railways had been rapacious,[39] paid little attention to the complaints of the railroad companies. The Foreign Office in fact expressed the belief that they "did better than any similar investment in South America, and operated as well as any private railway system in the world."[40]

The continuing negotiations over "conditions imposed upon" the British railroads were marked by the knowledge that the Dominions could not supply all of Britain's food needs, and that Argentine supplies were necessary. Therefore, the British did not wish to antagonize the Argentines to the point at which the British would lose their exports of manufactures to Argentina and the shipping, banking, and insurance business that accompanied it; nor did they wish to jeopardize other British holdings in Argentina. British representatives argued that favorable treatment of the railroads was necessary to obtain future British investment.

The British difficulties in small part stemmed from Argentine government actions. The government failed to introduce legislation to set aside Article 67 of the General Railway Act of 1891, which prevented the railroads from reducing their work expenditures by pooling traffic and redundant service. Instead, the government built up the line from San Juan to Mendoza in competition with a British line, and refused to allow the British to charge special rates to meet the competition. The director of a British railroad company forced action on this controversy on October 17, 1935, when he accused the Argentine authorities of "disloyalty" to their British friends. Translated into Spanish, this was rendered "desleal," which could also mean "a cheat" in Argentine usage.

In 1936, discussions of the possibility of nationalizing the British railways were begun.[41] On December 23, 1936, President Justo announced his plan for the gradual acquisition of the railroads, beginning with the above-mentioned acquisition of the Central Córdoba Railway for 10,000,000 pounds sterling, and continuing with further purchases whenever Argentine government finances permitted. President Justo struck what was to become the recurring theme in railroad controversies, and urged nationalization. He noted that

> in the frequent conflicts that have arisen with the employees of the privately-owned railways there is a growing difficulty in finding reasonable solutions to the differences between the parties, because the mass of workmen regard themselves as being exploited by foreign capital, the profit-seeking ambitions of which they blame for their economic situation; and owing to the hardships they have had to suffer for years past they have no disposition to attempt to overcome differences in a reasonable manner. It is felt among the workers that shareholders have no right to any dividend, and there is increasing resistance to contribute in any form at the expense of wages to the companies' fixed charges.[42]

Similarly, some years later, President Ortíz advocated nationalization because he

> thought the railways would have constant trouble with the men unless a situation was created whereby a strike would be regarded as an infringement of the country's patrimony. As far as the public are concerned, they must be given the idea that they had an interest in the railways and be induced to cherish them, as it were, as part of a necessity vital to the country's existence.[43]

Notably absent, then and later, was a scheme for profit sharing that might induce workers to increase productivity and thus create profits. The difficulties with labor, described by Justo, persisted even after nationalization.

Several suggestions were offered about the means of nationalizing the railroads. The British suggested a joint venture, with the Argentine government the minority stock holder. The British did not want the railroads purchased immediately, because their current value was low (Article 16 of the Mitre Law set the expropriation price of the railways at their recognized capital value plus 20 percent), and because this might have ended profits made on railroad operations. Substantial railroad profits were made on imported items, rather than on freight rates, as the railroad companies owned construction and equipment companies.

In 1938, the railroads were permitted to pool services and to reach price agreements. In June 1940, the railroads' attorney, Federico Pinedo, suggested that the Argentine government trade exports for blocked foreign credits, with the proviso that if it wished to do so, the government could take shares of foreign companies, rather than blocked credits, in payment. The railroads paid Pinedo 10,000 pounds sterling for his legal advice. Soon after, Acting-President Castillo appointed Pinedo Minister of Finance. In December, Pinedo made the same suggestion as part of his economic plan. He was accused of conflict of interest: his plan was not adopted, and he resigned.

There were, however, a number of mitigating circumstances to the conflict-of-interest charges levied against Pinedo. The details of his plan, in fact, followed suggestions made by the Institute of Transport Economics of the University of Buenos Aires. A measure similar to his proposal had been foreshadowed by the Anglo-Argentine Trade Agreement of 1939, which permitted the British to pay for meat in blocked sterling. Wright believes that this was done so that the Argentine government could build up credits to buy the railroads, although Weil states that the British refused to allow Argentina to use blocked funds. Further, a trade mission to Washington discussed with President Roosevelt the possibility of using United States credits to purchase the railroads; however, the desired arrangements were not obtained.[44]

The hostile political climate and war scarcities increased the railroads' difficulties. Equipment to replace the badly deteriorated physical capital was unavailable. Railroad consumption of petroleum and imported coal was restricted, and the government forced the railroads to burn maize, purchased at inflated prices from the government. Although a rate increase was granted, this was more than offset by forcing the railroads to return salary deductions to laborers. Finally, the railroads had to cut back services as an economy measure.

The road transport industry was also in difficulty because of limited imports, a circumstance which underscored Argentine dependence on foreign supplies for the most basic operations of its economy.[45] Anti-railroad sentiment was reinforced by hostility to the British-owned electric power and tramway companies.

The Argentine government's anxiety to retain British markets had influenced its treatment of the British-owned companies during the 1930s. The Compañía Argentina de Electricidad (CADE) was highly lucrative: its profits for 1933 were over 18 percent. Its contract provided that its installations were to pass free to the city government at the termination of the contract. Its British owners' desire to extend the contract is quite understandable, as was the popular desire for compliance with the contract. In 1936 the City Council voted to extend the contract to 1971, and to buy all of the company's buildings, properties and installations at its expiration.[46]

The case of the tramway company involved physical as well as financial impositions on Buenos Aires residents. The Anglo-Argentine tramway company provided service that relied on old and inadequate equipment. In 1928, Argentine taxi drivers began offering group service, a practice that rapidly expanded to the use of minibuses, known as *colectivos*. Within four years, one-quarter of the tram passengers had switched to colectivos, which travelled three times as fast as trams, and ran more frequently. But the British believed that transportation was a field for a natural monopoly, and that the unregulated colectivos constituted unfair competition, as the tramways both paid heavier taxes and had heavier expenses.

Opposition to the British was financed, in part, by the United States' General Motors, which wished to expand its sales of automobile chassis to Argentina.[47] Argentina, however, was responsive to British pressure: the Argentine government created a Transport Corporation that would aid the British tramway company, probably in exchange for a renewal of the Roca-Runciman Treaty, in 1936. The Transport Corporation legislation was passed by the Chamber of Deputies in September 1935, over Socialist opposition, and was passed by the Senate a year later, despite colectivo strikes, a government take-over of the colectivos, and mob violence against streetcars.[48] The Transport Corporation thus retained control of the major transport routes in Buenos Aires, and was given the right to confiscate the colectivos. The act was weakly enforced, however, and confiscation was not attempted until President Castillo took office. In 1942, the government ordered the owners of the colectivos to turn them over to the Transport Corporation, an act that was violently unpopular. The decrepit tramways had recently been described as

> large wooden boxes of loose metal, slack screws and rattling windows which traverse the city roaring and screaming like lions in a cage . . . Their progress over intersections of a line where streets cross is like the terrible battery of artillery and the rattling of machine-gun fire, every two or three minutes, day and night. And when a curve has to be negotiated, the antagonizingly high-pitched shriek, such as a rat might emit being squeezed on its tail, jars excruciatingly on the most tempered nerves.[49]

The colectivo owners went on strike as transport service deteriorated, and streetcars were attacked and burned. Although the colectivos were eventually turned over to the transport corporation, many were not put in service because the corporation lacked money to operate them. Overall transport service worsened. In 1943, the new Ramirez government ordered the transport company to stop the confiscation of colectivos, and appointed an interventor to take over the Transport Corporation. In 1944, the government ended the autonomy of the company for its failure to meet bond payments.[50]

In this atmosphere it was easy for Perón, who was appointed Chief of the Department of Labor and Social Security on October 27, 1943, to build up support among workers by forcing railroad companies to increase their pay (20 percent in 1944) and fringe benefits (a Christmas bonus, often equal to one month's salary). In addition, the government provided social security, clinics, and hospitals. Although rate increases and more favorable exchange rates were granted, the railroads had accumulated a deficit of almost 40 million pesos in 1944. By 1945, railroad service had deteriorated rapidly.

On September 17, 1946, a short-lived agreement was signed with the British, establishing a mixed company to acquire the British railroads. The new company was to be offered exemption from all taxes, the duty exemptions provided by the Ley Mitre, a guaranteed operating revenue, and a contribution from the Argentine government for modernizing the lines over a five-year period. The Argentine government retained the right to purchase shares at par from any shareholder until it gained full control of the railroads. The treaty was alarmingly close to the Pinedo plan, and Perón was severely criticized by Argentine nationalists.[51] The government responded by announcing its intention to purchase foreign-owned railways.

Two forces other than internal politics influenced Perón's change in policy. First, the longer that blocked sterling funds were not spent during the postwar inflation, the less their real value. Second, the United States opposed the treaty. The American Secretary of the Treasury told the British Chancellor of the Exchequer that a clause in the treaty violated the spirit of the United States' 1945 $4 billion loan to Britain. This clause provided that "if in any year the balance of payments with the sterling area be unfavorable to Argentina, Argentina may furthermore dispose freely, within said area, of its sterling balances for an amount equivalent to the deficit."[52] *The Economist* commented that

> It did not take long for the doctrinal experts in the U.S. Treasury and State Departments to detect the conflict between this clause and the provision of the Anglo-American agreement of December 1945, which lays it down that all releases from accumulated sterling balances must, within one year of the effective date of that agreement, "be freely available for current transactions in any currency area without discrimination."

On the other hand, *The Economist* continued, it would be difficult for Britain to settle with its creditors "if it is allowed to pay them off only in dollars or the equivalent."[53]

The Economist was correct; the rapid disappearance of her dollar reserves led Britain, after consultation with the United States, to decree the inconvertibility of the pound on August 20, 1947.[54]

It would have been difficult for war-torn Britain to supply Argentina with new capital goods in exchange for the blocked sterling balances. Only the sale of the railroads would eliminate the Argentine blocked sterling accounts and satisfy the United States, which had to be able to defend its loan to Britain against congressional critics. (It is ironic that United States analysts have criticized the purchase of the railroads as a waste of Argentine foreign exchange.) Moreover, Argentines feared that unless Britain and Argentina acceded to the United States' request, the United States might use the British-owned railroads as collateral for the British loan, thus substituting United States for British ownership of Argentine railroads.

In December 1946, Argentina purchased three small French-owned lines for 182,796,174 pesos. It took a month of negotiations to set the purchase price for the British lines: the Argentines claimed that since this was a matter of purchase, no expropriation, the Ley Mitre did not apply. In February 1947, a purchase price of 2,482,500,000 gold pesos (150 million pounds sterling) was agreed upon for the British railroad companies and associated properties: real estate, grain elevators, station buildings, and one oil refinery. Most of the purchase price came from blocked funds, the rest from future sales to Britain, to be regulated under a trade treaty, which was signed in February 1948. The railroads were finally transferred to Argentine ownership on March 1, 1948.[55]

Once the railroads were Argentine, Perón reequipped them, purchasing supplies from Britain, Canada, and the United States. (The number of railroad locomotives, wagons, and equipment, except for passenger cars, had been declining since 1931.) Between 1946–47 and 1955, the government acquired 441 locomotives, 4,139 of various kinds of freight cars, and 627 passenger cars. But during the next eight years, after the fall of Perón, locomotives and freight cars deteriorated more quickly than they were replaced: by 1963, there were 638 fewer locomotives and 14 fewer freight cars than in 1955; on the other hand, 1,352 additional passenger cars had been added.[56] Despite government purchases, in 1963, 91 percent of the steam locomotives were more than thirty years old, 29 percent of the diesel engines were badly deteriorated, most of the electric coaches were more than twenty years old, and half of them were in poor condition, as were 54 percent of the passenger trains and 46 percent of the freight trains.[57]

The poor condition of the railroads contrasted sharply with the improved condition of the highways. The plans of the early 1930s had been at least partially carried out: there were 25,857 miles of all-weather roads in 1945, 44,437 miles in 1950, and 50,378 miles in 1962. The metaled and improved road network had expanded 43 percent by 1975. The attractiveness of highway transport resulted in the fact that by 1975, 80 percent of the freight and 82 percent of the medium- and long-distance passengers traveled by road, while railroads carried only 8 percent of the freight and 15 percent of the passengers, the remainder traveling by ship and airplane.[58]

The decline in cargo carried by the railroads during the depression had brought with it a decline in railroad employment, which did not regain its 1930 level until 1946–47. Perón's reequipment of the railroads was accompanied by expanded employment, not all of which was needed to operate the railroads. In 1955, the railroads employed 209,854 persons; their numbers increased through 1959, when railroad employment reached 219,600, despite the fact that real wages in cash per worker were slightly higher in 1930 than during the depression or under Perón. This factor was offset for many workers by expanded fringe benefits, especially rent-controlled housing, which they would have had to leave if they changed jobs.[59] Real wages of railroad workers fell sharply from 1955 to 1959, but finally passed their 1930 level in 1963 (see Table 7.2). In comparison to real wages in the rest of the economy, the position of railroad workers improved, because real wages per capita fell for the economy as a whole during this period.

Given the relative advantages of a job on the railroads, the government was able to reduce railroad employment only by granting special incentives to workers who resigned. For example, by offering severance indemnification pay, and priority in low-cost housing, the government pensioned off 54,000 workers

Table 7.2 Real Wages Per Capita of Railroad Workers, 1930–1963.
(1943 prices)

Year	Real Wages per Railroad Worker	Index of Real Wages per Railroad Worker
1930	2,892	100.0
1935	2,725	94.2
1946	2,753	95.2
1955	2,632	91.0
1959	2,220	76.8
1963	2,991	103.4

SOURCE: Santa Cruz, *Ferrocarriles Argentinos*, p. 33; and Diz, "Money and Prices in Argentina," p. 126.

at the cost of 5 billion pesos. Railroad employment had been reduced to 243,777 by 1960, and to 150,244 by 1962.[60]

Unless propelled by foot pedal, railroads are not a labor-intensive activity. In the absence of adequate capital equipment, the amount of work that could be done was limited. The effective working day had declined to three hours by 1961, an indication of both the railroad workers' strength and the lack of better employment (and/or housing) opportunities elsewhere. The result of the use of the railroads to absorb unemployment is that in comparison to their profit from 1930 to 1945–46, they registered a deficit from 1946–47 to 1962–63, which, by 1961, was equal to one-fifth of the government's total expenses, or about 80 percent of its total deficit. If allowance is made for the facts that the railroads were supplied with fuel oil at reduced prices, that they did not make provision for amortization or for the funds they received from the treasury, and that they paid no taxes, the deficit was probably equal to nearly half the total government budget expenditures. (The political opposition to such proposed rationalizations as ending subsidized freight rates and reducing the inflated work force can be imagined.)

As the foreign railroads had been thought to be highly profitable and exploitative, it was predicted that strong demands, both for higher wages and more employment, would be made on them by labor. It is possible that an increase in railroad employment was less expensive than a welfare system or open unemployment and an unemployment insurance system would have been. If this was the case, Perón's expansion of railroad employment makes sense economically as well as politically. The difficulty with the situation was not necessarily that railroads employed redundant workers, but that the structure of fringe benefits tied them to a specific location, so that when it was finally possible for them to work in productive employment elsewhere, it was too expensive for them to move.

The Argentine government's railroad policies after World War II reflected the fact that there were a number of suppliers of the capital goods needed by the railroads, and that as long as Argentina had enough foreign exchange it could purchase required capital equipment. This was not the case in the petroleum industry. An additional point of difference between the railroad and petroleum situation is that while the laws regulating railroads in the Anglo-Saxon and Hispanic traditions are similar, they are markedly dissimilar with regard to ownership of the subsoil.

The development of Argentine petroleum extraction and refining also reflects the contrast between management by multinational and national corporations, and the central role of control of energy sources both in fact and in the ideology of the transformation of the economic structure of a developing nation. It also provides a major example of public policy formation when combined with foreign ownership.

Under Hispanic law, subsoil rights in land belonged to the king. But when the Latin American nations became independent in the nineteenth century, it was uncertain whether the national or provincial governments inherited the crown rights to the subsoil. The result was that Argentina had both public and private oil firms. The first attempt to produce oil in Argentina was made in 1865 in the Northern province of Jujuy, and was followed by other attempts in the North during the next forty years, all of which failed. Part of the difficulty lay in the undercapitalization of the firms, which lacked both funds and technical knowledge. Furthermore, not only was transport limited in the North, but no sooner had the railroads heard of a small share of domestic petroleum being sent to Buenos Aires than they raised their rates.[61]

On December 13, 1907, a new, major souce of oil was found at the port of Comodoro Rivadavia. Immediately, President José Figueroa Alcorta reserved 200,000 hectares of oil land for the nation by issuing a decree that prohibited private claims for mine ownership or exploration for five leagues around Comodoro Rivadavia.[62] In 1909, this action was modified to prohibit claims for a radius of five miles around each government well in public lands. The reserve was reduced to 5,000 hectares in 1910, and a limit for state exploration set at five years.

President Roque Sáenz Peña established a government bureau, the Dirección General de Explotación del Petróleo, to develop the Argentine government's oil deposits, but gave it only 500 paper pesos to carry out its work, which was to be financed from petroleum sales. The increase in funds for exploration until 1913 was insufficient. Nationalists assert that direct or indirect pressure from Great Britain, which supplied Argentina's imported coal, accounts for the government's inaction in developing its oil fields.[63] The honorary head of the Dirección General de Explotación del Petróleo denounced the menace of foreign development of Argentine oil:

> The public powers, with an incredible slowness and an inconceivable stinginess, have delayed six years before stating clearly and making known to the public the immense riches which the great oil fields of Comodoro Rivadavia represent. In the meantime, the reconnoitering cavalry have arrived: the "syndicating operators" who have monopolized the land of promise (more than 80,000 hectares in one syndicate), who have recruited a phalange of proselites, few of them conscious and the immense majority unconscious, making stockholders of "everyone from ministers to penpushers".... The preliminaries of conquest are those already employed in other places and presently in Mexico ... [including, an attempt to] discredit the Executive Power and the finances of the Nation, the negation ... that there has been sufficient work carried out at Comodoro Rivadavia during the last two years of the present administration to demonstrate that at last the country can dispose of combustible of its own ... [and the] ... repetition of the theory ... according to which the things and properties of

the greatest value of the Nation must be sold out to mercenary hands, because governments are poor administrators; a theory denied by the world.[64]

The publication of this report led President Sáenz Peña to order a detailed exploration of Comodoro Rivadavia, prohibiting, for the time being, claims to mines, and declaring void exploration permits not in conformity with the Mining Code. Private complaints led President de la Plaza (1914–16) to restrict this provision to national government lands. Provincial governments followed Sáenz Peña's precedent: Salta suspended private oil claims and established a reserved oil field in 1911; Santa Fe established a reserved field in 1913.

Ownership of tankers was central to autonomous oil development; if the government lacked them, foreign oil companies could control the oil industry by refusing to transport oil unless their terms were met, or could offset changes in conditions granted to them by an increase in oil tanker freight charges. As production increased, transport problems were ameliorated by use of a Navy oil tanker, and the renting of another oil tanker, with a purchase option, from the British. In 1914, however, the British refused to sell it, so orders for tankers were placed in the United States in 1915, while two engineers were sent to the United States to study their techniques in 1916.[65]

The outcome of the first decade of oil production in Argentina (1907–16) was that the government produced 293,551 cubic meters of oil, and private firms, 7,771 cubic meters, despite the granting of exploration permits covering 500,000 hectares. Arturo Frondizi (president, 1958–62) asserts that this occurred because rival interests were concerned with monopolizing permits, rather than exploring or exploiting oil properties. He adds that although the government aided private firms, the latter sabotaged government production.[66]

Standard Oil controlled a later stage of elaboration of petroleum: the import and marketing of petroleum derivatives through its West India Oil Company and its Compañía Nacional de Petróleo. Together, the firms controlled 95 percent of kerosene and 80 percent of gasoline consumption, and were able to set prices and to prohibit retailers from buying from other suppliers. From 1912 to 1915, the Compañía Nacional de

Petróleo obtained 6.3 million pesos profit on 7 million pesos of capital. In order to protect a petro-distillery, Congress had increased duties on refined petroleum from two to three gold centavos, but declared unrefined petroleum duty-free. Standard Oil imported a petroleum distillate duty-free under this law, easily transforming it to kerosene, which cost the treasury 16 million pesos in duties that should have been paid between 1905 and 1916. To end these practices, President de la Plaza issued a decree in 1915 which defined the characteristics of each oil product according to quantitative analysis, and approved a law which lowered the customs duty on kerosene and established duties on unrefined petroleum.[67]

The shortage of imported fuels during World War I gave a new impetus to Argentine government oil development.[68] President Hipólito Yrigoyen (president, 1916–22) wished to establish a petroleum policy based on: (1) the intensification of government oil exploitation for which funds were insistently demanded; (2) the principle stating that oil deposits are the property of the nation even when encountered in provincial jurisdiction, but authorizing the Provinces shares in the profits from oil produced in their territories; and (3) the maintenance of private enterprise—without permitting mixed (private and government) enterprise—and with a legal modification to insure government control over it.[69] This policy was not put into effect because Congress refused to enact the desired legislation.[70] The problem of congressional inaction persisted until 1930, as the Radical Party presidents carried the Chamber of Deputies, but not the Conservative Senate, with them. In the absence of new legislation, the president resorted to issuing decrees. In 1922, for example, the president decreed the creation of the Dirección General de Yacimientos Petrolíferos Fiscales under the Ministry of Agriculture. This became autonomous in 1923, and less subject to political shifts under Mosconi (1922–30).

The technical capacity of the Argentine oil industry increased: from 1914 on, oil was distilled into five subproducts, and a variety of technical improvements were initiated. Both government and private oil production increased (see Table 7.3), with the share of private enterprise rising to 23.4 percent in 1922.[71] The expansion of government production was limited

Table 7.3 Public and Private Argentine Oil Production, 1907–1946 (cubic meters)

Year	Percent Public	Percent Private	Total	Year	Percent Public	Percent Private	Total
1907			16	1927	60.0	40.0	1,372,020
1908			1,821	1928	59.7	40.3	1,442,063
1909			2,989	1929	58.4	41.6	1,493,067
1910			3,293	1930	57.9	42.1	1,431,107
1911			2,082	1931	46.9	53.1	1,861,413
1912			7,462	1932	43.2	56.8	2,088,831
1913			20,733	1933	42.3	57.7	2,176,559
1914			43,795	1934	37.5	62.5	2,229,714
1915			81,580	1935	41.5	58.5	2,272,977
1916	94.4	5.6	137,551	1936	46.4	53.6	2,457,545
1917	94.5	5.5	192,371	1937	48.5	51.2	2,600,107
1918	92.0	8.0	214,867	1938	52.7	47.3	2,714,823
1919	89.0	11.0	211,301	1939	54.9	45.1	2,959,168
1920	86.5	13.5	262,494	1940	60.5	39.5	3,276,496
1921	85.3	14.7	326,906	1941	63.6	36.4	3,499,757
1922	76.6	23.4	455,498	1942	64.9	35.1	3,768,547
1923	76.8	23.2	530,209	1943	66.7	33.3	3,948,412
1924	78.6	21.4	704,697	1944	66.9	33.1	3,852,088
1925	65.6	34.4	952,199	1945	67.5	32.5	3,637,521
1926	59.6	40.4	1,248,118	1946	68.3	31.7	3,307,219

Sources: Frondizi, *Petróleo y Política*; and Silenzi di Stagni, *El Petróleo Argentino*.

by the fact that Congress voted no funds for oil exploration between 1916 and 1922. Increases in capital came rather from sales, capital rising from 11,842,300 at the end of 1916 to 61,969,900 six years later.[72]

Existing petroleum laws lapsed in 1920, and it became possible for prospectors to acquire exploration rights from the government for ten gold pesos, and then sell them to private firms for 100,000 pesos.[73] The acquisition of exploration rights over vast areas limited the Y.P.F.'s action; in Jujuy, owners of exploration rights even claimed payments from the government railroads to operate in their territory.[74] As Congress failed to act, the president issued a series of decrees in 1924, which ordered vast government exploration for oil; during the exploration period, new private claims for exploration permits were suspended, both in government and in private lands. Norms were established for seeking claims in privately held land to ensure that the claims would be worked.[75] Santa Fe and Entre Rios reserved their entire territory, as did Salta and Jujuy.

The future development of Argentine oil policy was strongly influenced by the inept behavior of Standard Oil, which in 1922 refused to deliver gasoline for military airplanes without prior payment. The director of the Army Air Force, Enrique Mosconi, felt insulted by this procedure; his decision to fight the "predominance of foreign monopolies," and his publications on petroleum, led to his appointment as Director of the Y.P.F. from 1922 to 1930.[76] Mosconi at first believed that private oil firms should be maintained. By 1929, he stated that a mixed firm, composed of government and private Argentine capital, would provide the best means of developing the Argentine oil industry, because he believed that, while a government monopoly ran the risk of increasing costs, a mixed company would combine the benefits of the flexibility of a private firm with the guarantee given by the State. Mosconi added that poor public petroleum service and an increase in costs were preferable to "the excellencies which the organizations of foreign firms can offer, because they, in the end, export in the maximum degree the riches which are obtained from the deposits and generally constitute the seed of grave perturbations in the economic and political order." In 1928, he stated that as long as private Argentine capital would not invest in a mixed organization in petroleum, "there remains no other road to adopt than that of government monopoly ... in all the activities of this industry: production, elaboration, transport, and commerce."[77]

Mosconi initiated a price war with the trusts on August 1, 1929, and he believed he could win it only if a state monopoly were established. By 1936, the increased strength of the private companies led him to again favor the establishment of a mixed firm with a monopoly of oil development.[78]

The United States' reaction to Argentine oil policy provides an example of "imperialist" behavior. In April 1919, the State Department issued the first of its instructions to investigate reports of new oil developments. In 1920, it ordered that "all proper assistance and support" be given to agents of American oil companies operating in Argentina. Rumors of possible nationalization or a monopolistic grant to a foreign concern prompted the State Department to inform the Argentine government that a government or government-controlled monopoly "would violate the principle of reciprocity, would exclude American capital, and might reduce the flow of trade."[79]

American views did not change Argentine policy. Sr. Mosconi attempted to annul Standard Oil's 1920 concession in Salta, but Standard, which was represented by Rómulo S. Naón, the first Argentine Ambassador to the United States, won the case in 1932, after the fall of Yrigoyen and Mosconi's resignation. As a result, Standard's production in Salta quadrupled in the next four years, its share of total production rising from 76.4 percent in 1931 to 93.6 percent in 1934. Y.P.F. maintained its volume of output, while its relative importance declined.[80]

The program of strengthening Y.P.F. began with the reservation of land for its exploration and development. The government attempted to ensure the success of Y.P.F. by additional measures such as requiring the government railroads to purchase oil and derivatives from Y.P.F. in 1923; this requirement was extended in 1926 to all public bodies, although in practice, private firms were favored in the interior. A new distillery was constructed near Buenos Aires, with the result that Y.P.F. sold increasing amounts of derivatives, and less crude, with a corresponding increase in revenues.[81] Y.P.F. extended its control over Argentine oil policy by selling its own products, which had previously been sold by a private firm.

Petroleum product prices varied among the geographic regions, with eleven different prices being charged for gasoline in 1929. To some extent, price differences reflected different distances from oil distillation plants. Y.P.F. constructed a plant in Salta, which reduced its need for price differentials. In 1929, Y.P.F. lowered prices throughout Argentina, and in 1930 established a uniform price. As a result, private firms, which had to match Y.P.F. prices, concentrated their sales in the more profitable area of the Federal District and its environs. Frondizi estimates that oil price reductions saved Argentine consumers some 400 million pesos between August 1, 1931 and December 12, 1935. He asserts that in the absence of Y.P.F. action, gasoline prices would have risen as the price of the peso fell, a plausible assertion, considering that wholesale prices rose 10.5 percent during this period.[82]

The reduction in gasoline prices was a factor in the expansion of road transport which, beginning in 1931, was financed by a gasoline tax. Attempts to increase Y.P.F.'s control of oil production were defeated in 1929–30, when Yrigoyen's proposals to nationalize oil, and to import petroleum from Russia in exchange for Argentine goods, were not adopted.[83]

As the Y.P.F. price reductions implied an increase in its share of the market, its policy endangered the division of the Argentine petroleum market decided upon by the foreign oil firms in the Achnacarry Accord of September 17, 1928, under whose provisions Royal Dutch Shell, Standard Oil of New Jersey, and the Anglo-Persian Oil Company agreed to maintain their relative shares of oil markets. The Argentine gasoline market was assigned the following quotas, which applied until 1937: Standard Oil, 45.79 percent; Royal Dutch Shell, 27.65 percent; Y.P.F., 14.63 percent, and the remaining firms, most of which were British, 11.93 percent.[84] In a 1930 meeting to discuss European markets, the oil companes agreed to act together to control world oil supplies, which, according to Arturo Frondizi, implied a joint front against the expansion of Y.P.F.

The petroleum policies of the governments which followed Yrigoyen tended to increase the developmental work of Y.P.F. while yielding some existing fields to private oil companies. The government of Uriburu increased the reserve established in 1924 to include all of Tierra del Fuego and increased Y.P.F.'s legal powers and financial resources, while at the same time aiding private firms in Salta, Mendoza, and the Federal District. In 1930, competition increased between Y.P.F. and the foreign companies for control of the Buenos Aires gasoline market.

In 1915, an ordinance in the Federal District had set the terms for installation of gasoline pump stations: permission to operate the stations was to last for ten years, at the end of which the stations were to pass, without cost, to the ownership of the Muncipality. In addition, a distance of at least 400 meters was required between pumps. Upon the termination of the ten-year periods, Y.P.F. received the pumps. Y.P.F. was not subject to the 400 meter minimum distance requirement. But after Yrigoyen was overthrown, the new mayor of the Federal District extended the period during which companies could operate their gas stations; and in 1932, he eliminated the minimum distance requirement.

Later in 1932, rulings favoring private oil companies were contested by Socialist Councilmen, who passed an ordinance reinstating the oil regime that had existed under Yrigoyen. The mayor vetoed the ordinance, but later withdrew his veto. In 1936, the Buenos Aires City Council attempted to establish a Y.P.F. monopoly of gasoline supply for the city; but since part of the ordinance was vetoed by the mayor, the ordinance was suspended.

In 1932, a law (11.668) governing Y.P.F. was passed which recognized it as the government body charged with carrying out national oil policy. Its purpose was to study, explore, and exploit deposits of hydrocarbons that the State had or would acquire in the future, and to effect the industrialization, transport and sale of such products and their derivatives. In no case could the deposits, distilleries or oilpipes of Y.P.F. be alienated. Y.P.F. was exempted from import duties on its machines, materials, and equipment, and from national real estate and personal property taxes, but it was required to contribute at least 10 percent of its profits to the government. At various times this requirement was increased to 30 percent, a factor which limited the Y.P.F.'s capitalization.

President Justo had decreed the extension of oil reserves to all national territories in 1934; all of the provinces that were thought to contain oil reserved at least some of their oil land. In 1935, private firms were informed that if they wished to explore or exploit them, they would have to form mixed societies, and a code governing private oil firms was established under law 12.161. It recognized government ownership of petroleum deposits, permitted the formation of mixed societies, established new permanent oil reserves in Chubut and Neuquén, and maintained existing reserves. Both federal and provincial governments could establish temporary reserves for up to ten years. A tax on oil companies was levied for the first time; it was set at 12 percent of gross product. No other taxes were to be levied on oil.[85]

In 1935, the private oil companies began to import oil and dump it on the Argentine market, hoping to drive Y.P.F. out of business by a price war which included discounts and allowances to intermediaries. But the Argentine anti-trust law (11.210) was not used against the oil companies. Instead, President Justo issued a decree on July 20, 1936, which prohibited petroleum exports, and established import quotas which were to be set each quarter in accord with Y.P.F.'s proposals. These provisions were shifted by a regulating decree of August 7, according to which Y.P.F. was informed about private companies' imports.

The distribution of imported crude to private firms was to be by agreement with Y.P.F.; and sales of derivatives were to be by both Y.P.F. and private firms, based on agreements between them. Y.P.F. was not to make profits on imported oil products. It had reached an agreement with Standard Oil in 1936 that would enable it to purchase all of Standard Oil's installations in Argentina, but the purchase did not take place because Congress was unwilling to purchase Standard Oil. Instead, Y.P.F. reached an accord with Shell and Standard, on the distribution of the gasoline market, which was signed on June 28, 1937.

An accord with the small oil firms had been reached on September 29, 1936. Under this decree, Y.P.F. and the private oil firms agreed in 1936 and 1937 on the distribution of the gasoline market, establishing shares or promising not to change prices[86] (see Table 7.4). The attempt at industry self-regulation was similar to that established in the United States under the National Recovery Act. A curious result was that a government corporation (Y.P.F.) bound itself to arbitration in disputes with private firms.

The 1937 accord was maintained for ten years. One of the stipulations of the accord was that Y.P.F. production was limited by its final sales, and import of crude was reserved to specified private firms, except in exceptional circumstances.[87] The government therefore refused a private firm permission to import oil in October 1939, after the war broke out. Similarly, the 1937 accord limitation on Y.P.F.'s imports was interpreted to preclude its import of Mexican oil produced from Mexico's expropriated wells (some of which had been the property of the firms which signed the Argentine accord). Y.P.F. nonetheless increased its share of the market from 38 percent in 1939 to 68 percent in 1943, as World War II made it difficult to import crude. Although the formal accord terminated in 1947, Y.P.F. continued its policy of sharing the market with the private

Table 7.4 Distribution of the Argentine Gasoline Market According to the Agreement of June 28, 1937 (liters)

Company	Federal District	Interior	Total
Shell	38,370,000	166,000,000	204,370,000
Standard	71,850,000	215,704,696	287,554,696
Other private	55,143,820	104,295,304	159,439,124
Y.P.F.	134,643,000	179,000,000	313,536,180
Total (rounded)	300,000,000	665,000,000	965,000,000

Source: Frondizi, *Petróleo y Política*, p. 360.

companies, rather than carrying out the aggressive policies of 1928–30.[88]

This cautious policy was quite possibly the only one open to the government, which needed to maintain energy production. Y.P.F. could only expand production if foreign supplies became available. In practice, the United States was the only source of well-drilling equipment during the late 1940s. The United States, Great Britain, and the Netherlands set the following priorities for allocation of oil-drilling equipment: first, satisfaction of their own needs and that of their territories; second, concessions in areas that they controlled; third, areas with the highest yield per unit employed; and fourth, other countries. Argentina fell into the fourth category, and so had to wait to receive drilling equipment; an Argentine sourly remarked that under the quota system Argentine gold did it about as much good as that of King Midas.[89]

The scarcity of oil production equipment led the United States to establish the Petroleum Administration for Defense, which administered exports of American petroleum equipment. Because of the priority system that had been established, Y.P.F. had to submit the details of its operations to the Petroleum Administration for Defense in order to justify the use of the materials it requested. This, however, infringed on the secrecy of Argentine defense plans, and the Executive had to grant special permission to provide the information. United States restrictions were maintained until the end of 1953 on the export of various categories of petroleum equipment.[90]

The government responded to the energy shortage by seeking to develop all sources of energy. In 1943, it had created the Dirección Nacional de la Energía (D.N.E.) to coordinate the production, distribution, and consumption of all fuel in Argentina. In 1945, (autarchic) agencies, including Y.P.F., were placed under its control. In practice, the D.N.E. left Y.P.F. less autonomy to carry out its own development. Difficulty was encountered both in obtaining foreign exchange to import equipment (Y.P.F. by law could not export oil to obtain exchange), and in promoting personnel according to merit (the personnel policies of the successor organization of the Dirección

Nacional de la Energía, the E.N.D.E., were based on political rather than technical criteria).[91]

Since the Argentine economy grew rapidly under Perón, while oil production did not, the need for oil imports grew. This contributed to worries over national defense and finances. During the late 1940s and early 1950s, Argentina depended on imports for more than half of its oil supply. The international oil consortiums, rather than the Argentine government, controlled this supply, which, if interrupted, could paralyze the nation, a point that was stressed by Minister Barro.[92] This reliance on imports placed an increasing burden on the balance of payments: in 1957, petroleum imports were $300 million, about 23 percent of total imports and almost as much as the $340 million trade deficit, which, in turn, made the development of Argentine oil a prime concern of the government.

Y.P.F. had been unable to raise enough capital to finance a large expansion of domestic production; as a consequence, a variety of attempts were made to exploit Argentine oil wealth, under a series of controversial oil contracts with foreign oil firms.[93] After negotiations began in the mid-fifties, the Frondizi government announced in July 1958 that agreements in principle had been reached for foreign oil financing and investment of $1 billion dollars, with the goal of making Argentina self-sufficient in oil in three years. The announcement of the contracts caused an uproar, as Frondizi had formerly opposed foreign oil trusts and favored a government monopoly. His self-justification is as follows:

> It is said that the petroleum policy of the President was completely contrary to that which was sustained by citizen Frondizi in his book *"Petróleo y Política"*. . . . In the book I sustained the necessity of arriving at self-sufficiency of petroleum by means of a state monopoly. It was an idealistic and sincere thesis. When I came to power I encountered a reality which did not correspond to this theoretical posture. . . . The option for the citizen who occupied the Presidency was very simple: either he anchored himself to this theoretical position of past years and the petroleum would continue to slumber under the earth, or petroleum would be extracted with the aid of foreign capital in order to alleviate our balance of payments

and adequately nourish our industry. In a word, either the intellectual prestige of the author of *"Petróleo y Política"* would be saved, or the country would be saved.

I did not vacillate in placing the country above the self-love of a writer. I believe that any Argentine in my place would have proceded in the same way, unless he would have been a politician who would prefer to guard his electoral chances before those of the welfare and progress of his people. I maintained the fundamental objective which was self-sufficiency, but I rectified the means to achieve it.[94]

The contracts provided for participation of foreign oil companies in the development of Argentine oil, credit for the purchase of foreign drilling machinery and other equipment, and medium-term credit for the purchase of foreign oil. The contracts for foreign oil company participation in the development and production of Argentine oil were not concessions, which would have given the oil companies title to the oil: this was precluded by Article 40 of the 1949 Constitution, which transferred petroleum from the private property of the nation's provinces to the public property of the nation, making it an inalienable public good.[95]

Instead of granting concessions, the government leased or purchased the services of foreign companies, stipulating payment based on work done and adjustments to cover increases in cost caused by inflation. The government also employed foreign companies to manage the development of an area. In one case, the government was to pay for the cost of development and share profits, including foreign exchange savings, from production. In another, production and development were to be undertaken by a foreign firm at its own risk; the oil produced was to be sold to the government.[96]

Argentina did not become self-sufficient in oil production within the hoped-for three years. Nonetheless, by 1961, as production under the oil contracts rose, petroleum imports fell to one-fifth of Argentine oil consumption, 8.9 percent of merchandise imports, and 27.3 percent of the trade deficit.[97]

Not everyone was convinced that the results were worthwhile. The terms granted the oil companies under the contracts were sufficiently better than those prevailing in the rest of the world that rumors of bribery abounded: one persistent North American account was that government negotiators were so ignorant of the oil industry that the bribe that they accepted was too small. Another was that the terms were highly favorable, as the oil companies realized that they would be expropriated in the near future. The manner in which the contracts were drawn up was suspect: in closed negotiations without a call for public bids, and through the president's office, rather than the Y.P.F.

Critics of the mid-fifties' contracts had called attention to the freedom of companies to convert currencies to dollars and remit them at a time when the Argentine economy was characterized by multiple exchange rates and exchange controls. The government needed to strike a balance between control of the exchange market and reasonable repatriation of funds. In the 1958 lease-of-services contract signed with Dresser Industries, A.G., the company was assured of the conversion of its peso earnings at the free market rate. In a direct exploitation contract signed with the Pan American International Oil Company (a subsidiary of Standard Oil of Indiana), the company was guaranteed a fixed price of $10 per cubic meter, of which 60 percent was to be paid in dollars. At the free market rate, the peso share became convertible into dollars only with the permission of the Argentine authorities.[98]

The profit-sharing petroleum development contract signed with Loeb-Rhoades constituted the most sensitive provision of the contracts. The government agreed to reimburse Loeb-Rhoades for its costs. Although prior Y.P.F. approval was required for all subcontractors to whom any operations were assigned, the company maintained control—by means of an Operations Committee—as long as it had an investment to protect. This four-man committee was drawn up in order to control expenditures, with Loeb-Rhoades and Y.P.F. each naming two men. The Committee's chairman was to be named by the company as long as it remained a creditor; he was to cast the deciding vote in case of a tie. The Committee was to hold title to all land, equipment, and petroleum in the area, and was to retain exclusive control of all operations. These provisions were so broad that they were attacked as granting a concession in all but name. The payment to producing contractors of world prices without the normal government participation in profits was considered a sell-out, while exclusion of incentive provisions from the lease-of-services contracts was inefficient.

The government protected the companies from conflicts between domestic consumers and foreign producers by tying prices paid to the foreign companies to world prices for oil, and by safeguarding foreign investors against inflation. Y.P.F. was the major distributor of petroleum in Argentina, and it would pass on any increase in costs to consumers only if this was in accord with government policy.

The critics of the oil contracts appeared justified during the early 1960s; petroleum production rose in 1962, but remained steady from 1963 to 1966. The Government had cancelled the oil contracts on November 15, 1963, but permitted the companies to continue work pending settlement of financial claims.[99] The brief political stability of the late sixties led to substantial expansion: from 1966 to 1969 production increased 31 percent; there was a small balance of trade surplus; petroleum accounted for only 5.4 percent of total imports, but for 28 percent of oil consumption.[100] The relative strength of Argentine oil development enabled the government to nationalize (much of) the oil distribution network in the early seventies without fear of repercussions from foreign oil producers. As long as there is easy access to the capital goods needed for oil exploration and refining, Argentina will be able to control her petroleum industry. At the same time, the 1970s world petroleum situation has shifted the balance between those analysts who criticize development of high-cost capital-intensive activities in nations with small- and medium-sized markets, and those who stress the strategic importance of control of scarce resources and the possible sharp rise in prices when only a few producers control production of strategic goods. The rapid rise in oil prices, which severely limited the less developed nations' capacity to import a large volume of both oil and other commodities, makes the various steps taken to procure a secure supply of petroleum appear reasonable. In their absence, the

Chapter Eight: Economic Dependence and Independence in the Twentieth Century

ONCE UPON A time a noble family was blessed with a particularly healthy and intelligent son. The family therefore complained violently about "the ugly misshapen daughter that we are cursed with," in the hope that by denying the existence of their good fortune, neither God nor man would take it away.

Argentines resemble the noble family: they eat well; much of their economic history has been fortunate; yet their analysis is characterized by complaint. Gross national product grew at about 3.7 percent per year from 1900 to 1955, a rate of increase greater than that of France, the United Kingdom, Germany, the Netherlands, Switzerland, Denmark, and Norway, although below that of the United States, Canada, and Japan.[1] Many Argentines concentrated on comparisons to the latter group, and characterized both the level and structure of their own economic growth as inadequate. The complaints drew on the protectionist ideology of Alejandro Bunge and on resentment of oligarchs and foreigners. Although the share of manufacturing and services in gross domestic product increased, the best-known government policies were directed to international trade and agriculture. This resulted in accusations that foreigners and their local allies attempted to protect their trade in the export of primary products and the import of manufactures, thus limiting Argentine industrial development and fostering Argentine economic dependence upon the supply of foreign exchange. When foreigners invested in manufacturing and services, they were said to favor other foreign-based firms in Argentina, and to base their decisions on the welfare of the parent firm, rather than that of the firm's Argentine branch or the Argentine nation.

The debate over the role of foreigners and allied groups has continued into the 1970s, because it is part of the continuing struggle about which group represents the national interest, as well as about the distribution of income and wealth. The political aspects of class and regional conflict dominated Argentina during the early twentieth century, as the vote was extended first, in 1911, to all men who registered for compulsory military service and then, in 1949, to women by the new Constitution. From the mid-thirties, struggle for control of the economy has overshadowed attempts to control Argentina's weak political parties. Foreigners and their local allies have shared in the struggle for economic control. Blaming them for Argentine economic difficulties is inconsistent with Argentina's long-run success in increasing income and the share of manufacturing and services in gross domestic product, but it is consistent with the continuing wrangle over the distribution of income and wealth.

A brief indication of ways in which foreigners could influence the economy is indicated by their ownership of factors of production and by their trade relationships with Argentina. During the nineteenth century, until the first World War, Argentine land was owned by Argentines. Immigrants were almost 10 percent of the population, while more than one-half of the capital was provided by foreigners. Throughout the twentieth century, land ownership was concentrated in Argentine hands. After World War I, immigration fell by 75 percent, and continued to decline. By the 1960s, immigrants provided just over 10 percent of the labor force.

As Argentina developed, she supplied most of her own investment needs. From 1922 to 1929, only 17 percent of new investment came from foreign sources; this fell to 13 percent in the Great Depression, 2 percent under Perón, and less than 2 percent thereafter. Similarly, as the size and complexity of the economy grew, Argentine dependence on international trade decreased. Exports comprised more than 25 percent of gross domestic product from 1900 to 1922; 25 percent from 1922 to 1929; 20 percent during the Great Depression; 9 percent under Perón; and only 6 percent by the 1970's.[2]

The share of imports in gross domestic product was similar to that of exports. A point to which I shall return is that at times foreign nations refused either to let Argentina use her blocked sterling balances, or purchase certain categories of goods, so that the composition as well as the level of imports influenced the Argentine economy.

Finally, international trade could influence economic activity if government spending were made possible by the receipt of taxes on trade, or if the money supply varied directly with the level of foreign exchange, as it would under a gold standard. In Argentina, customs revenues at first were of substantial importance, providing 56 percent of government income from 1900 to 1913, 48 percent during World War I, 56 percent during the 1920s, 51 percent during the Great Depression, 25 percent from 1940 to 1942, 10 percent under Perón, 6 percent from 1956 to 1962, and 2 percent during the 1960s. Yet even this link is weaker than it seems: foreign exchange became available to Argentina through loans and investment, as well as through trade, while when the government needed to spend money, it did so whether or not revenues were available from customs receipts. This is borne out by the fact that from 1909 to 1954, the correlation between real foreign exchange and real government spending was negative, while that between the real money supply and real government spending was positive. The fact that the gold standard had broken down is evidenced by the negative correlation between the level of real foreign exchange and real money supply.

The plausibility of blaming foreigners for Argentine economic difficulties varies strikingly during the twentieth century. From the turn of the century to the 1920s, complete economic autonomy was not a national goal because Argentines wanted to continue to attract investments from the United Kingdom and continental Europe, and to continue to export to them. As long as the Argentine economy appeared to be profitable, foreign loans and investment supplemented Argentine financial resources. At the turn of the century, foreign investment accounted for half of total investment; 80 percent of this was British. Argentine reliance on the United Kingdom for loans and investment indicates dependence on a single nation rather than integration into the world economy.

This was not because the United Kingdom tried to keep other nations out, but because Argentina was unable to attract much interest in its financial paper and investment opportunities on the continent.

There were some complaints about the situation. Professor Eteocle Lorini wrote:

> All the industrial, commercial, agricultural and mining companies which furnish our Argentine statistics bear the foreign mark *limited,* so that one ends by getting the impression that one is studying a purely English colony, for one finds *limited* upon all species of manufactures, *limited* after the statements of capital, all undertakings are *limited,* insurance is *limited,* the circulation and distribution of Argentine wealth is *limited.*[3]

The force of Lorini's analysis was lessened by the declining importance of foreign investment. While 84.2 percent of the owners of Argentine industries in 1895 were foreign, their proportion had declined to 64.5 percent by 1913. It is often the case that foreign investors from capital-rich nations can afford to invest in capital-intensive industries as part of their many investments, in contrast to local investors from capital-scarce nations, who instead distribute their investments among labor-intensive activities. In Argentina, however, the fact that many of the foreign owners had immigrated to Argentina with limited funds led to a different distribution of economic power than that often associated with economies dominated by foreign investment. Foreign owners were important in both the clothing industry, which employed the smallest amount of capital per worker (see Table 8.1), and in the metallurgy industry, which required substantial capital per worker. There was no significant relationship between the importance of foreign ownership and the amount of capital per worker, and the number of workers per firm in 1913.

Both the amount of capital and the number of employees per firm increased between 1895 and 1913; development was limited by modern standards. On the average, more than ten workers per firm were employed only in chemicals and graphic arts in 1895; and only in construction, chemicals, and "other"

Table 8.1 Capital, Employees, and Ownership of Argentine Firms, 1895 and 1913

	Capital per Firm[a]	No. of Empl.	Cap.[a]/Empl.	% Ownership		
				Arg.	Foreign	Mixed
1895						
Total	12,795.1	6.6	1,938.7	15.7	84.3	
Food	16,483.5	6.6	2,497.5			
Clothing	7,997.0	5.7	1,367.9			
Construction	11,765.3	7.7	1,528.0			
Furniture	10,185.9	5.6	1,818.9			
Art and ornament	9,029.4	2.7	3,344.2			
Metallurgy	8,371.4	4.6	1,819.9			
Chemical	40,701.8	14.9	2,731.7			
Graphic arts	21,100.3	11.9	1,773.1			
Other	33,776.9	8.8	3,838.3			
1913						
Total	36,648.2	8.4	4,362.9	32.3	64.5	3.1
Food	40,234.6	7.1	5,666.8	37.9	57.9	4.2
Clothing	14,147.5	8.2	1,725.3	15.0	83.6	1.5
Construction	25,190.2	10.2	2,469.6	25.8	71.8	2.4
Furniture	14,104.6	6.5	2,169.9	23.6	74.0	2.4
Art and ornament	14,604.7	4.3	3,396.4	25.4	72.8	1.8
Metallurgy	32,861.1	9.0	3,651.2	20.4	76.6	3.0
Chemical	67,041.6	17.6	3,809.2	24.2	66.1	9.7
Graphic arts	22,920.3	9.2	2,491.3	39.4	56.5	4.1
Textiles	14,004.5	6.3	2,222.9	91.4	8.0	.7
Other	436,056.5	30.1	14,486.9	39.6	52.0	8.4

SOURCE: Ministerio de Agricultura, Dirección General de Comercio e Industria, *Censo Industrial y Comercial de la República Argentina, 1908–1914* (Buenos Aires, 1915).
[a]In nominal pesos.

industries in 1913.[4] Before the First World War, the most profitable enterprises, agriculture, and the milk and sugar industries, were controlled by Argentines. In the rest of the economy, the patterns of foreign ownership that were to mark Argentine economic history were already in evidence: British dominance in utilities, and United States investment in import-substituting and export-promoting industries, such as meat packing, sheepskin processing, shoe and sewing machine factories, chemicals, and petroleum. Europeans concentrated in the quebracho industry.[5] British performance in the utilities was criticized justifiably. Concern about dependence on foreign owners grew when the owners were absentee, rather than immigrant, and when they formed a highly visible nucleus of dominant firms in an industry. As their importance increased, German and American capital came under attack.

On the other hand, there was little concern about either the structure or the terms of trade (prices of exports divided by prices of imports) before the First World War. Argentina's five main trading partners, Great Britain, France, Germany, Italy, and the United States, accounted for half of Argentine exports, and one-quarter of Argentine imports, while Argentina accounted for only 2½ percent of their trade. If disputes were to arise, Argentina would have little bargaining power. This was much more important in the early 1900s, when exports accounted for 25 percent of gross domestic product, than it has been since 1955, when exports have accounted for only 6 percent of gross domestic product.

The circumstances of Argentine trade were favorable at the beginning of the century; terms of trade improved 25.8 percent from 1892–99 to 1900–12. Argentines did not suggest that Europe was so rich that a larger share of each additional dollar of imports would be spent on machines rather than food, so that food prices would fall and terms of trade move against Argentina. Agricultural exports were promoted, and effective tariff protection was given to industry. The importance of Great Britain as a source of trade and investment declined until the Great Depression (see Table 8.2). Argentina's ability to increase its economic output and to diversify its productive structure and trading partners, from the beginning of the century until the Great Depression, indicates that during this period Argentina was integrated into the world economy in conditions in which a strong sense of national self-interest guided decision making.

Argentine economic policy was designed to function in pre-World War I conditions. Argentina was on the gold standard; as a result, international trade was central to both money supply, and, through customs receipts, to government revenues.

On the other hand, most American economists say that the performance of a modern economy is determined by the level of demand. The components of demand are consumption, investment, and government spending, plus foreigners' spending on

Table 8.2 Percentage Distribution of Argentine Imports and Exports According to Trading Partner 1900–1904 to 1950–1953

| | Imports | | | | | |
	Britain	France	Germany	U.S.A.	Italy	Other
1900–04	33.1	9.0	13.5	12.4	10.9	21.1
1905–09	33.8	9.8	14.5	13.7	9.0	19.2
1910–14	32.8	9.3	16.6	14.3	8.5	18.5
1915–19	25.7	5.6	.6	31.9	6.7	29.5
1920–24	23.4	6.0	10.8	25.0	6.5	28.3
1925–29	17.5	6.0	11.5	24.6	8.7	28.7
1930–34	22.4	5.7	10.2	15.3	9.5	36.9
1935–39	22.2	4.7	9.6	15.6	4.5	43.4
1940–44	17.9	.6	.3	26.1	.4	54.7
1945–49	11.9	3.3	.1	27.9	6.5	50.3
1950–53	7.9	8.3	7.6	18.2	4.6	53.4

| | Exports | | | | | |
	Britain	France	Germany	U.S.A.	Italy	Other
1900–04	16.6	14.5	12.2	4.6	2.3	49.8
1905–09	17.6	10.7	11.4	4.6	3.8	51.9
1910–14	25.9	8.6	11.4	7.6	3.1	43.4
1915–19	31.0	11.7	.2	21.1	5.2	30.8
1920–24	25.4	6.3	7.2	10.8	3.6	46.7
1925–29	27.6	6.6	12.1	8.8	5.4	39.5
1930–34	37.4	7.2	8.3	6.5	4.3	36.3
1935–39	33.4	4.9	7.4	11.5	3.5	39.3
1940–44	36.0	1.2	—	26.1	—	36.7
1945–49	25.7	5.7	1.4	13.5	5.1	48.6
1950–53	17.2	6.3	5.1	20.6	5.2	45.6

SOURCES: Vásquez-Presedo, *El Caso Argentino,* and *Anuario del Comercio Exterior,* several issues.

goods and services exported from a nation, minus a nation's spending on imports. The first three items are strongly influenced by nationally controlled fiscal and monetary policy. The latter two are strongly influenced by foreign nations' policies.

In attempting to isolate the effects of foreign-influenced from domestic-influenced policies, note that the foreign-influenced variable (real foreign exchange level) moves in the opposite direction from the domestic-influenced variables (fiscal and monetary policy).[6]

In evaluating the effect of domestic and foreign-influenced policy variables on the economy, it is necessary to take other factors which influence economic performance into account. These can be grouped into expectations, and good or bad luck years. In many systems of economic analysis, the interest rate is used to represent market evaluations of risk, and therefore expectations. There are two reasons for not using the interest rate in this manner in the Argentine case. The first is that for many years, the official interest rate was set by the government. The second is that the real rate of interest is determined by world as well as Argentine conditions, so that a change in the interest rate reflects factors other than expectations in Argentina. In the regression analysis introduced in this chapter, the Argentine presidency, rather than the interest rate, is used as a variable which reflects Argentine expectations. This is done because Argentines' economic behavior often reflects their faith in the president: they invest, or withhold investment, and raise prices and wages, or keep them level, based on their evaluation of the president, his program, and his ability to enforce it. Who is president corresponds to Argentine expectations of the immediate future; it has a significant relationship to Argentine economic performance.

Good or bad luck years include those historical accidents that were outside the control of domestic or foreign economic policy makers, which influenced Argentine economic performance. These were World War I, the years of extreme shipping shortages in World War II, drought, and the Great Depression. Thus, the discussion of Argentine economic relationships with the rest of the world is necessarily complex, and includes an analysis of historical accident, policy variables influenced by domestic and foreign economic decision makers, and Argentine expectations.

Before the First World War, Argentina was part of Britain's unofficial empire. Although this relationship had been weakened by the Argentine financial difficulties of the 1890s, Britain was still Argentina's most important trading partner before World War I. The hypothesis that trade with Great Britain was an important but not unique determinant of Argentine economic activity is partially supported by the fact that before World War I, Argentine gross domestic product was more strongly correlated with Argentine government spending than with United Kingdom imports from Argentina.[7] As merchandise imports comprised one-quarter of Argentine gross domestic product before World War I, their sudden unavailability, due to the lack of shipping to Europe during the war, was an economic disaster for Argentina, whose income fell from 4,875 million gold pesos in 1913 to 4,213 million in 1917 (see Table A.I).[8] To some extent, the United States supplied goods previously obtained from the United Kingdom, France, and Germany; western world production was directed to the war effort, and little attention was paid to supplying nonbelligerents. Although the value of Argentine exports rose from 500 to 672 million gold pesos from 1913 to 1918, the value of imports fell from 497 million gold pesos to an average of 344 million from 1914 through 1917. Prices of imports rose more rapidly than prices of exports, and in consequence, terms of trade fell 13 percent from 1914 to 1915–18; the reduction in the volume of imports was greater than the reduction in their value.

This decline in the volume of imports constituted a shortage of real goods and services which would have led to inflation even if the money supply had been held constant. The imported nature of the Argentine inflation of 60 percent during World War I is underscored by the fact that the money supply increased only 45 percent. It fell from 949.0 million pesos in 1912 to 788.4 million in 1914, regaining the prewar level only in 1917, and reaching 1,148.7 million in 1918, which was 21 percent above the 1912 level. Average annual government income fell from 325 million pesos during 1910–13 to 248 million in 1914–18. The greatest shortfall occurred in customs receipts, which fell from 61 percent of government income in 1910 to 45 percent in 1917.

During the war, an estimated 16 percent of the labor force was unemployed. The government attempted to provide jobs despite the shortfall in income, but we are uncertain as to the amount of government spending. Contemporary sources indicate that government spending fell from 409 million pesos in 1910–13 to 401 million in 1914–18. Current revisions based on United Nations estimates indicate an increase of real government spending of 19 percent between 1913 and 1918. The gap between government receipts and expenditures was covered by borrowing. The deficit (using the contemporary sources) rose from 35 percent of income in 1910 to 61 percent in 1914–18. Government borrowing did not take the form of a major increase in the public debt. The government relied on loans from the banks, with the result that funds remaining for loans to the private sector fell.[9] In the Banco de la Nación, loans for agriculture, stock raising, commerce, and industry comprised 80 percent of the Bank's portfolio in 1914, but only 57 percent in 1918. The per capita level of bank loans was below the prewar level until 1918; the fall in the availability of credit paralleled the course of the economy.[10] Nonetheless, in the absence of a greater availability of imports, or of Argentine ability to produce goods previously imported, it is not clear that increased credit to the private sector would have increased its output.

Expansion in government activity and money supply was strongest under President Hipólito Yrigoyen, who first governed from 1917 to 1922. His expenditures are attributed to political needs rather than to economic theories by friends and enemies alike. Social acts were far more prominent than economic actions, as indicated by both the conservative Finance Minister Federico Pinedo, and the Peronist Finance Minister Alfredo Gomez Morales, in their evaluation of President Yrigoyen.[11] According to Pinedo, "Yrigoyen was not a statesman, but a demagogue. One of the social conquests was to make the oligarch and plutocrat Joaquin Anchorena wait in the waiting room while receiving the rabble-rousing Sailor García." Alfredo Gomez Morales states:

> Yrigoyen's government in the First World War was, in economics, a disaster. His ideas were like those of any other *estanciero,* although more paternalist and humane. . . . During the war, flour was scarce, while enormous quantities of wheat were in the port to be sent abroad. No one conceived that it was possible to dictate a law retaining the amount needed for domestic consumption. Free trade required that wheat be allowed to leave as it [free trade] was sacrosanct. That was when they initiated Radical Bread, made with bran.* [12]

*Based on interviews carried out in Spanish in 1971 by investigators of the Instituto Torcuato Di Tella. The translations are mine. Note that Sr. Gomez Morales read and corrected the transcripts of his interview; Sr. Pinedo died before doing so. In accordance with the rules governing the use of this material, I have paraphrased his remarks, which, although placed in quotes to identify them, are not intended as literal quotations.

Although economic policies largely reflected political considerations, the policies adopted strongly influenced the nation's economic performance. The impact of these policies, and of the regimes which made them, is subjected to econometric analysis in the section that follows. The results of the analysis vary strikingly, depending upon how much control over the economy is attributed to presidential decision making. If we hold the incrementalist belief that current actions are influenced strongly by past commitments, then only the percentage change in levels of any category of expenditure can be influenced by presidential action; the level of expenditure reflects the dead hand of the past as well as current commitments. If we do not hold an incrementalist view of presidential decision making, then it would have to be argued that although presidential decisions in the past, as well as in the present, affected economic performance, when a single individual had been president for many years, the level of expenditure, rather than changes in the level, captures the effect of presidential action.

I have suggested that fiscal and monetary policy, international trade, the president, and good or bad luck years together determine the level of Argentine economic output. In this analysis, fiscal policy is represented by the level of real government spending; monetary policy, by the level of the real money supply; and international trade, by the level of real foreign exchange. Dummy variables are established for the presidency, and for good or bad luck years (see the definitions attached to Table 8.3). When the incrementalist interpretation of Presidential decision making was used in my first analysis (the relationship between a percentage change in each of the variables and a percentage change in real gross domestic product was examined for 1914–54),[13] I found that the percentage change in real government spending, a constant term, a percentage change in real money supply, and the presidencies of Yrigoyen and Alvear make a positive and significant contribution to the explanation of percentage change in real gross domestic product. Wage shares increased strongly during these presidencies, and this may have generated favorable expectations about the sale of Argentine goods, thus stimulating

Table 8.3 Determinants of Real Gross Domestic Product 1914–1954

GDPMN	R²/SEE	TXR	MONEYREL	GOVREAL	TIME	X6	X7	X8	X9
OLS	0.9967	−8189	4.559*	0.9289	298.0*	866.6	1569.	232.0	530.1
DW = 2.10	469.6	−0.8133	2.996	0.9073	3.688	1.775	2031	0.2416	0.5049
	X10	X11	X12	X13	X14	Constant			
	1372.		2223	3766*	−791.2*	3167.*			
	1.153		1.807	2360	−3.784	3.008			

LG	R²/SEE	LT	LM	LGV	X6	X7	X8	X9	X10
OLS	0.9950	0.1813E-01	0.1684*	0.6406*	0.8395E-01*	0.1328*	0.9257E-01	0.1025	0.1108
DW = 2.08	0.3258E-01	07847	3.395	8128	2.378	2.630	1776	1.887	1.695
	X11	X12	X13	X14	Constant				
	0.9013E-01	0.1062E-01	−0.7291E-01	−0.6680E-01*	3.965*				
	1.249	0.1185	−0.6240	−5.023	7.087				

GDPMN	R²/SEE	MNXCGR	MONEYREL	GOVREAL	TIME	X6	X7	X8	X9
OLS	0.9967	−9.637	4.595*	0.8735	229.6*	8345	1509.	212.7	471.6
DW = 2.09	4664	−1.020	3.062	0.8687	3.784	1.716	1960	0.2311	0.4619
	X10	X11	X12	X13	X14	Constant			
	1306.		2230.	3801*	−812.5*	3224*			
	1.122		1.838	2.397	−3.859	3.123			

LG	R²/SEE	LMNXR	LM	LGV	X6	X7	X8	X9	X10
OLS	0.9950	0.9475E-02	0.1672*	0.6349*	0.8516E-01*	0.1341*	0.8689E-01	0.9862E-01	1.1082
DW = 2.11	0.3281E-01	0.4527	3.336	7.906	2.395	2.633	1.676	1.786	1.625
	X11	X12	X13	X14	Constant				
	0.9199E-01	0.1252E-01	−0.7002E-01	−0.6775E-01*	4.045*				
	1.267	0.1384	−0.5949	−4.833	7.213				

GDPMN

GDPMN	R²/SEE	IRD	MONEYREL	GOVREAL	TIME	X6	X7	X8	X9
OLS	0.9969	−15.69	4.152*	0.6966	320.9	829.3	1336.	−267.7	44.18
DW = 2.25	4553	−1.557	2754	0.7130	4.045	1.786	1.754	−0.2704	0.4173E-01

	X10	X11	X12	X13	X14	Constant
	9490.	1072.	1951.	3730.*	−765.1*	3215.*
	0.8130	0.8716	1.615	2414	−3.838	3.347

LG

LG	R²/SEE	LI	LM	LGV	X6	X7	X8	X9	X10
OLS	0.9949	−0.3356E-02	0.1698*	0.6225*	0.8479E-01*	0.1309*	0.7150E-01	0.8195E-01	0.9628E-01
DW = 2.13	0.3287E-01	−0.3287	3.390	8.133	2.381	2.552	1.191	1.367	1.454

	X11	X12	X13	X14	Constant
	0.9215E-01	0.1445E-01	−0.6834E-01	−0.7026E-01*	4.164*
	1.266	0.1599	−0.5802	−5.610	8.089

SOURCE: Cortés Conde, Gorostegui de Torres, and Halperin Donghi, *Evolución de las Exportaciones Argentinas*; International Monetary Fund, *Balance of Payments Yearbook*; BCRA, *La Evolución de la Balanza de Pagos*.

NOTE: Variable X 14, "bad luck years," includes World War I, the years of the worst shipping shortages of World War II, drought years, and depression years. Results similar to those obtained using X 14 were also obtained when either X 16 or X 17 were substituted for X 14. X 16 included World War II, drought, and depression years (1914–17, 1930–33, 1938–45, 1949, 1952, and 1954); X 17 included World War I, and 1930–54, all of which had some degree of trade limitation. X 14 was chosen as the variable to be discussed in the text as the best results were obtained by its use.

E-01 indicates that the decimal point should be read as one place to the left; E-02 indicates that it should be read as two places to the left.

Definition of Variables

GDPMN	Gross Domestic Product, in 1943 pesos.
LG	Percentage Change of GDPMN. (logarithm).
TXR	Total Foreign Exchange Income, in 1943 pesos.
LT	Percentage Change of TXR.
MONEYREL	Money Supply, in 1943 pesos.
LM	Percentage Change of MONEYREL.
GOVREAL	Government Expenditure, in 1943 pesos.
LGV	Percentage Change of GOVREAL.
MNXCGR	Export Income, in 1943 pesos.
LMNXR	Percentage Change of MNXCGR.
IRD	Import Expenditure, in 1943 pesos.
LI	Percentage Change of IRD.

Dummy Variables

TIME	Time.
X6	1923–28 (Alvear).
X7	1929–30 (Yrigoyen).
X8	1931–32 (Uriburu).
X9	1933–38 (Justo).
X10	1939–41 (Ortiz).
X11	1942–43 (Castillo).
X12	1944–46 (Farrell).
X13	1947–54 (Perón).
X14	1914–17, 1930–33, 1938, 1943, 1945, 1949, 1952, 1954 (bad luck years).

growth. Indirect evidence for this hypothesis stems from the fact that the wage share contributes significantly to the explanation of the output level of selected mass consumption goods, whose output increased strikingly under Yrigoyen and Alvear.

Bad luck years are negative and significant contributors to the explanation of the percentage change in real gross domestic product. It should be noted that including bad luck years in the model does not significantly improve the explanation, but does significantly increase the importance of the presidency. It is also striking that neither the percentage change in total foreign exchange income, in income from export receipts, or in expenditure on imports, is significantly related to the percentage change in real gross domestic product, which would have been the case if Argentina had depended upon imported supplies to maintain output for the entire 1914–54 period.

If the incrementalist view of presidential decision making is correct, then, except for the 1920s, little that the presidents did other than effect the changes in the real level of foreign exchange, money supply, and government spending, had a significant effect on changes in the real level of gross domestic product. When we examine the relationship of the variables by subperiod, the pattern that emerges indicates the increasing importance of a percentage change in real government spending in explaining a percentage change in Argentine gross domestic product until 1944. After World War II, the percentage change in real export earnings was a significant determinant of real economic growth, but it was less significant and had a lower weight (see Appendix C) in explaining the growth rate than did percentage change in real government spending. Throughout the 1914–54 period, the percentage change in real government spending was more significant than the percentage change in other policy variables, and had a greater weight in explaining percentage increases in real gross domestic product.

The percentage change in real money supply is the second most important explanatory economic policy variable for a percentage change in real gross domestic product. For the period as a whole, the percentage change in real export earnings is not a significant determinant of the percentage change of real gross domestic product.

I used a nonincrementalist interpretation of presidential decision making in my second analysis. In order to ensure that the variable for presidency measures the net impact of policy making (as distinct from the trend of the economy), a variable for time is included in the regression model. The results of an analysis examining the effect of levels of variables on the level of real gross domestic product are strikingly different from those reported above. The most important contribution to the explanation of real gross domestic product is bad luck years, which are negative and significant. Positive and significant contributions to the explanation of real gross domestic product are made by time, a constant term, money supply, and the presidency of Perón, under whom wage shares increased strikingly. Indeed, Perón declared in 1945 that he was not a fascist but a follower (*partidario*) of Hipólito Yrigoyen.[14] If we set the criterion of significance at the 10 percent level, then the presidencies of Alvear (1923–28), Yrigoyen (1929–30), and Farrell (1944–46) are positive and significant. Once again, neither total foreign exchange, export earnings nor import expenditures are significant.

An examination of the relationship between the levels of the policy variables and the level of real gross domestic product for 1914–54 indicates that the order of significance of their contribution to the explanation of real gross domestic product is real government expenditure, real money supply, and real exchange income. The same is true for percentage changes of the policy variables and percentage changes in real gross domestic product. Percentage changes in total foreign exchange receipts are significant contributors to the explanation of percentage change in real gross domestic product in the post-World War II period. The level of real export earnings is a significant contributor to the explanation of the level of real gross domestic product during the Great Depression, although the level of foreign exchange is not, which at least in part explains the government's concern with maintaining traditional exports.

In interpreting the importance of the presidencies, the incrementalist view is adopted for all presidencies except that of Perón. Since Perón held office for a dozen years, the nonincrementalist interpretation seems appropriate for that period.

As his predecessors held office for relatively short periods of time, the incrementalist view appears appropriate for the pre-Peronist period. This evaluation is applied throughout the rest of this analysis.

In the 1920s, the advent of peace increased the availability of imports and decreased the importance of foreign exchange availability. The impact of level and percentage change of real government spending outweighs that of either real money supply or real export earnings, neither of which are significant.

Within the context of a somewhat reduced influence of foreign trade on the economy, the problem of dependence on a single trading partner increased: Britain took twice its prewar share of Argentine exports. Britain's low economic growth, combined with Argentine difficulties in selling her exports to other nations, may have placed an implicit limit on Argentine growth.

On the import side, to the extent that Argentina could be forced to buy goods from Great Britain, she was saddled with inappropriately designed goods at high prices, because they were designed for an economy with British rather than Argentine factor proportions. Britain had large supplies of labor relative to capital, especially when compared to the United States; factor proportions within Britain did not encourage the development of capital-intensive technology. In the United States, as in Argentina, labor was comparatively scarce, and capital-intensive technology was therefore more profitable than in Britain. Moreover, Argentina and the United States had similar agricultural conditions; United States agricultural equipment was suited to Argentine agriculture. In the case of railroads, Britain was a nation of high population density, short distances, and intense use of railroads, and it therefore relied on heavy steel rails. Steel, however, is expensive. The United States had large distances, a population density lower than Britain's, and a more moderate and seasonal use of rails for agricultural shipments, and therefore relied on light-weight steel rails. American conditions were similar to those of Argentina; British conditions were not. Thus, similar factor proportions in the United States and Argentina contributed to an Argentine preference for American capital goods, and the

United States therefore replaced Britain as the leading source of imports (see Table 8.2).

Argentina's difficulties in marketing her exports stemmed from the fact that while her economy was complementary to Great Britain's, it was competitive with that of the United States and food-producing European nations. Argentine exports to the United States increased at the beginning of the war by "concentrating on the shipment of hides, wool, linseed, and quebracho. United States demand for these goods was certain to diminish after the war ended. On the other hand, the promising sales of corn and meat that had become important in 1914 ... fell to almost nothing due to the revival of United States agricultural production."[15] During 1914–18, although the value of United States–Argentine trade increased, its volume declined.

After the war, both the United States and Argentina were caught with unsalable surpluses of cattle. The United States producers and the U.S. Department of Agriculture obtained high tariffs on raw material products and sanitary restrictions regulating their trade in 1921 and 1922. European nations were concerned with self-sufficiency and raised their tariffs. Great Britain enacted a limited imperial preference on trade in manufactures and semi-manufactures in 1921. Although these restrictions did not affect Argentine goods, Great Britain threatened to extend such restrictions to Argentine products as well.[16]

After the war, few of the Argentine industries that had begun to develop with government aid were strong enough to extract protection from newly available imports. Many firms disappeared. Nonetheless, economic structure did not immediately revert to its prewar channels. Argentina's trading partners took advantage of new situations. Exporters who desired to protect their markets against those Argentine firms operating behind protective tariff barriers invested in Argentina in order to maintain their market. In some cases, Europeans copied American products and sold them at lower prices, while the establishment of United States manufacturing firms in Argentina provided a market for American exports. Nor was American investment confined to manufactures: in 1929,

United States direct investments in Argentina, excluding the value of petroleum deposits still in the ground, were estimated at $331,819,000 distributed among 99 firms, which included utilities, $147,736,000; manufacturing, $82,008,000; selling, $52,908,000; petroleum, $29,811,000; and miscellaneous, $19,-256,000.[17] (An additional $20,000,000 should be added to allow for U.S. loans to and investments in Argentine controlled enterprises.) Further, Argentine government loans were sold in New York, rather than London. Thus, while the United States dominated foreign loans to and investments in Argentina, and sales of many goods to Argentina, Great Britain continued to dominate the market for Argentine exports.

The increasing dependence of Argentina on Great Britain during the late twenties was underscored by Sir Malcolm Robertson, British Ambassador to Argentina, who remarked that "Without saying so in as many words, which would be tactless, what I really mean is that Argentina must be regarded as an essential part of the British Empire. We cannot get on without her, nor she without us." His views reflected the fact that Britain took almost 30 percent of Argentine exports, but Argentina bought only 20 percent of her imports from Britain. Thus, Argentine reliance on Britain for export sales had doubled since the beginning of the century, while imports from Britain had fallen by one-third.

Yet Argentina's ability to import from any nation depended upon her ability to export; although imports were 20 percent of gross domestic product, they had, as we have seen, a smaller role in determining Argentine economic performance than either Argentine monetary or fiscal policy. Nonetheless, the shock of World War I led many Argentines to believe that the size of international trade was crucial to Argentine economic performance. Since Argentina sold primarily to Great Britain, Argentine-British trade relations were central to Argentine trade policy; British economic conditions, which influenced British trade with Argentina, therefore were thought to influence Argentine economic growth. British purchases from Argentina were 6.5 percent of gross domestic product during the 1920s.

The course of Anglo-Argentine trade relations varied strikingly during this decade. The initially weakened postwar economic relations between Britain and Argentina are reflected in a lower correlation between United Kingdom imports from Argentina and Argentine gross domestic product: 0.81 for 1918–24 compared to 0.94 for 1900–13. As dependence on sales to the United Kingdom increased during the twenties, this correlation rose to 0.93 for 1925–29. Yet the limited reliance of the Argentine economy on British economic conditions is indicated by the fact that Britain's real income did not regain its prewar level until 1927; the Argentine economy recuperated by 1918.[18]

When changes in income were great, however, they led to a change in the level of international trade and Argentine economic activity. This relationship was strongest during the Great Depression, when British imports from Argentina fell, as did Argentine gross domestic product.[19] Similarly, when United Kingdom prices fell, so did Argentine, despite the fact that Argentina experienced uneven increases in the money supply and in government spending. In these circumstances, it is reasonable to speak of the impact of an imported deflation, just as, when the prices of imports rise and domestic prices follow, we speak of an imported inflation.

Although the close relationship between British trade and income, and that of Argentina, gave the impression that Argentina was increasingly within Britain's economic sphere, Britain was far from happy with the fact: Argentina ran a consistent surplus in her balance of trade with the United Kingdom. Starting with World War I, Argentine merchandise imports from Great Britain were less than merchandise exports, except for 1922–23. Argentina's payments for British goods were 38 percent less than British payments for Argentine goods in 1914–21; 15 percent less in 1923–26; 46 percent less in 1927–29; 45 percent less during the thirties; 62 percent less during the forties, and 41 percent less during the early fifties. During the 1920s, Britain tried to increase its sales to Argentina by urging "Buy from those who buy from us!" as a principle of international trade, a policy first advocated by the British Ambassador in 1926. By threatening to treat Argentina more severely than the Commonwealth nations unless a series of trade concessions was granted, Britain laid the groundwork for the Roca-Runciman Treaty (May 1, 1933).

Citizens of both nations claimed that they were cheated under its provisions, which guaranteed Argentine sales of chilled beef to Britain at mid-1932 levels in exchange for arrangements that funds arising from such sales be substantially spent in Great Britain.[20] Trade policy was buttressed by exchange controls, and by other policies which successfully favored Great Britain: "Whereas practically the totality of imports from Britain received official exchange, not more than half of those from the United States . . . were covered in this manner."[21] As a consequence, imports from Great Britain rose from 17.5 to 22.2 percent of the total from 1929 to 1939. Exports to Great Britain rose from 32.1 to 35.9 percent. The key item in trade relations with Great Britain during this period is that from 1934 to 1936, Great Britain purchased 98.6 percent of Argentine exports of chilled beef, 77.0 percent of frozen mutton and lamb, and 76.8 percent of the frozen pork exports.[22] Despite the very great dependence of the cattle industry on British markets in foreign trade, roughly three-quarters of Argentine beef was consumed within the nation in 1935. The share of domestic consumption of all meats in total production rose from 49 percent in 1920–24, to 56 percent in 1925–29, to 60 percent in 1930–34, and to 62 percent in 1935–39. The decreasing importance of meat exports in total meat production is one reason why the Roca-Runciman Treaty was criticized. Supporters of the treaty are well aware that Britain accounted for 7 percent of Argentine gross domestic product during the Great Depression. Nonetheless, it is true that the level of government spending was more important than international trade in determining the performance of the Argentine economy.[23]

Nonetheless, the government was preoccupied to a great extent with obtaining income; it stated that unless interest and amortization payments were maintained, it would be unable to market either its domestic or foreign debt. The breakdown of international trade made it difficult to maintain payments; the government therefore repatriated part of the foreign debt, saving an estimated 70,201,000 pesos that otherwise would have been sent abroad.[24] Yet, only moderate benefits were obtained from foreign lenders and investors, whose investment in Argentina continued, but did not keep pace with domestic growth: foreign ownership fell to 10.5 percent of total investment. Since international capital markets were of limited value as a source of funds during the depression, there was increasing pressure to create resources locally.

The result was that the Argentine economic new deal was a curate's egg: good in spots, bad in others. Even in those instances where economic policies were a success, they were a psychological failure. The government's contempt for both intellectual and political opposition, coupled with respect for foreigners, fed the flames of xenophobia (see chapter 4). It was increasingly practical to enforce xenophobic policies, as the outside world had increasingly little to offer.

The partial restraint that had been imposed during the depression was loosened as World War II began. The lack of imported supplies, coupled with the need to maintain economic activity, gave rise to increases in money supply and government spending that led to an inflation that predates Perón.

The Argentine government has been accused of negligence in maintaining high levels of foreign exchange, when it should have spent its exchange on stockpiling imports of vital supplies as the war approached. This charge should be modified by the fact that many policy makers expected Germany to win the war rapidly, in which case supplies could have been maintained and stockpiling would have wasted exchange and damaged the exchange rate.[25] In many respects, the economic impact of World War II was similar to that of World War I, with two significant exceptions: Argentines were certain that they did not wish to lapse again into vulnerability to outside forces at the end of the war, while Americans were certain that Argentines were fascists who should be punished. With respect to vulnerability through international trade, it was clear that Argentina would continue to need foreign supplies. Yet in 1951, Gomez Morales castigated previous regimes for lacking an independent economic policy:

> Argentina, before the Peronist Revolution, without doubt had its political objectives, although they appeared blurred by a conception lacking realism and neutralized by the lack of a positive policy on international affairs. This is even more true

in the economic sphere, since it would be difficult to achieve any fundamental objective without first achieving economic independence. . . .

What did the Great Powers want from us? To maintain us in our condition of producers of cheap raw materials and consumers of expensive manufactures. To maintain us in our character of exporters of *regalias* [roughly, "royal benefits"], dividends, incomes, and other services to feed the coffers of the great foreign capitalist consortiums.[26]

The official Argentine policy was that the World War II and the postwar policy of the Allies, which focused on provisioning the Allies and rebuilding Europe, also tended to force less developed nations into a status quo of raw materials producers, and, *pari passu,* to prevent their industrialization. Gomez Morales noted that Adam Smith and Jean Baptiste Say thought that the United States should confine itself to agricultural production; he found Allied advice to Argentina equally enlightened.[27] In a moderate mood, Gomez Morales stated in 1971 that "We interpret economic independence not as autarchy, but the retention of decision making."[28]

During the war, it was not possible to buy scarce materials. The same was true immediately after the war, when United States production was used to rebuild Europe: Argentina could not obtain goods, even by paying for them. Reserves were used to cancel the foreign debt—as Central Bank President Prebisch had proposed—as there was no way that they could be used to supply the country with anything other than war surplus. This at least eliminated interest and amortization payments on the foreign debt, which freed a substantial part of export earnings for current imports. Thus, telephones and other basic public services were purchased from their foreign owners. There was no choice about the purchase of railroads (see chapter 7). A British representative indicated that Argentina's blocked sterling reserves were to be considered Argentina's contribution to the war effort, to help to save the free world.

With respect to American attitudes, although diplomats assured Argentines of the United States' good will, the American Congress was interested in farm bloc votes, and continued to be hostile to Argentina; Americans generally thought Argentines were dictatorial and pro-Nazi. In the postwar period, Argentina was punished by the administration of Marshall Plan expenditures in Europe in ways that limited European purchases of Argentine goods. United States Department of State officials alleged at least thirty instances of outright discrimination against Argentina by European Cooperation Administration officials. Moreover, E.C.A. officials told Argentina that a percentage of any dollars spent in Argentina under the Marshall Plan would have to be returned to the United States to pay outstanding debts. This situation was slightly alleviated by the United States Army, which purchased Argentine meat without stipulating how the dollars be spent by Argentina.[29]

The situation was particularly acute because President Perón believed that the United States Secretary of State George C. Marshall, and Ambassador James Bruce, had stated that the United States expected to buy Argentine surpluses to supply Europe; however, the United States converted the Marshall Plan into a vehicle for disposing of United States farm surpluses. Argentina, therefore, had "agricultural surpluses and a shortage of exchange."[30] The United States also prevented the British from paying their debts to Argentina with Marshall Plan aid, and forced Argentina to use her blocked sterling balances to purchase outmoded British-owned Argentine railroads (see chapter 7). Moreover, the United States also opposed, unsuccessfully, the Anglo-Argentine Trade Pact of 1949, under which Argentina and Britain exchanged meat and petroleum. As in the case of opposition to the Miranda Eady agreement, this stemmed from United States and British adherence to the Geneva agreement favoring multilateral trade, although at the time the Anglo-Argentine pact was signed, the United States was not able to supply Britain with meat, while Britain and Argentina lacked the dollars to buy American products. Moreover, the United States' adherence to multilateralism was unreasonable both because Argentine ability to trade with the United States was limited by the inconvertibility of Argentine balances of the pound sterling, and because American farmers were opposed to the sale of Argentine agricultural products in the United States.[31] Restrictions on foreign trade were so severe that, with respect to foreign markets, Argentina was faced with virtually wartime conditions until 1953.

According to Alfredo Gomez Morales, Argentina's strong reserve position during these years was more apparent than real, since these were not free reserves which could be used immediately.

Argentines believed that various joint purchase arrangements by the Allies resulted in single (Allied) purchasers and many sellers in various commodity markets; this market structure benefited the single purchaser. In order to obtain better terms, the Argentine State Trading Institute (I.A.P.I.) was created so that "a single purchaser would be faced with a single seller."[32] Unfortunately, Argentine difficulties in selling exports were intensified by the pricing policies of the I.A.P.I., which hindered production at home by low prices to producers, and sales abroad by high foreign sales prices. This is in contrast to Uruguayan policies and performance.[33] However, United States agricultural surpluses and pricing policies would have hindered Argentine sales even without the political conflict between the two nations. To some extent, therefore, Argentina's postwar difficulties in obtaining foreign exchange stemmed not from the dependence of a weak nation on stronger partners, but from an unsuccessful attempt to set prices. Although Argentine Central Bank President Miranda suggested in May 1948 that I.A.P.I. was needed to bargain against such groups as the International Food Council, and that Argentina had quite as much right to I.A.P.I. as the United States did to its own various agricultural support programs, the majority of international trade was returned to private hands in February 1949.[34] The shortage of foreign exchange was mitigated, to some extent, during the Korean War, when Central Bank President Alfredo Gomez Morales believed that maintenance of reserves was a key to obtaining foreign loans. In order to maintain reserves, he converted dollars into gold, and told the military that no dollars were available for imports, which could only be obtained by use of bilateral conventions. Reserves were thus maintained at 40 percent of imports.[35] Because government attempts to obtain foreign exchange by setting the prices of exports had failed, the government obtained a $125 million credit from Eximbank to Argentina; it covered the amount owed in the United States by Argentines. The government attempted to create an economic climate that would attract foreign capital by purchasing foreign firms when enough exchange was available (rather than expropriating them without compensation), and by regulating them when it was not. For example, the foreign-owned electric firm, CADE (which supplied Buenos Aires), was not expropriated by Perón, who did not want to purchase a plant that already was installed in Argentina. An agreement was reached with CADE, and the government focused its attention on the development of the electric grid in the interior, using the government firm, Agua y Energía Eléctrica. CADE was not permitted to expand outside of Buenos Aires, "to make its negotiating attitude more flxible." CADE had to increase its services in Buenos Aires to maintain its concession. It attempted to make the government responsible for the credits used to import the equipment needed for expansion. In this case, the plant would have been paid for by higher rates, guaranteed by the government, and the profits would have gone to CADE. The government countered by expanding the electric plant owned by the government, and then renting that plant to CADE. An agreement was worked out which set the rate of profit and evaluated the firm's capital. This agreement was set aside for one that was more favorable to CADE after the overthrow of Perón.[36]

In 1953, the government established a law (no. 14222) governing foreign investment, and granted carefully negotiated contracts to foreign oil companies. In 1949, the government began negotiations with foreign oil firms, because its own oil firm, Yacimientos Petrolíferos Fiscales (Y.P.F.), supplied only one-half of Argentine oil needs. The Anglo-Argentine Trade Pact bound Argentina to purchase British-produced petroleum from the Middle East. When a British official complained that Argentina failed to fulfill "promptly and completely" the Andes Pact of February 1948 or the Anglo-Argentine Trade Pact of 1949, the *Financial Times* of London suggested:

> If a satisfactory settlement on these questions cannot be reached without undue delay, the Government should withdraw the facilities Argentina secures under the pact for purchasing fuel supplies in the sterling area. At this point, Argentina is most vulnerable. It may be arguable whether the Argentine can find markets in other countries for its meat supplies, but it is certain that the country cannot afford to lose access to sterling area petroleum. There is no other available source from which the supplies needed to keep Argentine industry in full operation can be obtained outside the dollar area. With virtually no gold reserve and little prospect of earning more hard currencies, Argentina is not in a position to satisfy its requirements in that direction. Use of this "sanction" may entail some risk of being temporarily deprived of Argentine meat supplies. But . . . Argentine shipments now account for only 20 percent of Britain's total meat imports, we need have no qualms on that score.[37]

As Argentina fell behind in its payments to Britain (some £500,000 in debt was outstanding by March 31, 1950), the British National Coal Board suspended shipments of coal to the Argentine railways,[38] thereby underscoring Argentina's need for domestic sources of power.

In seeking foreign contracts, the Argentine government would not grant concessions, which were prohibited by Article 40 of the Constitution. An exploration contract was suggested to Esso and Shell, and was rejected on the grounds that to accept such a contract would leave them open to similar restrictions by other nations.[39] A number of Argentine officials were assigned to study Mexican oil policy; as a result of these studies Argentina began negotiations with more than twenty smaller oil firms.

The government wanted a contract signed with Y.P.F. which provided for exploration outside of zones where Y.P.F. had already found oil, and for any oil found to be sold to Y.P.F.

After this was achieved, in a contract with a subsidiary of Standard Oil of California, Esso and Shell entered into negotiations in 1955 with the government. Gomez Morales thought that a mixed society of Argentine and foreign entrepreneurs, with Argentina holding majority control, was an excellent solution.

An insight into the basis of Perón's foreign economic policy is provided by his Economy Minister's criticism of the alternatives. He categorized as "xenophobic" attempts to carry out development alone,[40] while also criticizing as insufficient the policy of President Frondizi's economic adviser,[41] Rogelio Frigerio, of "opening the door to foreign capital [and] establishing a simple set of priorities." Gomez Morales believed that policy agreements must be set investment by investment, with great care for the details. Otherwise, book increases in capital rather than real business would be attracted, and tariff and exchange protection would be required. Summing up his attitude, Gomez Morales said that "it is necessary to attract foreign capital, but also to act with great perspicacity, thinking that foreign capital will not come here as a benefactor; on the contrary, it will extract from the country all that it can. It is a question of finding conditions so that it can come to do business, yes, but dirty business, no. . . ."[42]

Other aspects of foreign economic relations followed a similar pattern of careful choice in establishing ties with outside economic groups: Argentina did not join the International Monetary Fund because it wished to maintain its bilateral trade treaties. Although exchange levels recovered, dependence on foreign loans and investment increased after the overthrow of Perón because the economy increased in complexity, the need for imports began to increase, and it was difficult to replace these new imports by domestic production. The Argentine economy's ability to increase its productive capacity is indicated by the share of imports in the supply of gross fixed investment, which increased from 11.7 to 19.2 percent from 1950 to 1963 (see Table 8.4).

The combination of exchange scarcity and increasingly complex economic structure increased Argentine economic dependence after 1955.[43] The difficulties engendered by

Table 8.4 Imports as a Share of Various Output Categories 1950–1963

Category	1950 (Percent)	1953 (Percent)	1963 (Percent)
Intermediate demand	3.7	3.4	4.2
Final demand	1.6	1.6	5.0
Personal consumption	—	.7	1.4
Government consumption	—	—	1.8
Gross Fixed investment	—	11.7	19.2
Value of production	2.8	2.7	4.5

SOURCE: BCRA, *Transacciones Intersectoriales de la Economía Argentina:* 1950; *ibid.,* 1953; *ibid.,* 1963.

exchange scarcity were compounded by the fact that the new government joined the International Monetary Fund and ended bilateral agreements, which meant that outstanding sums had to be paid immediately in currency rather than in sales of goods in the future. Other indications of increased economic dependence after 1955 are the fact that foreign firms increased their participation in the 100 largest manufacturing firms from 14 percent in 1957 to 50 percent in 1966; these were in the most rapidly growing sectors of industry. Foreign banks raised their share of Argentine bank loans from 16.0 percent in 1966 to 22.3 percent in 1970, and their share of deposits from 31.6 percent to 40.5 percent during this period. Their loans were greatest to industries dominated by foreign firms. Argentines complained that these banks used deposits by Argentine firms to finance foreign competition.

The material presented in this and earlier chapters indicates that foreign influence in the Argentine economy was greatest at the beginning of the twentieth century, and after World War II. Despite the importance of foreigners for specific activities at various times, to the extent that the economy can be controlled by the use of economic policy variables, Argentine influence on the economy has been greater than that of foreigners: first, by sheer size of the domestic market compared to that of foreign trade; second, by predominantly Argentine ownership of factors of production; and third, by the Argentine government's ability to use a variety of instruments of control. It has influenced the distribution of real profits between sectors and has regulated conditions of foreign entry into these sectors, whether as investors or as suppliers.

In the end, foreign influence over the economy depends upon foreigners' ability to cut off supplies. This would be crucial if Argentina were a small nation incapable of manufacturing its own capital goods or other necessary imports, and of operating at full capacity. Imported machines are so often set up for markets larger than Argentina's that excess capacity typified Argentine industry. As substantial economic growth during many periods when imports were scarce indicates, the economy often had great room to expand with existing plant and equipment. When capacity was fully utilized, and scarcity of imports began to matter, the difficulty at times lay as much in Argentine exchange allocation policy (in the 1930s) as it did in foreign unwillingness to supply selected capital goods (World War II and the immediate postwar period). As a result, Argentina's complex international economic relations cannot be characterized as consisting of a one-sided economic dependence.

Chapter Nine: Conclusion

ECONOMISTS CLAIM THAT they can analyze, for any economy, three basic questions: what goods are produced, how they are produced, and for whom they are produced. In Argentina in the twentieth century, the answers to these three questions were determined by a combination of world events, government policy, and consumer demand. Argentines attempted to produce a range of goods which, in their view, would ensure Argentine economic independence; they were limited in their ability to do so by the active intervention of the British and United States governments. On the other hand, the range of consumer goods produced within Argentina was widened by Argentine government-imposed import quotas and exchange control.

In Argentina, government limitation on the importation of cheap foreign equipment has resulted in the high cost of capital goods. At the same time, frequent change of policies has increased the risk of and decreased the investment in capital goods. Consequently, goods are produced in a more labor-intensive manner than would otherwise be the case.

Finally, goods are produced for anyone who can buy them: the government, corporations, and individuals. When the government has pursued a policy of high employment, a wide variety of consumer goods has been produced. When the government has followed a policy of economic contraction, the fall in private demand has been as anticipated: but worse, as unemployment has increased, the infant mortality rate has risen. This has happened because urban Latin Americans feed their children infant formulas and powdered milk bought in stores, instead of nursing them. When unemployment increased, poor families had less money to spend, and added more water than before to infant formula and powdered milk. In consequence, the children were severely malnourished, and the mortality rate far higher than it would have been either if the government had had better policies or if Argentines had nursed their children.

Over the long run, government policy was more successful in maintaining enough food at low prices than it was at providing sufficient low-cost housing either by its own construction or by freeing rents, interest rates, and the use of mortgage bonds so that the private sector would build enough low-cost houses. The lack of low-cost housing was reinforced by the fact that construction was begun for high-cost housing which was not always either completed or rented. Investment in construction often took the place of investment in stocks, and was speculative rather than responsive to past patterns of real profits for each of the sectors of the economy.

Finally, the questions asked here can be asked with reference to regions as well as income classes. Buenos Aires has been favored above all other regions. In the provinces, there has been little relief by use of peaceful means, and an increasing use of violence. Had the provinces been richer, they might have lost more people to car accidents each year. As it is, they increasingly lose them to terror and counterinsurgency. Only redress of regional and class imbalances, and consistent application of policy, would improve Argentine chances for more rapid economic development, and the substitution of death by auto accident for death by politically inspired terror.

Appendix A: The Regression Model Used in Chapter Two

The model used in chapter 2 is based on the adaptive expectations model developed by Mark Nerlove.[1] His basic assumption is that output in a given year reflects the ability of producers to adjust output which obtained in the past to a desired level. As Nerlove points out, for the model to work, it must be assumed that in one period, the economy is in equilibrium.

Producers respond to profits (see chapter 2, note 9). As profit levels change, producers adjust their output in an attempt to reach a new equilibrium position in which the rate of return on investment in any activity, adjusted for risk, is the same as that in any other activity. Producers typically do not supply all of their own financial needs, but also use funds raised from banks, other financial intermediaries, stock markets, and suppliers. Each of these would be loathe to invest funds where the rate of return on investment was less than could be obtained elsewhere. Thus, the assumption of capital mobility does not require that each producer be able to produce each of the alternative products under consideration for investment, but only that lenders be aware of their many opportunities.

For any sector of production, therefore, this year's output is a result of the producers' wish to adjust their output to a new desired level of production, and of the lenders' wish to adjust the distribution of their loans between sectors so that a maximum return is earned. The actual difference between this year's output and last year's, depends upon the difference between desired output for this year, and that of last year, and the time it takes to reach the desired level of output, as shown in equation (1):

$$Q_t - Q_{t-1} = \&(Q^*_t - Q_{t-1}).$$

Q_t is actual output in time t, Q_{t-1} is output in time $t - 1$, Q^*_t is desired output in time t, and & is a coefficient of adjustment, used to estimate the time it takes the economy to reach desired levels of output.

The desired level of production depends on the change in real profits in each sector.[2] My initial assumption is that the change in real profits in each sector (each sector is denominated by the subscripts 1 through 9) in the last period, P_{t-1}, indicates the profit pattern that investors believe will prevail at the end of the production period. This will give the correct ordering of profits between sectors, as I assume that in the initial period, profits on investment adjusted for risk are equal. Moreover, in the Argentine case, 1960 was used as a base year. Change in real profits, therefore, was equal to zero in 1960. There is evidence that actual profits in the cattle industry were zero and that in the economy as a whole, before adjustment for risk, profits were low. After adjustment for risk, they may have been close to zero in 1960. The change in real profits, therefore, is probably fairly close to the level of real profits, adjusted for risk, in Argentina from 1950 to 1969. (The change in real unit profits for each sector is shown in Table A.2.)

I have stated that under my initial assumption that past profits will prevail, P_t is set equal to P_{t-1}. The result is equation (2), which states that desired output depends upon changes in past profits in each of the sectors (written as $P_1 \ldots P_9$):

$$Q^*_t = a + bP_1 + cP_2 + dP_3 + eP_4 + fP_5 \\ + gP_6 + hP_7 + iP_8 + jP_9 + ut.$$

Substituting the right hand side of (2) into (1), we obtain equation (3):

$$Q_t = \&a + \&bP_1 + \&cP_2 + \&dP_3 + \&eP_4 + \&fP_5 + \&gP_6 \\ + \&hP_7 + \&iP_8 + \&jP_9 + (1 - \&)Q_{t-1} + \&ut.$$

The interesting feature of this regression is that it permits the estimation of the time that is needed by the economy to respond to changes in alternate profits. If & equals one, then actual output equals desired output. If & equals one-half, adjustment takes place within two years. If & equals .33, it takes about two and a half years for the changes in output to equal the desired changes in output. The regression coefficients reported in Table A.1—the regression coefficient of Q_{t-1} is equal to $(1 - \&)$—imply that agriculture and mining adjust to desired levels within two years: both commerce and transportation adjust within two years to desired levels of output, and manufacture adjusts in about two and a half years. The remaining sectors had longer periods of adjustment.

A long period of adjustment can reflect either institutional blockages to mobility, or a long maturation time for investment with heavy capital requirements. In the latter case, a long period of adjustment does not imply an inefficient response to profit alternatives. It is particularly plausible in the case of the electricity industry, which needed a long time to realize its capital-intensive projects. Delivery of electricity was marked by shortages, brownouts, and breakdowns throughout the period.

The longer the time it takes to reach desired levels of output, the less rewarding such shifts in resources are likely to be. In general, as economies become more developed, the increasing technological complexity of operation and the greater capital intensity of technique of production imply that increasing lengths of time will be required to reach desired levels of output. This is consistent with Dr. Reca's findings that the speed of adjustment of agricultural production has decreased from 1924–44 to 1945–65.[3] The implications of the coefficients of adjustment reported above are that it will take the economy at least two to three years to adjust to profit changes imposed by the government in an attempt to direct economic activity. Further, given the technological reasons for the length of time it takes to respond fully to profit signals, there is little reason to believe that the government could, by direct operation of the economy, achieve desired changes faster than the private sector. This may be one reason that direct

Table A.1 Determinants of Real Gross Domestic Product 1950–1969

1.	AGRV	R^2/SEE	A1	PA	PMN	PMF	PEL
	OLS	0.9895[a]	−0.5160[a]	211.8[a]	10.149	241.2[b]	10.242
	Q' = 2.27	1.85	−3.940	3.806	1.811	2.332	1.398
2.	MNV	R^2/SEE	MN1	PA	PMN	PMF	PEL
	OLS	.9984[a]	.524[a]	250.0[b]	−2.926	393.493[b]	62.385[a]
	Q' = .77	3.5696	6.644	3.183	− .282	2.565	3.826
3.	MFRV	R^2/SEE	MFR1	MAG	MNP	MFP	MEL
	OLS	0.9941[a]	0.8290[a]	0.6493	0.0453	0.1975	0.4213
	Q' = 1.62	3.544	7.201	1.012	0.2446	1.652	1.178
4.	ELV	R^2/SEE	ELI	AG2	MN2	MF2	EL2
	OLS	0.9989[a]	0.9167[a]	−31.17	−0.311	−90.69	21.93
	Q' = 2.17	3.131	10.99	− 0.3424	−1.028	− 0.6313	1.371
5.	CONV	R^2/SEE		AGRU	MNU	MFRU	ELU
	OLS	.9578[a]		222.78[b]	27.4[c]	205.66	23.59
	Q' = 2.14	5.07		2.66	1.89	1.08	1.33
6.	CMXV	R^2/SEE	CMX1	MAG	MNP	MFP	MEL
	OLS	0.9959[a]	0.8333[a]	0.7643[c]	0.1856	0.0978	0.2165
	Q' = 2.02	1.824	8.996	2.304	1.948	1.603	1.061
7.	TRANSV	R^2/SEE	TRANS1	MAG	MNP	MFP	MEL
	OLS	0.9981[a]	0.8737[a]	0.1652	0.763	0.1684[b]	0.0751
	Q' = .84	1.2481	11.80	0.7213	1.167	4.005	0.5179
8.	FNXV	R^2/SEE	FNX1	AG2	MN2	MF2	EL2
	OLS	0.9992[a]	0.7139[a]	80.56[b]	−4.824[b]	124.6[b]	11.15[a]
	Q' = 2.79	0.6538	9.653	3.440	−2.504	3.071	3.967
9.	SVSV	R^2/SEE	SVS1	PA	PMN	PMF	PEL
	OLS	0.9995[a]	.959[a]	42.841[b]	−0.851	73.224[b]	7.180[b]
	Q' = 1.01	0.549	16.342	2.502	−0.531	2.478	3.182

[a]Significant at the 1 percent level of probability.
[b]Significant at the 5 percent level of probability.
[c]Significant at the 10 percent level of probability.

Definition of Variables

AGRV	Volume of Agricultural Output
MNV	Volume of Mining Output
MFRV	Volume of Manufacturing Output
ELV	Volume of Electricity Output
CONV	Volume of Construction Output
CMXV	Volume of Commercial Output
TRANSV	Volume of Transportation Output
FNXV	Volume of Financial Output
SVSV	Volume of Services Output
A1	AGRV lagged one year
MN1	MNV lagged one year
MRF1	MFRV lagged one year
EL1	ELV lagged one year
CMX1	CMXV lagged one year
TRANS1	TRANSV lagged one year

PCON	PCMX	PTR	PFN	PSV	CONSTANT
27.146	48.088	98.901[a]	10.847	183.964[a]	150.261[a]
1.341	.877	3.637	.902	3.586	11.477
PCON	PCMX	PTR	PFN	PSV	CONSTANT
15.561	349.014[a]	159.415[a]	−16.414	349.266[a]	74.583[a]
.502	3.816	3.518	− .802	4.377	7.966
MON	MCM	MFN	MSV	MTR	CONSTANT
−0.2357	0.5969[a]	1.278	0.3615	0.7337	25.99
−0.8446	2.697	1.323	0.0857	1.523	2.081
CO2	CM2	TR2	EN2	SV2	CONSTANT
23.65	−100.9	−12.13	−45.77[b]	−85.05	25.73[b]
0.7779	−1.068	− 0.2562	− 2.409	− 0.9289	2.440
CONU	CMXU	TRA1	FNXU	SVSU	CONSTANT
−71.41	420.62	132.18	54.11[b]	415.18[a]	100.56[a]
− 1.70	1.08	1.33	2.46	5.35	29.09
MCN	MCM	MFN	MSV	MTR	CONSTANT
−0.2661	0.6251[a]	1.778[b]	−1.390	0.3447	21.16[c]
−1.878	5.324	3.567	−0.6688	1.424	2.184
MCN	MCM	MFN	MSV	MTR	CONSTANT
−0.1772	0.2824[b]	0.3280	1.663	0.5229[b]	19.06[c]
−1.768	3.650	0.9609	1.081	3.123	2.472
CO2	CM2	TR2	FN2	SV2	CONSTANT
36.08[a]	66.45[b]	47.89[a]	6.394	63.90[b]	31.76[a]
5.575	2.537	3.519	1.476	2.520	4.144
PCON	PCMX	PTR	PFN	PSV	CONSTANT
8.572	31.779	18.454[c]	7.389[b]	80.908	7.822
1.577	1.718	1.894	2.389	1.703	1.320

FNX1	FNXV lagged one year
SVS1	SVSV lagged one year
AGRU	Change in real unit profits of agriculture
MNU	Change in real unit profits of mining
MFRU	Change in real unit profits of manufacture
ELU	Change in real unit profits of electricity
CONU	Change in real unit profits of construction
CMXU	Change in real unit profits of commerce
TRANSU	Change in real unit profits of transportation
FNXU	Change in real unit profits of finance
SVSU	Change in real unit profits of services
PA	AGRU lagged one year
PMN	MNU lagged one year
PMF	MFRU lagged one year
PEL	ELU lagged one year
PCON	CONU lagged one year
PCMX	CMXU lagged one year
PTR	TRANSU lagged one year
PFN	FNXU lagged one year
PSV	SVSU lagged one year

AG2	AGRU lagged two years
MN2	MNU lagged two years
MF2	MFRU lagged two years
EL2	ELU lagged two years
CO2	CONU lagged two years
CM2	CMXU lagged two years
TR2	TRANSU lagged two years
FN2	FNXU lagged two years
SV2	SVSU lagged two years
AG3	AGRU lagged three years
MN3	MNU lagged three years
MF3	MRFU lagged three years
EL3	ELU lagged three years
CO3	CONU lagged three years
CM3	CMXU lagged three years
TR3	TRANSU lagged three years
FN3	FNXU lagged three years
SV3	SVSU lagged three years
AG5	AGRU lagged five years
MN5	MNU lagged five years
MF5	MFRU lagged five years
EL5	ELU lagged five years
CO5	CONU lagged five years
CM5	CMXU lagged five years
TR5	TRANSU lagged five years
FN5	FNXU lagged five years
SV5	SVSU lagged five years
MAG	The sum of AGRU × its regression weight through AG5 × its regression weight
MEL	The sum of ELU × its regression weight through EL5 × its regression weight
MNP	The sum of MNU × its regression weight through MN5 × its regression weight
MFP	The sum of MFRU × its regression weight through MF5 × its regression weight
MCN	The sum of CONU × its regression weight through CO5 × its regression weight
MCM	The sum of CMXU × its regression weight through CM5 × its regression weight
MFN	The sum of FNXU × its regression weight through FN5 × its regression weight
MSV	The sum of SVSU × its regression weight through SV5 × its regression weight
MTR	The sum of TRANSU × its regression weight through TR5 × its regression weight

Table A.2 Change in Real Unit Profits of Economic Sectors, 1950–1969, From Levels Prevailing in 1960

	AGRU	MNU	MFRU	ELU	CONU
1950	−0.217391	0.706522	−0.010870	0.195652	0.282609
1951	−0.144000	0.160000	−0.032000	−0.064000	0.176000
1952	−0.122581	0.187096	−0.038710	−0.129032	0.174193
1953	−0.071006	0.035502	−0.011834	−0.147929	0.106509
1954	−0.109890	0.241758	−0.021979	−0.093407	0.197802
1955	−0.149254	0.169154	0.014926	−0.054726	0.179105
1956	−0.099206	0.226190	−0.023810	−0.115080	0.250000
1957	−0.042623	0.226230	−0.042623	−0.288524	0.121312
1958	−0.067146	0.225420	−0.021583	−0.131894	0.127098
1959	0.084223	0.088968	−0.003559	−0.223013	0.053381
1960	0.0	0.0	0.0	0.0	0.0
1961	−0.118613	0.077555	−0.000912	0.093978	0.107664
1962	−0.104181	0.156627	0.003544	0.049610	0.131113
1963	−0.027147	0.180609	−0.006094	0.089751	0.093629
1964	0.106614	−0.010879	−0.033072	−0.063969	0.037859
1965	−0.015327	0.081403	0.001703	−0.011921	0.156335
1966	−0.095371	0.158026	−0.030219	0.089271	0.212919
1967	−0.126726	−0.004454	−0.052561	0.205567	0.254788
1968	−0.111044	−0.040636	−0.094951	0.230940	0.219473
1969	−0.089720	−0.060935	−0.115701	0.079626	0.241869

	CMXU	TRANSU	FNXU	SVSU
1950	−0.021739	−0.032609	0.597826	0.043478
1951	0.048000	−0.064000	0.496000	0.0
1952	−0.019355	0.032258	0.406451	0.038709
1953	−0.106509	0.029586	0.443787	0.065089
1954	−0.126373	0.010989	0.505494	0.104395
1955	−0.119403	−0.039801	0.537314	0.124378
1956	−0.055556	0.059524	0.400793	0.031746
1957	−0.036065	0.134426	0.409837	−0.009836
1958	−0.057554	−0.002398	0.330935	0.076739
1959	0.022539	−0.052194	−0.109134	−0.055753
1960	0.0	0.0	0.0	0.0
1961	−0.055657	0.031022	0.085766	0.120438
1962	−0.109851	0.043940	0.098512	0.141035
1963	−0.108587	0.139612	−0.018837	0.053186
1964	−0.118364	0.061793	−0.027850	0.069626
1965	−0.136580	0.020436	−0.055177	0.146117
1966	−0.163848	0.156917	−0.092875	0.231771
1967	−0.142985	0.197995	−0.077951	0.250334
1968	−0.140817	0.250654	0.078254	0.263730
1969	−0.120935	0.254953	0.191588	0.280934

NOTE: Calculated from price indices with a 1960 base. See Definition of Variables, Table A.1.

ownership of the economy was not a major feature of any of the government's plans before 1970.

The speed of adjustment estimates presented here are based upon equation (3). Although this is the form of the regression model from which it is easiest to calculate the speed of adjustment, it is not always the form of this model which provides the best estimate of output in a given sector. As a check, regressions were estimated, successively, for each sector, setting P_t equal to P_t, P_{t-1}, P_{t-2}, P_{t-3}, P_{t-4}, P_{t-5}, and P_{t-6}. As noted in the text, setting anticipated profits, P_t, equal to those which actually prevailed, P_t, does not imply a belief in crystal ball gazing. Instead, it indicates a belief that businessmen can easily predict profit patterns during a year, because such patterns are heavily influenced by government activities, and government policies are known. Evidence supporting this evaluation is given by the fact that in four out of nine cases, the regression model using last year's changes in alternate profits predicts less of the variance in output than does the model using current changes in alternate profits. However, the use of current changes in real profits gave the best prediction of output only for the construction sector. The time period of changes in real profits included in the regression which predicted output best was one year in the past for agriculture, mining, and service, and two years in the past for electricity and finance. The best estimate for manufacture, commerce, and transport was obtained using the weighted sum of changes in alternate profits for the past five years; the weights were taken from the regression equation for each of these years.

The hypothesis that investors were tied to a sector, rather than being mobile between sectors, was tested by including changes in real profits for each sector for several time periods, and no changes in real profits of other sectors, in the regression equation. Past changes in real profits of a sector predict less of the variance of a sector's output than do the regressions described above; investors are therefore mobile between sectors.

One way in which the estimates of output might be improved is by the inclusion of variables which represent the effect of uncertainty. This can be done by utilizing information on both the level and structure of interest rates. These variables were not included in the final version of the regression, as the government-regulated interest rates differed from those that prevailed on the market; there is no accurate series available on those interest rates that actually were paid. Nonetheless, the rate of interest and the term structure of interest rates were included in a trial run, in case there was some relationship between regulated rates and those that actually prevailed. The structure of interest rates was measured by the ratio of the 30–, 180–, and 360-day interest rate to the 90-day rate; the level was represented by the 180-day rate. In the cases of electricity, commerce, and construction, the regression results were significantly improved if the variables for level and term structure of interest were included.

There are two sectors for which the results of the regression equations require comment: construction and agriculture. The former is presented here, the latter in Appendix B. In the case of construction, a regression equation leaving out past output, and including current changes in real profits, gives the best prediction of current construction output. This is in part because construction activity is speculative. In much of Latin America, and certainly in Argentina, construction activity often is undertaken instead of investment in the stock market. This is because of a well developed market for residential and industrial buildings. Yet the speculative nature of this investment is evident from the large number of high-rent residential buildings that are either incomplete, or completed, but not rented. Nonetheless, the increase in value even of uncompleted or unrented buildings makes the enterprise worthwhile. At the same time, the private sector cannot respond fully to the potential demand for housing, because the government's regulates interest rates, modifies (and, at times, suppresses) mortgage bonds, establishes rent control, and subsidizes housing. If the government were able to provide for the nation's housing needs, the private sector's inability or unwillingness to supply all the housing that the government believes is required under its conditions, would be of limited importance. However, the government apparently lacks the funds, and the private sector the incentive, to invest in the amount of housing that would be enough to satisfy the needs of Argentines of all income classes.

Thus, we find that the unusual form of regression equation obtained for the construction sector is consistent with conditions that are less typical of a market economy than are those in other sectors of the Argentine economy. This is both because of the importance of the level and structure of interest rates for the construction sector, and because of the use of this sector as a supplement to the stock market.

Finally, there are some technical features of this model that differ from the original model proposed by Nerlove. In his model, desired output was measured by the level of inputs the producers used. As Nerlove studied agricultural output, the input he considered was land. This is reasonable if the proportions of land, labor, capital, and other inputs are constant throughout the period studied. If technology changes, and factor proportions with it, the amount of land brought into production is not a consistent measure of producers' intentions. Such changes in technology occurred in the Argentine case. An alternate measure of producers' intentions to produce a desired output which could be used for all sectors was therefore sought.

In equilibrium, factors of production are employed up to the point where the additional rate of profit earned as a result of using the factor is just equal to the additional rate of profit earned on using any other factor. Output reflects the combined use of all inputs, in whatever proportion they were used; actual output appears more reasonable an index of the level of inputs used in an attempt to reach a desired output than does the quantity of any single input. In equation (3), therefore, past output—rather than an index of past input—whether of land or any other factor of production, appears in the right hand side of the equation. This is consistent with the frequently heard comment that current production is strongly influenced by that which was obtained last year.

A technical problem is raised by the inclusion of last year's output in a regression equation used to predict this year's output, because technically imperfect regression statistics, which overstate the significance of various of the explanatory variables, may result. The usual way out of this difficulty is to recast the regression equation, either in first differences, or in logarithms. It is not appropriate to do either in this case, as it would destroy the economic meaning of the regression used here, which involves adjustment to levels.

Moreover, technical tests carried out to determine the validity of the results reported here indicate that autocorrelation of the residuals is not significant at the five percent level of probability for a majority of the regression equations reported. Positive autocorrelation of the residuals is suspected for the regressions for mining and for transport. In the case of transport, the substitution of a regression equation utilizing one year's past profits, rather than several, might eliminate this problem. In the case of mining, no immediate solution suggests itself. I prefer to use a model that corresponds to the way decisions are actually made, and be cautious in relying on the results, rather than to use a system with technically better statistics, but little economic meaning. I therefore believe that the regressions where autocorrelation of the residuals is suspected are worth the benefit of the doubt.

Appendix B: The Regression Model Used in Chapter Four

The regression model used to explain the impact of government policies on the volume of agricultural production, is presented in chapter 4, and is similar to the one in chapter 2. In the model in chapter 4, it is assumed that investors can invest in any of nine agricultural activities, or in nonagricultural activities, and that their investment is determined by changes in real profits. The agricultural activities analyzed are the production of cereals and flax, forrage crops, oilseeds, industrial crops, fruits and flowers, vegetables and legumes, cattle, wool, and milk. The investment opportunities available are represented by changes in real profits of forrage crops, oilseeds, industrial crops, fruits and flowers, vegetables and legumes, cattle, wool, milk, corn, wheat, and nonagricultural activities. As in the case of the model presented in chapter 2, it was assumed that it takes time for businessmen to adjust their production to changing real profit opportunities; for this reason, the previous year's output was included in the regression.

It was believed that the regression model would work less well for agriculture than for other activities because weather conditions strongly influence agricultural output. Weather was not included in the model, because it cannot be changed by government policy makers. Finally, it has been argued that farmers are less able to diversify their investment than other investors, and that as the farm population rose, increased agricultural activity would take place, and agricultural output increase. An alternate series of regressions was therefore run, in which advantage was taken of the almost perfect correlation between population and time. Time was used as a representative of population, and was included, in addition to the output and profit variables already mentioned. The following paragraphs describe the regression procedure applied to each group of agricultural products.

In the case of cereal and flax, the best estimate of output is provided by last year's changes in real profits, last year's output, and population (see Table B.1). An alternate regression was run, in which costs to produce wheat were used in deriving the change in real profit index; the results, however, were poorer than those obtained when the change in alternate real profit index was constructed using the gross domestic price deflator to represent costs. Either wheat production costs are not typical of the cost of producing other grains or flax, or the index of the cost of wheat production is inaccurate.(The change in real unit profits for each agricultural activity and for nonagricultural activities is shown in Table B.2.)

In the case of forrage crops, the best prediction of output is given by last year's output and changes in real profits. The best prediction of oilseed output is given by last year's output and last year's change in real profits. The best prediction of industrial crop output is given by last year's output, changes in real profits three years ago, and population. The three-year lag reflects the cultural practices used for sugar cane and grapes, whose output is difficult to increase in a shorter period of time, although it could, of course, be decreased without a time lag. The best prediction of the output of fruits and flowers is provided by last year's output, this year's changes in real profits, and population. The best estimate of vegetable and legume production is given by last year's output and this year's changes in real profits. The best estimate of wool production is given by last year's output, changes in real profits four years ago, and population. The best prediction of milk production is given by last year's output, changes in real profits this year, and population; the regression, however, is not significant.

The significance of population in the regression equations supplements Reca's finding that the ability to shift land resources in response to price changes was less under Perón than during preceding periods. The products for which popula-

Table B.1 Determinants of Agricultural Production by Product, 1950–1969

Cattle Slaughter, Based on Reca's Data

Dependent Variable	Estimated Coefficient	t
Constant	−41.2856	−41.0630[a]
Herd, Reca 1	0.9886	51.3799[a]
Change in Real Profits:		
Forrage crops 1	−9.7259	−8.1585[b]
Oilseeds 1	−1.0347	−3.8771
Industrial crops 1	−4.6702	−7.2331[b]
Fruits and flowers 1	3.9119	9.6309[b]
Vegetables and legumes 1	−4.0330	−5.1757
Cattle 1	−2.9884	−4.7989
Wool 1	1.7674	5.0990
Milk 1	19.3100	11.8668[b]
Wheat 1	−10.7115	−10.6833[b]
Corn 1	6.8492	15.2894[a]
Nonagricultural	54.2238	7.6780[b]

General table note is below.
R-squared = 0.9999[c]
Durbin-Watson statistic (Adj. for 0 Gaps) = 2.8256
Number of observations = 16
Sum of squared residuals = .0039
Standard error of the regression = 0.0623

Cattle: Natural Increase

Independent Variable	Estimated Coefficient	t
Constant	0.0768	0.3603
Herd, Reca 1	0.2136	53.7076[a]
Change in Real Profits:		
Forrage crops 1	2.9433	11.6744[b]
Oilseeds 1	0.5369	9.5131[b]
Industrial crops 1	1.2671	9.2797[b]
Fruits and flowers 1	−0.4626	−5.3783
Vegetables and legumes 1	−1.5149	−9.1927[b]
Cattle 1	−1.2076	−9.1644[b]
Wool 1	−0.6279	−8.5660[b]
Milk 1	−2.7957	−8.1239[b]
Wheat 1	2.4160	11.3304[b]
Corn 1	−1.0207	−10.7739[b]
Nonagricultural	−17.4299	−11.6701[b]

R-squared = 1.0000[c]
Durbin-Watson statistic (Adj. for 0 Gaps) = 2.8255
Number of observations = 16
Sum of squared residuals = 0.0002
Standard error of the regression = 0.013

NOTE: See Appendix B for detailed interpretation of results, and p. 269 for an explanation of how the Index of Change in Real Profits was constructed.

Number after independent variable name indicates number of periods the variable was lagged. "Past Output" is output, usually lagged one year.
[a]Significant at 5% level. [b]Significant at 10% level. [c]Significant at 1% level.

Cattle Herd

Independent Variable	Estimated Coefficient	t
Constant	129.4060	5.1367
Herd, Jarvis 3	−0.2798	−1.1616
Change in Real Profits:		
Forrage crops	−30.2183	−3.4696
Oilseeds	−16.1196	−3.8694
Industrial crops	−0.5399	−0.0699
Fruits and flowers	−63.2229	−4.4463
Vegetables and legumes	104.1902	4.2245
Cattle	11.2580	1.1592
Wool	31.1484	9.4870
Milk	46.6849	3.7385
Wheat	−63.0342	−7.6250
Corn	2.3114	0.5692
Nonagricultural	320.9956	3.8843

NOTE: The three-year lag for herd gave the best fit in the Jarvis series. The limited degrees of freedom mean that the regression is best viewed as descriptive and that the usual measures of significance should not be applied.
R-squared = 0.9973
Durbin-Watson statistic (Adj. for 0 Gaps) = 3.3697
Number of observations = 14
Sum of squared residuals = 1.28007
Standard error of the regression is 1.13140

Cattle Herd

Independent Variable	Estimated Coefficient	t
Constant	40.5946	15.3340[a]
Herd, Reca 1	0.2467	4.8816
Change in Real Profits:		
Forrage crops 1	10.6443	3.3993
Oilseeds 1	1.1221	1.6007
Industrial crops 1	5.3128	3.1325
Fruits and flowers	−4.2830	−4.0144
Vegetables and legumes 1	3.8228	1.8677
Cattle 1	3.5014	2.1406
Wool 1	−1.8230	−2.0023
Milk 1	−20.2903	−4.7471
Wheat 1	11.4866	4.3372
Corn 1	−6.9822	−5.9337
Nonagricultural 1	−55.0474	−2.9675

R-squared = 0.9997[c]
Durbin-Watson statistic (Adj. for 0 Gaps) = 2.8254
Number of observations = 16
Sum of squared residuals = .0268
Standard error of the regression = 0.163653

Table B.1 (continued)

Wool Output

Independent Variable	Estimated Coefficient	t
Constant	119.1426	8.4446[a]
Past output 1	−0.1587	−0.9653
Change in Real Profits:		
Forrage crops 4	−1.3570	−0.1582
Oilseeds 4	−3.8635	−1.7602
Industrial crops 4	12.4213	1.7237
Fruits and flowers 4	−31.1738	−3.4665[b]
Vegetables and legumes 4	59.1416	4.9603[a]
Cattle 4	16.4949	2.1197
Wool 4	22.0062	6.3853[a]
Milk 4	−6.7464	−0.4754
Wheat 4	−1.4211	−0.2645
Corn 4	−3.9006	−0.9136
Nonagricultural 4	268.0720	4.0813[b]
Population	−0.2801	−1.0737

NOTE: Population and Constant are not lagged. Past output is output lagged one year. Other independent variables are lagged four years.
R-squared = 0.9948[c]
Durbin-Watson statistic (Adj. for 0 Gaps) = 2.8306
Number of observations = 16
Sum of squared residuals = 2.00474
Standard error of the regression = 1.00118
$Q' = .014$ (modified Von Newmann ratio)

Forrage Crops

Independent Variable	Estimated Coefficient	t
Constant	115.9700	4.7414[c]
Past output 1	−0.3070	−1.2604
Change in Real Profits:		
Forrage crops 1	42.9840	−1.1862
Oilseeds 1	−29.3499	−1.9784[b]
Industrial crops 1	0.3372	0.0113
Fruits and flowers 1	−162.9028	−3.6042[a]
Vegetables and legumes 1	273.1804	3.7666[a]
Cattle 1	5.5525	0.1215
Wool 1	43.8327	2.3080[b]
Milk 1	−101.8154	−1.7672
Wheat 1	−76.9419	−2.5620[a]
Corn 1	−55.5229	−2.3232[b]
Nonagricultural 1	−378.5527	−0.9618

R-squared = 0.9478[c]
Durbin-Watson statistic (Adj. for 0 Gaps) = 3.2771
Number of observations = 19
Sum of squared residuals = 389.034
Standard error of the regression = 8.05226
$Q' = 2.19$

Table B.1 (continued)

Vegetable and Legume Output

Independent Variable	Estimated Coefficient	t
Constant	98.7839	6.2870[c]
Past output 1	0.0337	0.1931
Change in Real Profits:		
Forrage crops	−93.7168	−4.2520[c]
Oilseeds	−16.4118	−1.9252
Industrial crops	34.9578	1.7788
Fruits and flowers	−11.1990	−0.3690
Vegetables and legumes	85.0510	1.9449
Cattle	152.6577	5.4287[c]
Wool	31.3116	3.0889[a]
Milk	43.5533	1.1069
Wheat	−24.2750	−1.5707
Corn	33.5612	1.8714
Nonagricultural	1636.2266	6.0660[c]

R-squared = 0.9620[c]
Durbin-Watson statistic (Adj. for 0 Gaps) = 2.7213
Number of observations = 19
Sum of squared residuals = 185.757
Standard error of the regression = 5.56412
Q' = 2.98

Fruit and Flower Output

Independent Variable	Estimated Coefficient	t
Constant	97.1330	3.5353[a]
Past output 1	−0.3232	−0.6093
Change in Real Profits:		
Forrage crops	−66.3386	−2.5420[b]
Oilseeds	−1.3481	−0.1563
Industrial crops	−26.5513	−1.2097
Fruits and flowers	−7.3947	−0.2545
Vegetables and legumes	2.9205	0.0675
Cattle	−3.5780	−0.1210
Wool	12.1617	0.8885
Milk	93.2137	2.2153[b]
Wheat	−16.6377	−0.9831
Corn	16.2108	0.9907
Nonagricultural	350.1179	1.1944
Population	3.1366	2.0836[b]

R-squared = 0.9831[c]
Durbin-Watson statistic (Adj. for 0 Gaps) = 2.4712
Number of observations = 19
Sum of squared residuals = 150.648
Standard error of the regression = 150.48904
Q' = 2.88

Table B.1 (continued)

Cereals and Flax Output

Independent Variable	Estimated Coefficient	t
Constant	176.7959	5.3102[c]
Past output 1	−0.6513	−2.7856[a]
Change in Real Output:		
Forrage crops 1	−168.6809	−2.4034[b]
Oilseeds 1	−54.5558	−2.9337[a]
Industrial crops 1	−12.5278	−0.3990
Fruits and flowers 1	−179.2540	−3.4299[a]
Vegetables and legumes	315.2419	3.3564[a]
Cattle 1	51.2382	0.8514
Wool 1	60.8207	2.2029[b]
Milk 1	31.9149	0.3840
Wheat 1	−125.5822	−2.9377[a]
Corn 1	−1.2829	−0.0472
Nonagricultural 1	−60.1116	−0.1122
Population	−2.2966	−1.4133

R-squared $= 0.9516$[c]
Durbin-Watson statistic (Adj. for 0 Gaps) $= 2.2760$
Number of observations $= 19$
Sum of squared residuals $= 363.119$
Standard error of the regression $= 8.52196$
$Q' = 1.12$

Oilseed Output

Independent Variable	Estimated Coefficient	t
Constant	108.6811	3.7357[c]
Past output 1	−0.0035	−0.0131
Change in Real Profits:		
Forrage crops 1	−54.0829	−0.8415
Oilseeds 1	−11.7117	−0.5445
Industrial crops 1	39.0192	0.8695
Fruits and flowers 1	−128.1772	−2.1170[b]
Vegetables and legumes 1	188.3787	1.8937
Cattle 1	78.8642	1.2802
Wool 1	64.3102	2.4010[b]
Milk 1	121.9175	1.0286
Wheat 1	−111.9772	−2.7533[a]
Corn 1	−5.9869	−0.1501
Nonagricultural 1	1301.9463	2.2406[b]

R-squared $= 0.9009$[a]
Durbin-Watson statistic (Adj. for 0 Gaps) $= 1.9514$
Number of observations $= 19$
Sum of squared residuals $= 924.148$
Standard error of the regression $= 12.4107$
$Q' = 1.71$

Table B.1 (continued)

Industrial Crop Output

Independent Variable	Estimated Coefficient	t
Constant	99.8319	4.7731[a]
Past output 1	0.0160	0.0901
Change in Real Profits:		
Forrage crops 3	116.0138	4.0240[a]
Oilseeds 3	5.2204	0.6837
Industrial crops 3	17.3119	1.0410
Fruits and flowers 3	−39.7826	−1.6050
Vegetables and legumes 3	−17.1631	−0.3944
Cattle 3	−79.9890	−3.1945[a]
Wool 3	−17.8490	−1.5986
Milk 3	−48.8125	−1.1824
Wheat 3	52.6524	2.8383[b]
Corn 3	−58.1105	−4.0764[a]
Nonagricultural 3	−933.7649	−3.6722[a]
Population	2.0497	2.8419[b]

R-squared = 0.9891[c]
Durbin-Watson statistic (Adj. for 0 Gaps) = 3.3157
Number of observations = 17
Sum of squared residuals = 39.2491
Standard error of the regression = 3.61705
Q' = 2.11

Milk Output

Independent Variable	Estimated Coefficient	t
Constant	40.4505	1.1003
Past output 1	0.5838	1.5127
Change in Real Profits:		
Forrage crops	11.5638	0.4375
Oilseeds	6.7805	0.8923
Industrial crops	−35.9250	−1.9125
Fruits and flowers	27.4276	1.0516
Vegetables and legumes	−51.6081	−1.2829
Cattle	−48.7197	−1.6743
Wool	−13.8805	−1.4177
Milk	20.0768	0.5057
Wheat	19.1984	1.2999
Corn	−15.9083	−1.0896
Nonagricultural	−524.0735	−1.7954
Population	0.3743	0.5267

R-squared = 0.7648[c]
Durbin-Watson statistic (Adj. for 0 Gaps) = 2.3352
Number of observations = 19
Sum of squared residuals = 122.554
Standard error of the regression = 4.95084
Q' = .66

Table B.2 Change in Real Unit Profits for Variables Used in Table B.1

	Forrage Crops	Oilseeds	Industrial Crops	Fruits and Flowers	Vegetables and Legumes	Cattle
1950	0.231335	-0.432757	-0.251900	-0.032117	-0.144554	-0.483427
1951	-0.002861	-0.349346	-0.021787	0.285054	-0.329270	-0.392739
1952	0.039032	-0.476229	-0.162854	0.186566	-0.052257	-0.310125
1953	-0.312733	-0.494257	-0.144935	0.111152	-0.106369	-0.242291
1954	-0.241549	-0.522116	-0.143400	0.413388	0.088568	-0.274653
1955	-0.089090	-0.428221	-0.066770	0.287730	0.004065	-0.343218
1956	-0.190545	0.122217	0.004931	0.287330	0.079204	-0.402797
1957	-0.194255	0.174725	0.312446	0.358320	0.089970	-0.454634
1958	-0.319185	-0.156558	0.164859	0.141483	-0.043631	-0.360512
1959	-0.107393	0.909992	-0.116222	-0.300756	-0.111206	0.100893
1960	0.000001	0.000001	0.0	0.000001	0.0	0.0
1961	-0.089521	0.340492	-0.035459	-0.094724	0.047250	-0.170100
1962	-0.062875	-0.021147	-0.140704	-0.248945	-0.073360	-0.247777
1963	-0.189575	0.322108	-0.314477	-0.265062	0.005717	-0.149777
1964	-0.353961	0.199366	-0.319152	-0.535636	-0.179248	0.163588
1965	-0.291066	-0.142774	-0.248532	-0.385939	-0.287288	0.135782
1966	-0.152714	-0.067192	-0.228516	-0.039940	-0.037602	-0.086119
1967	-0.226855	-0.165765	-0.324585	-0.291820	-0.067381	-0.107514
1968	-0.223446	-0.151158	-0.323453	-0.027457	0.089440	-0.147133
1969	-0.246560	-0.068411	-0.288153	-0.136493	0.314348	-0.175349

	Wool	Milk	Wheat	Corn	Nonagricultural	Time
1950	0.140944	-0.213749	-0.214542	0.468224	0.047882	1.000000
1951	0.746870	-0.314286	-0.377480	-0.070500	0.032839	2.000000
1952	-0.381381	-0.234846	-0.345228	0.045197	0.024681	3.000000
1953	-0.290631	-0.284739	-0.059132	-0.057245	0.018637	4.000000
1954	-0.317776	-0.327225	-0.145509	-0.154034	0.027250	5.000000
1955	-0.244579	-0.216418	-0.229828	-0.298515	0.035717	6.000000
1956	0.114300	-0.163941	-0.114128	-0.100004	0.021659	7.000000
1957	0.307275	-0.199424	-0.236206	0.212555	0.008705	8.000000
1958	-0.053941	-0.233009	-0.248715	-0.122034	0.013423	9.000000
1959	-0.023144	-0.162463	-0.251484	0.379339	-0.018039	10.000000
1960	0.0	0.0	0.0	0.0	0.0	11.000000
1961	-0.082252	-0.042473	0.096856	0.080139	0.021608	12.000000
1962	-0.047100	-0.123839	0.065243	0.326879	0.020289	13.000000
1963	0.307409	-0.231378	0.251107	0.465251	0.005568	14.000000
1964	0.229701	-0.172716	0.259818	0.030918	-0.021068	15.000000
1965	-0.087491	-0.201837	-0.193732	-0.012770	0.002924	16.000000
1966	-0.129860	-0.103544	-0.201803	-0.068378	0.017227	17.000000
1967	-0.220492	-0.144620	0.023073	0.127515	0.023370	18.000000
1968	-0.271878	-0.062696	0.022651	-0.096111	0.018529	19.000000
1969	-0.296521	0.074252	0.058675	0.140239	0.014363	20.000000

tion is significant in the regression equation tend to be those associated with family farms.

It is essential to subdivide the agricultural sector into crops and cattle, as the output of each responds to changes in real profits in different ways. Most notably, when cattle profits increase, herds are built up that same year, and cattle slaughter decreases. Cattle slaughter increases as a result of herd build-up several years after the initial favorable profit pattern. Crop output, on the other hand, increases as profits increase. While this general analysis holds, it is modified by the change in profits that can be earned in other sectors. Thus, if cattle profits rise, the slaughter rate might not fall if, instead of holding cattle off the market for herd increase, cattlemen slaughtered cattle and invested the proceeds earned in another, more lucrative, activity.

Similarly, the different technical characteristics of crop and cattle production require that past output, used in the crop regressions, be replaced by herd size in the cattle regressions. In the case of cattle, prior herd increases are associated with increases in current slaughter, natural increase of herd, and gross cattle output (defined as slaughter plus herd). The sign for last year's herd size in the regressions is positive, as the herd in fact is a capital good in the production of cattle. For crops, however, past output, except for a small fraction used as seeds, is not a capital good. Instead, it is often the case that a high output results in a "glut on the market," and therefore in profits that are lower than expected. As a result, farmers reduce output of the crop in question the following year. As expected, the sign on last year's output is negative in many of the regressions for crops.

Three different sources of data were used in carrying out regression analysis for the cattle industry; the best results are presented here. The use of different sources of data was necessary because the Central Bank's figures have been criticized for insufficient adjustment for cattle smuggling, which was probably more than 3 percent of the gross output for the period as a whole. Following the sharp decline in cattle profits in 1966, smuggling probably reached 50 percent of the slaughter. Alternate regressions therefore were run using data provided by Dr.

Reca and Dr. Jarvis. There is some difficulty in using the alternate series, as they contain data for fewer years than the Central Bank series. Reca's data covers 1950–64; estimates were made for 1965 and 1966, and incorporated into the regression. Jarvis' data runs from 1950 to 1966.

In the regressions using Dr. Reca's data for natural increase, a perfect correlation was obtained, in which natural increase depended upon last year's herd and last year's change in real profits. The regression using Dr. Reca's data indicates that virtually all herd size is predicted by last year's herd and last year's changes in real profit opportunities. The adjustment from actual to desired herd size was more rapid than that reported for nonagricultural sectors, which indicates that the very wealthy cattlemen were sensitive to profit opportunities. This result differs from popular propoganda, which often states that rich, absentee cattlemen are indifferent to profits. On the other hand, changes in real profits have a somewhat lower level of significance in the regression for cattle than they do for other sectors of the economy. Thus, because of the technical characteristics of the cattle industry, cattlemen can change output more rapidly than can entrepreneurs in other sectors; they are not indifferent to changes in real profit opportunities. However, such changes determine cattle output less than they do in many other economic sectors. The Jarvis regression implies a three-year cycle for the size of cattle herds and a somewhat greater sensitivity to real profit opportunities. The Jarvis-based regression, however, predicts herd size less well than does the Reca-based regression.

The regressions for cattle production perform better than those for crop production; this reflects both the lesser sensitivity of cattle than crops to weather conditions, and the fact that the index of change in real profits is more accurate for cattle than for crop production. This is because agricultural wages as a share of average wages fluctuated sharply from 1950 to 1969. Cattle production, which had very low labor requirements, had changes in real profits close to those in the index for the cattle sector. On the other hand, crop production was characterized by higher labor requirements than cattle production. It was not possible to shift techniques of production rapidly in the short run. The cost of producing crops varied more than the cost of producing either cattle or nonagricultural products. In consequence, the index constructed to represent change in real profits, which does not take into account differences in wage rates between sectors, is less accurate for crop production than for other activities. Despite this defect, the regressions are significant at the 1 percent level, and confirm the results reported by Dr. Reca.

A technical problem is raised by the inclusion of last year's output in a regression equation used to predict this year's output, because technically imperfect regression statistics, which overstate the significance of various of the explanatory variables, may result. The usual way out of this difficulty is to recast the regression equation either in first differences or in logarithms. It is not appropriate to do either in this case, as it would destroy the economic meaning of the regression used here, which involves adjustment to levels.

Moreover, technical tests carried out to determine the validity of the results reported here indicate that autocorrelation of the residuals is not significant at the 5 percent level of probability for the majority of the regression equations reported. Positive autocorrelation of the residuals is suspected in the case of wool. For cattle, there were insufficient degrees of freedom to carry out the BLUS test for autocorrelation for the regressions using Reca and Jarvis data. As further data becomes available, it will be possible to carry out this test. In the interim, it seems reasonable to expect that the absence of positive autocorrelation typical of the majority of regressions presented for agriculture will also obtain for cattle, and that the cattle regressions therefore should be given the benefit of the doubt.

Appendix C: A Skeleton Key
to Regression Equations
and Correlation Coefficients

Regression equations are used to present and analyze the relationship between two or more variables. In some cases, the relationship between two variables can be represented by a diagram (see page 266); in this case, the relationship can also be represented by an equation, $Y = a + bX$. This equation indicates that the value of Y is always equal to amount a or more. The constant is called a. Y is a when X is equal to zero. Y can take values greater than a; Y increases as X increases by an amount proportional to X. The proportion b in the equation is referred to as the "weight" of X. In the equation $Y = 2 + .1X$, Y equals 2 when X equals zero; Y is 2.2 when X is 2, etc. In the equation $Y = 2 - .1X$, Y is 2 when X is zero, Y is 1.8 when X is 2, etc. Additional variables which influence Y can be included in the regression; e.g., $Y = a + bX_1 + cX_2 + dX_3$. In this case, b is the weight of X_1, c is the weight of X_2, and d is the weight of X_3.

In practice, the relationship between X and Y may not be exactly that indicated by the equation $Y = a + bX$. Individual observations may cluster around the line described by $Y = a + bX$, rather than coincide with it. The value of Y estimated by $Y = a + bX$ may not be identical with the observed value of Y as indicated in Figure 2. For example, at point m, m is the observed value of Y and n is the value of Y predicted by the equation for the corresponding value of X. Thus, in describing the relationship between variables, economists usually write regression equations as, for example, $Y = a + bX + e$, where e indicates an error term showing that the value of Y is not identical to that predicted by the equation $Y = a + bX$.

In discussing statistics from a regression equation, we say that a variable makes a positive and significant contribution to the explanation of the behavior of a dependent variable (e.g., X makes a positive and significant contribution to an explanation of Y) when a positive change in X is associated with a positive

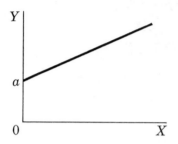 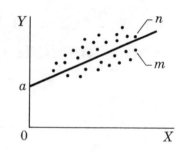

change in Y. It is negative if a decrease in X is associated with a decrease in Y, and it is significant if tests of the relationship between X and Y indicate that the relationship could have occurred by chance only five times out of one hundred, for example. In this case, we say that the relationship is significant at the 5 percent probability level.

A number of terms are used to describe the variation in the values of a variable such as gross domestic product. A rough measure of variation is the "range," which is the absolute difference between the smallest and highest gross domestic product. Because the range only describes the two extreme values of the gross domestic product, alternative measures are used to describe the variation in its value. The variance is the mean of the squared deviations of individual observations of gross domestic product from its mean. This variance can be separated into two components. Gross domestic product can be computed from a regression equation, as in the example above; similarly, the variance of the computed gross domestic product can be calculated. The computed gross product is not identical to the observed gross product. The difference between the two is termed the "residual"; its variance can also be calculated. The variance of gross domestic product is equal to the variance of the computed gross domestic product (called the "explained variance"), plus the variance of the residual (called the "unexplained variance"). The larger the share of variance of gross domestic product accounted for by the explained variance, the better the explanation.

t statistics are used to indicate the chance that the relationship between an independent variable (X) and a dependent variable (Y) are significant. Statistical tables are used in evaluating *t*; in the case that there are thirty or more observations, *t* is usually significant if it is equal to two or more. If there are less than thirty observations, *t* must be considerably greater than two to be significant. Those variables for which *t* is significant at the 5 percent probability level have been starred throughout the tables.

"D. W." refers to the Durbin Watson coefficient, which is used in the technical analysis of time series; for a detailed explanation, see any introductory text on econometrics.

The correlation coefficient measures the degree of relationship between two variables. If the two variables are related so that increases in the value of X are associated with increases in the value of Y, and there is no fluctuation in the relationship between X and Y, there is a perfect correlation between the variables. It is reported as +1. If increases in the value of X are associated with decreases in the value of Y, and there is no fluctuation in the relationship between X and Y, there is a perfect negative correlation between them; it is reported as −1. If there is no tendency for high values of X to be associated with high values of Y or for high values of X to be associated with low values of Y, there is no relationship between them; this is reported as 0. The values found in practical work fall somewhere between these limits, approaching unity in cases where the degree of relationship is high.

Notes

Chapter Two: Economic Theory and Argentine Economic Growth

1. Randall, "Inflation and Economic Development in Latin America: Some New Evidence," pp. 416–24.

2. See also Eshag and Thorp, "Economic and Social Consequences of Orthodox Economic Policies . . ."

3. See Quintana, *Development Problems in Latin America;* and Prebisch, *The Economic Development of Latin America.*

4. See Powelson, "The Terms of Trade Again."

5. See, for example, the works of Hirschman, Mamalakis, Di Tella, and Diamand.

6. Shackle, "Keynes and Today's Establishment in Economic Theory . . . ," p. 516.

7. The problem of variation within a presidency is not great because of the short duration of many presidencies: very great policy variation led to the overthrow of the president.

8. Past inputs and expected alternate profit opportunities are included in the analysis of Argentine output presented in this chapter and in Appendix A. Regression analysis is the technique used to obtain the information presented in the text.

9. Reca, *Price and Production Duality Within Argentine Agriculture,* pp. 62–65.

10. Fienup, Brannon, and Fender, *Agricultural Development of Argentina,* pp. 78–79.

11. Computed as (index of sectoral price minus index of gross domestic product price) divided by index of gross domestic product price. In the case of cattle, the change in profit was the same as absolute profit, since 1960 apparently had a zero profit for this sector.

Changes in profit opportunities are crucial in determining the structure and level of economic growth. An index of change in real unit profits is constructed by using an index of sectoral prices at factor cost as an estimate of change in sectoral receipts. Thus, where there is a difference between what the consumer pays and what the producer receives, due, for example, to the imposition of a sales tax, the use of the figure for what the producer receives is appropriate. The impact of the sales tax therefore is not included separately; the change in real profit index, therefore, includes the effect of government policy.

The gross domestic product price index is used as an estimate of costs. The result is an index of change of sectoral profit compared to a base year, for which the change of sectoral profit index is zero. However, in inflationary conditions, the index is biased upward over time. The sectoral profit index is therefore deflated by dividing it by the gross domestic product price index.

If too few sectors are chosen, the model will not represent choices open to investors. Worse, the sectors will not be homogeneous in their responses to economic variables. If too many sectors are used, the assumption that the gross domestic product price index is a reasonable approximation of an index of sectoral costs breaks down: very small sectors may require inputs whose prices change at rates quite different from the average price change.

The profit index is an index of unit profits. If it can be assumed that there is a well-functioning stock market which gives businessmen an investment choice among sectors, and that the payback period is the same for investment in each sector, then the unit profit index approximates the index of the profit rate for each sector.

This analysis is extended to the Brazilian economy in Randall, "Inflation and Economic Development in Latin America: Some New Evidence," pp. 317–22.

12. Biggs, *Devaluations, Inflation and Relative Price Changes for Agricultural Exports.*

13. The correlation between real gross domestic product and the government share of real product is −.93.

14. The elasticity of reserves with respect to the price of currency was perverse (.27) from 1950 to 1960. Randall, "Inflation and Economic Development in Latin America, 1950–1960," p. 423.

15. Technically, as long as the relative profits for livestock are favorable, and the discounted present value of anticipated profits on the sale of calves plus the final sale of the cow are greater than the present value of the sale of the cow, increases in output are diverted to inventory (cow) build-up, rather than used for sales to domestic consumers or for exports.

16. A statement that analyzes the 1948–64 policy cycle, using formal techniques of economic analysis, is provided by Miguel Sidrauski, in "Devaluación, Inflación y Desempleo," pp. 79–108, as follows:

1) For a devaluation to improve the balance of trade in a situation of constant real income, the money wage has to rise by less than the rate of exchange. When the elasticity of supply of the international sector is lower than the elasticity of supply of the domestic sector, as seems to be the case in Argentina, this implies that the "real wage" has to fall. 2) If the central bank follows a policy of maintaining a constant level of employment, the reduction of real wages may be difficult, as money wages will adjust, thereby partially offsetting the devaluation. 3) The partial adjustment of the money wages after devaluations explains why Latin American nations did not obtain substantial improvements in their balance of payments after large devaluations. 4) The large international sector income of the Latin American countries renders difficult the use of variations in the exchange rate in order to equilibrate the balance of payments. The greater this sector the greater will be the impact of devaluation on price level, and thereby on money wages, hence mitigating the effect of the devaluation. 5) According to classical analysis, devaluation will have an expansionary effect on the economy. Thus, in order to avoid inflationary pressures, the devaluation has to be accompanied with a restrictive monetary and fiscal policy. In general, a devaluation which takes place in an inflationary environment will have to be accompanied by a substantial increase in the normal quantity of money, if

unemployment is to be avoided. Fears of inflation on the part of the Central Bank may induce a smaller than required increase in the quantity of money causing a drop in real income. 6) The fact that some of the devaluating countries experienced a decline in their level of activity after the devaluation has been attributed by other authors not to the inadequacy of monetary and fiscal policies, but to the fact that the devaluation in general causes a redistribution of income towards the non-wage earning population that has a lower than average marginal propensity to consume. Reasonable values were given to the relevant parameters, and it seems as though this alternative hypothesis cannot by itself explain the drop in employment after devaluation. The hypothesis that monetary policy was too restrictive can provide the additional required explanation."

17. The distribution of profits among sectors explains 98.6 percent of gross domestic product. Randall, "Personal Income Distribution and Investment in Argentina, 1950–69," paper presented at the meetings of the Latin American Studies Association, November 15, 1974.

Chapter Three: Income Distribution, Consumption, and Investment

1. Kuznets, "Quantitive Aspects of the Economic Growth of Nations."

2. The estimates for 1914–35 are derived from the indices of salaries and occupation for Buenos Aires, and are linked to the 1935 wage figures provided by the Ministerio de Asuntos Económicos. From 1935–69, wage data are from the Ministerio de Asuntos Económicos; ECLA/CONADE worksheets; and from ECLA, *Statistical Bulletin for Latin America,* vol. 9 (1972).

3. Horowitz, "High Level Manpower in the Economic Development of Argentina," pp. 1–36; and Organization for Economic Cooperation and Development, *Education, Human Resources and Development.*

4. Edel, "Regional Integration and Income Distribution: Complements or Substitutes?" pp. 185–202.

5. See Appendix B.

6. Samuel A. Morley and Gordon W. Smith, *The Effect of Changes in the Distribution of Income on Labor, Foreign Investment and Growth in Brazil,* Program of Development Studies Paper no. 15, Rice University (Summer 1971).

7. See chapters 5, 8; and, among others, ECLA, *Economic Development and Income Distribution in Argentina,* pp. 48, 244, 269.

8. ECLA, *Economic Development and Income Distribution in Argentina,,* p. 7.

9. Various studies indicate that the adjustment period in Argentina is less than one year. The most recent statement is in Lucas, "Some International Evidence on Output-Inflation Tradeoffs," See also Friend, *The Propensity to Consume and Save in Argentina,* p. 4. Tests of several forms of consumption function yield results similar to those presented here. See n. 13.

10. Friend, *The Propensity to Consume and Save in Argentina.*

11. The revisions were based on the use of 1935–39 price weights. Detailed adjustments were made using data provided in Elias, *Estimates of Value Added, Capital and Labor.*

12. Kuznets, *National Product Since 1869* (New York: National Bureau of Economic Research, 1946).

13. Randall, "Personal Income Distribution and Investment in Argentina, 1950–69," Paper presented at the meetings of the Latin America Studies Association, November 15, 1974.

14. The same is true when the logarithm of inflation was introduced into the estimates.

15. Friedman, *A Theory of the Consumption Function*.

16. Gregory King's estimate was used as the basis of the calculations. King's estimate is reprinted in Mathias, *The First Industrial Nation*, p. 24.

17. Komiya, "The Supply of Personal Savings," pp. 157–81.

18. Burmeister and Taubman, "Labour and Non-Labour Saving Propensities," pp. 78–89.

19. ECLA, *Economic Development and Income Distribution in Argentina*. Estimates are presented in this study of the effect of changes in prices of various categories of goods on real income by quintile, and of various government policies on redistribution of family income. There were, however, not enough data to incorporate these effects into this chapter.

    Kuznets also notes that evidence for the United States is that "a large proportion of savings to finance private (and other) capital formation originates not in the income from assets (too often viewed as the *only* source of national savings) but in compensation of employees and income of entrepreneurs, particularly the former. Indeed, judging by the estimates for recent years, no more than half of the household savings to finance capital formation can be credited to household income from assets net of taxes." Kuznets, *Modern Economic Growth*, pp. 175–76.

20. Note that this result was obtained using a behavioral equation. The net domestic capital formation variable was obtained by subtracting amortization at historic cost as a percent of net remuneration of capital and enterprise from gross domestic capital formation as a percent of gross domestic income. This estimate of net domestic capital formation yielded better results than any other, and lies between the traditionally computed estimates of net domestic capital formation as a percent of gross domestic income, using either amortization at historic cost or at replacement cost as a percent of gross domestic income. For detailed comparisons, see the version of this chapter presented as a paper at the 1974 meetings of the Latin American Studies Association.

21. Heilbroner, *Understanding Macroeconomics* p. 94. Includes undistributed corporate profits and depreciation allowances.

22. See Kuznets, *National Product*.

23. ECLA, *Economic Development and Income Distribution in Argentina,* pp. 211–12.

24. Kuznets, *National Product*.

25. See chapters 2 and 5.

26. ECLA, *Economic Development and Income Distribution in Argentina*, p. 213.

27. See chapter 6; and David Felix, various works, on the problems associated with manufacturing when tariffs are levied on inputs used in manufacturing as well as on the finished good.

28. A United Nations study indicates that the degree to which this is true will probably be influenced by whether the corporation is owned by private domestic stockholders, a government, foreign entrepreneurs, or some mixed arrangement. For example, see "Public Enterprises: Their Present Significance and Their Potential in Development," *Economic Bulletin for Latin America,* January–June 1971, pp. 1–70.

29. ECLA, *Economic Development and Income Distribution in Argentina,* p. 264.

30. As noted in chapter 4, firms finance themselves during an inflation by delaying tax payments to the government. Estimates of redistributive effect are taken from ECLA, *Economic Development and Income Distribution in Argentina,* p. 261.

31. *Ibid.,* p. 265.

32. *Ibid.,* pp. 73, 152–55.

33. O'Donnell and Linck, *Dependencia y Autonomia.* The fact that imports are less strongly related to capital formation than withheld profits suggests that an examination of the determinants of imports, and in particular, the import intensity of the different consumption bundles consumed by the various income classes, would not significantly add to our knowledge of investment patterns.

Chapter Four: Money and Banking

1. Randall, *A Comparative Economic History of Latin America,* ch. 3.

2. Prebisch, *Conversaciones con el doctor Raúl Prebisch.*

3. On related points, see Charles Arthur Jones, *British Financial Institutions in Argentina, 1860–1914* (Ph.D. dissertation, Cambridge University, 1973). Under British copyright, this cannot be quoted.

4. "Crop financing through exchange market: briefly, it is customary for the cereal exporters, the heaviest sellers of exchange, to offer sterling futures (usually 90-day sight bills) some two or three months in advance of the time when they can actually deliver bills and documents to the banks. To avoid taking an exchange position, which is speculative, the banks must sell future exchange for about the same maturity or if futures are not in offer, spot exhanges will be sold as cover. If the bank does not have credit balances in London at the time of the spot sale, it arranges for sterling overdrafts. These overdrafts upon which the interest rate is included in the future exchange quotations run until such time as the local seller of sterling delivers his documents to the local bank and that bank in turn forwards them to its London correspondent, where the bills are accepted by the drawee, discounted by the London correspondent, and credited to the account of the Buenos Aires bank in cover of the overdraft. Thus the local banks, in effect, draw on the funds of the London money market. This method is not bound to be employed, however, as in 1928, for example, money was in abundance at such attractive rates, following two successful crop years, that the cereal exporters arranged part of their financing locally." (Uncitable U.S. source.)

In 1933, a grain law made the purchase and sale of wheat a government monopoly. It set minimum prices, so farmers could sell certificates of sale to the government or to an exporter. These certificates became the base of rural credit; moreover, the government built grain elevators. Gravil, "Intervención estatal."

5. Williams, *Argentine International Trade under Inconvertible Paper Money,* p. 156.

6. For details, see Randall, *A Comparative Economic History of Latin America,* Chap. 7.

7. Soares, *Economía y Finanzas de la Nación Argentina,* pp. 9–22.

8. Cited in Peters, *Foreign Debt of the Argentine Republic,* p. 64. See also Prebisch, *Conversaciones con el doctor Raúl Prebisch,* p. 9.

9. Prebisch, *Conversaciones con el doctor Raúl Prebisch,* pp. 6–8.

10. Peters, *Foreign Debt of the Argentine Republic,* p. 59.

11. *Revista de Ciencias Económicas* (1932), translated by Halperín. Prebisch published bank statistics separately for each of these three groups in the 1928 *Anuario* of the Sociedad Rural Argentina.

12. Halperín, *The Behavior of the Argentine Monetary Sector,* p. 157.

13. David Rock, *Politics in Argentina, 1890–1930: The Rise and Fall of Radicalism* (London and New York: Cambridge University Press, 1975), pp. 223–25, 253.

14. Permission was obtained to cite the official, but not to give details on the source.

15. *Ibid.*

16. Pinedo, *Interviews,* pp. 65–70.

17. Prebisch, *Conversaciones con el doctor Raúl Prebisch.*

18. *Ibid.,* 1:9–10.

19. Pinedo, *En Tiempos de la Républica,* 1:148.

20. *Ibid.,* ch. 10; and Bunge, various works.

21. Halperín, *The Behavior of the Argentine Monetary Sector,* p. 4.

22. Halperín, *ibid.,* and BCRA, *Memoria Anual,* various issues.

23. Halperín, *The Behavior of the Argentine Monetary Sector,* pp. 92–105.

24. *Revista Económica Argentina.* Statistics published in various issues.

25. Pinedo, *Nuestro Problema Monetario,* 1:60 and 2:136.

26. Pinedo, *Interviews,* p. 68.

27. Pinedo, *En Tiempos de la República,* pp. 117–18, cites Marx from "Zur Kritik."

28. Pinedo, *Interviews,* pp. 65–70.

29. Pinedo, *En Tiempos de la República,* pp. 148–49; Prebisch, *Interviews;* Federal Reserve Bank of New York, memo. These sources give different estimates of the peso amount received. The peso-sterling conversion rate governing the unblocking loan was stipulated in the agreement. As a repurchase clause was not included in the agreement, the bonds remained on the London exchange.

30. A. Hueyo, *La Argentina en la Depresión Mundial,* pp. 176–77.

31. *Ibid.*

32. Pinedo, *En Tiempos de la República,* p. 160. The foreign expert's criticism of the final draft is in *Economic Review* (July 1934), 3:118–19. Prebisch states that Radical Lisandro de la Torre opposed a Central Bank controlled by the government because of what happened in 1890, while Pinedo believed that a Central Bank would be

expansionist, and attacked this aspect. He nonetheless projected the Banco Central de la República Argentina, as the Caja de la Conversión no longer existed. Prebisch, *Conversaciones,* p. 68.

33. Pinedo, Interview, *Esto Es,* p. 3.

34. The text of the law is given in Ministerio de Educación, *Regimen Bancario Argentino,* pp. 1098 ff.

35. Prebisch, *Conversaciones con el doctor Raúl Prebisch,* p. 4a; Pinedo, *En Tiempos de la República;* Randall, *Comparative Economic History of Latin America.*

36. Prebisch, *Conversaciones con el doctor Raúl Prebisch,* p. 12.

37. *Economic Review* (July 1934), 3:119.

38. Prebisch, *Conversaciones con el doctor Raúl Prebisch,* p. 12.

39. Banco de la Nación Argentina, *Revista Económica* (July–September 1934), 3:78, cited in Halperín, *The Behavior of the Argentine Monetary Sector,* p. 221.

40. For examples of nineteenth-century government aid to insolvent banks, see Randall, *A Comparative Economic History of Latin America,* ch. 7.

41. Pinedo, *Interviews,* pp. 76–77.

42. *Ibid.*

43. Halperín, *The Behavior of the Argentine Monetary Sector,* pp. 220–23; Prebisch, *Conversaciones con el doctor Raúl Prebisch;* Diz, "Money and Prices."

44. Prebisch, *Conversaciones con el doctor Raúl Prebisch,* 1:9–10.

45. Pinedo, *Interviews,* p. 72.

46. *Ibid.,* p. 73.

47. Prebisch, *Conversaciones con el doctor Raúl Prebisch,* 1:9.

48. The Central Bank's proposal of selling treasury bills was opposed by some bank directors, who thought that the public would reduce its bank deposits to pay for them. But this view proved too narrow because the Treasury used the funds received in making payments and the funds returned to the banks, which, in time, were convinced of this. It was also feared that new treasury notes would attract an even greater inflow of foreign funds. In this case, however, purchasers of treasury notes bought foreign exchange futures to avoid the risk of devaluation. The Central Bank asked banks and exchange brokers to stop these transactions. Prebisch, *Conversaciones con el doctor Raúl Prebisch,* 2:7a–12a.

49. BCRA, *Annual Report* (1938), p. 28, cites the *Annual Report of the Minister of Finance* (1937), vol. 1, p. 41. Earlier material: budget information from Herschel and Itzcovitch, "Fiscal Policy in Argentina," p. 100. BCRA, *Annual Reports* (1937), p. 24; (1938), p. 22 (Page numbers refer to English translation published by the bank.) Prebisch, *Conversaciones con el doctor Raúl Prebisch,* 2:27a–29a.

50. Prebisch, *Conversaciones con el doctor Raúl Prebisch,* 2:22a.

51. BCRA, *Annual Report* (1937), p. 20.

52. BCRA, *Annual Report* (1939), p. 36.

53. BCRA, *Annual Report* (1940), pp. 1–8.

55. BCRA, *Annual Report* (1940), pp. 8–10.

56. Prebisch, *Conversaciones con el doctor Raúl Prebisch,* 2:36a.

57. BCRA, *Annual Report* (1941), p. 1.

58. BCRA, *Annual Reports* (1942), p. 80; (1943), p. 14. See also Pinedo, *Siglo y Medio;* he notes that from 1934 to 1938, 82 percent of government spending was covered by resources, but from 1939 to 1943, only 66 percent (p. 118).

59. BCRA, *Annual Report* (1942), pp. 12, 31.

60. See Cafiero, *Cinco Años Después,* p. 246.

61. BCRA, *Annual Report* (1944), p. 4.

62. BCRA, *Annual Report* (1945), pp. 9–10 (my translation).

63. BCRA, *Memoria Anual,* pp. 61–63; Ministerio de Educación, *Regimen Bancario Argentino,* pp. 1074–75.

64. Halperín, *The Behavior of the Argentine Monetary Sector,* p. 223.

65. Cafiero, *Cinco Años Después,* p. 263. The bank was called Instituto de Inversiones Inmobiliarios.

66. Halperín, *The Behavior of the Argentine Monetary Sector,* pp. 223–24.

67. Altimir, Santamaria, and Sourrouille, "Los Instrumentos de Promoción Industrial," pp. 724–25; and Gomez Morales, *Política Económica Peronista,* p. 141.

68. Gomez Morales, *Interviews,* p. 56. Note: The Instituto Ganadero Argentino also financed part of Argentine agriculture. Gomez Morales, *Política Económica Peronista,* p. 50.

69. Gomez Morales, *Interviews,* pp. 59–60.

70. *Ibid.,* p. 55.

71. *Ibid.,* p. 56.

72. Gomez Morales' memoirs give a figure of $100 million. BCRA, *Memoria Anual* cites $125 million.

73. Gomez Morales, p. 58.

74. Gomez Morales, *Política Económica Peronista,* p. 32; Peterson, *Argentina and the United States,* p. 468.

75. Gomez Morales, *Interviews,* pp. 61–63.

76. *Ibid.,* pp. 67–71.

77. *Ibid.,* pp. 71–73.

78. Halperín, *The Behavior of the Argentine Monetary Sector,* p. 227; Pinedo, *Siglo y medio de economía Argentina,* p. 131: "The result of this reform, which put all the management of money and credit in the hands of the government, was that shortly the gold began to disappear as if by enchantment, and simultaneously money proliferated in an unheard of manner" (my translation). Note: Gold was used to lower foreign claims on Argentines. For details, see BCRA, *Memoria Anual* (1948), p. 11.

79. BCRA, *Memoria Anual* (1946), p. 21.

80. Moyano Llerena, "La Devolución de los Despositos."

81. See p. 72. Overall growth 1943–55 computed in 1935–39 pesos; growth 1955–67 in 1960 pesos.

82. BCRA, *Memoria Anual* (1949), p. 4.

83. Moyano Llerena, "La Devolución de los Despositos."

84. Article 4, cited by Moyano Llerena in "La Devolución de los Depositos." Reserve requirements refer to the share of demand deposits and savings deposits at commercial banks that must be kept by the commercial bank in the form either of vault cash or of deposits at the central bank. Basic reserve requirements are those levied in general, set as a percentage of the deposit category. Marginal reserve requirements are those set as a percentate of a deposit category, to be applied on all deposits above a given monetary level. For example, to curb bank credit expansion, a central bank could set basic reserve requirements as 25 percent of demand deposits, and 100 percent of all deposits above those held as of the date the marginal requirement went into effect. Other forms of this requirement apply marginal requirements to all deposits that are a given percent above those held the date the marginal reserve requirement went into effect.

85. For earlier worries about this, see Moyano Llerena, "La Devolución de los Depositos," p. 152. In Argentina, only 40 percent of the money is held as demand deposits.

86. Randall, "Economic Development Policies and Argentine Economic Growth," pp. 129–30; and BCRA, *Memoria Anual* (1956), pp. 39–40.

87. Randall, "Economic Development Policies and Argentine Economic Growth," p. 132.

88. Samuel Itzcovitch, *Analisis de la Estructura Financiera Argentina, 1955–1965,* (Buenos Aires: Instituto Torcuato Di Tella, Centro de Investigaciones Económicas, 1968), p. 17.

89. Díaz Alejandro, *Essays on the Economic History of the Argentine Republic,* pp. 373–74, 387.

90. Dagnino Pastore, *Ingreso y Dinero,* 2:64, 98, 131, 352. See criticism of policy in Eshag and Thorp. See also Olivera, "Aspectos Dinámicos de la Inflación Estructural," "El Dinero Pasivo," "A Note on Passive Money, Inflation, and Economic Growth," and "On Structural Inflation and Latin-American 'Structuralism'"; Solís and Ghighliazza, "Estabilidad económica y política monetaria."

Chapter Five: Agriculture

1. Randall, *A Comparative Economic History of Latin America,* chap. 7.

2. Mulhall, *Handbook of the River Plate.*

3. Ortiz, *História Económica de la República Argentina,* 2:119.

4. Randall, *A Comparative Economic History of Latin America,* chap. 7.

5. Giberti, "Desarrollo Agropecuario," p. 99.

6. *Ibid.,* p. 119; and Cortés Conde, "Regimen de la Tierra en Argentina," pp. 74–76.

7. Coní, "Apuntes para la História de la Colonización en la Argentina," pp. 29–39.

8. *Ibid.,* p. 32.

9. *Ibid.,* p. 34.

10. Solberg, "Rural Unrest and Agrarian Policy in Argentina," pp. 21, 28.

11. In addition, a 1922 land reform was enacted which affected 20 million acres in peripheral areas. White, *Argentina.*

12. Fienup, Brannon, and Fender, *The Agricultural Development of Argentina,* p. 302; Taylor, *Rural Life,* p. 191.

13. Taylor, *Rural Life in Argentina,* pp. 198–9; and Pla, "Propiedad Rural," p. 55.

14. CEPAL, *El Desarrollo Económico de la Argentina,* p. 155; and CIDA, *Tenencia de la Tierra y Desarrollo del Agrícola Argentina,* p. 32. The 1960 figure is the percent of land held in units typified as "multifamiliar grande."

15. Cortés Conde, "Regimen de la Tierra en Argentina," p. 75.

16. Ortiz, *Historia Económica de la República Argentina,* 2:121–23; and CIDA, *Tenencia de la Tierra y Desarrollo Socio-Económico del Sector Agrícola Argentina,* pp. 138–39.

17. CEPAL, *Desarrollo Económico de la Argentina,* p. 155. See also for discussion of rental of government owned land.

18. Gomez Morales, *Interviews.*

19. Gomez Morales, *Política Económica Personista,* p. 147; Ortiz, *Historia Económica de la República Argentina,* 2:121–23; CIDA, *Tenencia de la Tierra y Desarrollo Socio Económico del Sector Agrícola Argentina,* pp. 138–39.

20. Giberti, "El Desarrollo Agropecuario."

21. Farmsworth and Kevarkian, *Argentina, Competitor of United States Agriculture.*

22. Cafiero, *Cinco Años Después,* p. 439.

23. CIDA, *Tenencia de la Tierra y Desarrollo Socio-Económico del Sector Agrícola Argentina,* pp. 98–106.

24. Jarvis, *Supply Response in the Cattle Industry.*

25. Farmworth and Kevarkian, *Argentina, Competitor of United States Agriculture,* pp. 39–43.

26. Rennie, *The Argentine Republic,* pp. 310–37; Scobie, *Argentina,* p. 234.

27. Fienup, Brannon, and Fender, *The Agricultural Development of Argentina,* p. 306.

28. Jarvis, *Supply Response in the Cattle Industry,* p. 15.

29. de Obchatko, *Factores Limitantes a la Introducción del Cambio Tecnologico,* p. 133.

30. SRA, *Anuario* (1928), p. 99; and Randall, *A Comparative Economic History of Latin America.* In 1930, these figures include taxes on land, agricultural production, and consumption of sugar, alcohol, and wine in the agricultural grouping, following Prebisch's analysis. If additional sales tax on tobacco, figures 8 percentage points higher; part of the sales tax is paid in part by the producer, who receives lower prices than he would if there were no tax, and in part by the consumer who pays more than he would in the absence of the tax.

Other group is tax on commerce, industry, and professions, other consumption, civil, commercial, legal. *Revista Económica Argentina,* November 1932.

31. Reca, *Price and Production Duality within Argentine Agriculture,* pp. 10–11.

32. *Ibid.,* p. 16.

33. Jarvis, *Supply Response in the Cattle Industry.*

34. Reca, *Price and Production Duality within Argentine Agriculture,* pp. 21–22; República Argentina, Poder Ejecutivo Nacional, *Periodo 1932–1938;* vol. 1, *Hacienda;* vol. 10, *Agricultura.*

35. The Minister of Hacienda, on November 29, 1933, stated that the entire economy was interconnected and Argentina needed to depend on itself, not on foreign markets. Public works were to be undertaken by means of government finance; production of imports that were no longer available was to be stimulated; colonization of agricultural lands was advocated; and depreciation might be acceptable, as the cost of living was not much influenced by import prices. Mini-sterios de Hacienda y Agricultura, *El Plan de Accion Economica Nacional* (1934), pp. 80, 87.

36. Reca, *Price and Production Duality within Argentine Agriculture,* p. 27; Prebisch, *Interviews.*

37. Pinedo, Interview, *Esto Es,* p. 2.

38. Reca, *Price and Production Duality within Argentine Agriculture,* pp. 26–30.

39. República Argentina, Poder Ejecutivo Nacional, *Periodo 1932–1938,* vol. 10.

40. República Argentina, Ministerios de Hacienda y Agricultura, *El Plan de Acción Económica Nacional,* p. 156.

41. Gomez Morales, *Política Económica Peronista,* p. 87. Under Perón, the various regulating boards were placed under the Central Bank in 1946, and were then in 1949 transferred to the Finance Ministry.

42. Solberg, "Rural Unrest and Agrarian Policy in Argentina," p. 21.

43. SRA, *Anuarios* (1929), p. 19, and (1951–52).

44. Solberg, "Rural Unrest and Agrarian Policy in Argentina," p. 23.

45. Rennie, *Argentine Republic,* p. 239.

46. Fienup, Brannon, and Fender, *The Agricultural Development of Argentina,* p. 211.

47. Arkes, *Bureaucracy, Marshall Plan, and the National Interest,* pp. 165–66, 208–9, 236–41, 259–62, 274, and 328; Peterson, *Argentina and the United States.*

48. Reca, *Price and Production Duality within Argentine Agriculture,* pp. 35–40. Exchange reserves in 1948 were $143 million (gold), and $115 million convertible foreign exchange at the end of the year.

49. *Ibid.,* pp. 40–1.

50. See also Gomez Morales, *Política Económica Peronista,* pp. 146–47; and Cafiero, *Cinco Años Despues.* Banco de la Nación credit increased from 990 million pesos to 1,730 pesos. Details of exchange rates applied to agricultural exports are given in Farmsworth and Kevarkian, *Argentina, Competitor of United States Agriculture,* p. 25.

51.   Age of Machinery, End of 1948 (% distribution)

Type of Machinery	Before '36	'36–'40	'41–'45	'45 & after
Tractors	40	27	17	16
Plows	64	23	10	3
Harrows	47	35	13	5
Sowing Machines	56	28	13	3
Harvesting Machines	55	31	7	7
Various	85	8	5	2
Totals	57	27	11	5

SOURCE: SRA, *Anuario* (1949).

Evidence that Peron's policy was carried out is given in the following table:

Argentine Tractor Imports (1922–51)

Yearly Averages of:	
1922–30	1,853
1937–39	3,137
1946–50	4,119
1948	10,163
1949	2,622
1950	3,789
1951	6,629

SOURCE: SRA, *Anuario* (1952), p. 10. See also ECLA, *El desarrollo económico de la Argentina,* addition 4, p. 126. Mimeo.

52. SRA, *Anuario* (1949), p. 3.

53. BCRA, 1960 base year, gives the smaller figure; CEPAL, which used 1960 weights, gives the larger figure.

54. Gomez Morales, *Politica Económica Peronista,* p. 65.

55. BCRA, 1960 weights.

56. Fienup, Brannon, and Fender, *The Agricultural Development of Argentina,* p. 108.

57. *Ibid.,* pp. 155–66; and de Janvry, *A Model Case of Economic Stagnation.*

58. Fienup, Brannon, and Fender, *The Agricultural Development of Argentina,* p. 168; Farmsworth and Kevarkian, *Argentina, Competitor of United States Agriculture,* p. 40.

59. Fienup, Brannon, and Fender, *The Agricultural Development of Argentina,* pp. 171–72.

60. República Argentina, Poder Ejecutivo Nacional, *Período 1932–1938,* vol. 10.

61. Weil, *Argentine Riddle,* p. 52.

62. Gomez Morales, *Politica Económica Peronista,* p. 147.

63. Fienup, Brannon, and Fender, *The Agricultural Development of Argentina,* pp. 105–7.

64. *Ibid.,* p. 209.

65. *Ibid.,* p. 211.

66. Lucio Graciano Reca, Interview, July 1971.

67. This, and the following, from República Argentina, Poder Ejecutivo Nacional, *Período 1932–1938,* vol. 10, and Smith, *Politics and Beef in Argentina,* chaps. 6–8, p. 144. Note: of 15 percent from Argentine frigoríficos, 4 percent was accounted for by existing Argentine firms, the remaining 11 percent by newly created national firms.

68. During 1936–37, this included subsidy payments by the Argentine government (from the profits derived from exchange control) on meat exports tó the United Kingdom. This had become desirable in order to offset, in part, at least, the imposition by the British government of an import duty on beef under the provisions of the Argentine-U.K. trade agreement of December 1, 1936. The payments were made to meat exporting companies, and were maintained through mid-1937. "Argentina and its Tariff," August 26, 1944, pp. 9–10.

69. Reca, *Price and Production Duality within Argentine Agriculture,* p. 14.

70. Fienup, Brannon, and Fender, *The Agricultural Development of Argentina,* p. 69.

71. *Ibid.,* pp. 68–73.

72. *Ibid.,* p. 78.

73. Reca, *Price and Production Duality Within Argentine Agriculture,* p. 93.

74. Fienup, Brannon, and Fender, *The Agricultural Development of Argentina,* pp. 119–20.

75. To some extent, Argentine production of yerba maté resulted from a provision of the 1926 land law, which required that those holding concessions allowing them to work on public lands in Misiones, must plant 75 percent of the land with yerba. As a result, yerba production provided the area's economic base. The nationalist economist Alejandro Bunge noted that Misiones bought more cows than Brazil, but Argentina feared Brazilian failure to buy Argentine wheat, despite the fact that the Brazilian flour industry was protected and expanding. *Revista Económica Argentina* (October 1933), p. 281.

76. Fienup, Brannon, and Fender, *The Agricultural Development of Argentina,* p. 115.

77. *Ibid.,* p. 117.

78. *Ibid.,* p. 225.

79. *Ibid.,* p. 248.

80. *Ibid.,* p. 260

81. *Ibid.,* p. 269.

82. *Ibid.,* pp. 272–73.

83. *Ibid.,* p. 311.

84. *Ibid.,* p. 188.

85. *Ibid.,* pp. 211–12.

86. *Ibid.,* p. 213.

87. *Ibid.,* p. 212.

88. Andruchowicz, *Use and Productivity of Resources in the Corn Producing Area.*

89. Fienup, Brannon, and Fender, *The Agricultural Development of Argentina,* pp. 274–75.

90. Cited in part in *Wall Street Journal,* July 16, 1975, p. 27.

Chapter Six: Manufacture

1. Eduardo Jorge argues that if small firms are included, then industrial concentration in the modern sector is less than Dorfman asserts. Jorge, *Industria y Concentración Económica,* p. 176.

2. Villanueva, "El Origen de la Industrialización Argentina," p. 462. Villanueva stresses the basis for growth laid in the 1920s, rather than the shock of the Great Depression of the 1930s, in his discussion of Argentine industrialization.

   A light increase in protection on paper, iron and steel, and other metal manufactures, and electrical machinery and supplies, occurred in the 1920s. For a comparison of 1909–27 tariff duties, see Díaz Alejandro, *Essays on the Economic History of the Argentine Republic,* p. 290.

3. Ferns, *Britain and Argentina in the Nineteenth Century,* pp. 326, 331.

4. Martinez, on the other hand, indicates that although the East-Center had 84.2 percent of Argentine agricultural wealth, this was only 20 percent greater than the national average on a per capita basis. Martinez and Lewandowski, *The Argentine in the Twentieth Century,* p. 372.

5. Brodersohn, "Historical View of Regional Implications in National Development," p. 8.

6. Ramos Mexia, *A Programme of Public Works and Finance,* p. 5.

7. Brodersohn, "Historical View of Regional Implications in National Development," p. 8.

8. Ramos Mexia, *A Programme of Public Works and Finance,* p. 29.

9. Brodersohn, "Historial View of Regional Implications in National Development," pp. 4–5.

10. Randall, *A Comparative Economic History of Latin America,* chap. 7; Tornquist, *The Economic Development of the Argentine Republic,* pp. 28–36.

11. Randall, *A Comparative Economic History of Latin America,* chap. 7; Díaz Alejandro, *Essays on the Economic History of the Argentine Republic,* p. 214. These developments are reflected in a relatively low capital/output ratio.

12. Solberg, "The Tariff and Politics in Argentina," pp. 261–62.

13. *Ibid.,* p. 264.

14. Randall, *A Comparative Economic History of Latin America,* chap. 7; Solberg, "Tariff," p. 267.

15. Solberg, "The Tariff and Politics in Argentina," p. 271.

16. *Ibid.* President Yrigoyen's position, however, was that "our tariff protection should be limited to those industries which are capable of promoting the general welfare of the country and of cheapening articles of general consumption, and should

not be such as to render difficult the importation of foreign merchandise." Cited in E. Gallo, *Agrarian Expansion and Industrial Development*, p. 19. Initial source: H. O. Chalkey, U.K. Commercial Attache, *Parliamentary Papers*, "Overseas Trade Reports," vol. 42, 1920.

17. Bunge, *Industrias del Norte*, p. 190.

18. Solberg, "The Tariff and Politics in Argentina," p. 274.

19. Cited in Villanueva, "El Origen de la Industrializacíon Argentina," p. 468.

20. Brodersohn, "Historical View of Regional Implications in National Development," pp. 8, 10, 14.

21. Significance tests run (X^2) based on various censuses, support this theory.

22. SRA *Anuario* (1928), p. 76. See also chapter 2.

23. Solberg, "The Tariff and Politics in Argentina," p. 277.

24. Cited in Solberg, "The Tariff and Politics in Argentina," p. 283. Initial source is Malcolm Robertson, "The Economic Relations between Great Britain and the Argentine Republic," *International Affairs*, 9:228. Lord D'Abernon was head of the negotiating team.

25. Techint, *Boletin Informativo*, p. 12.

26. Díaz Alejandro, *Essays on the Economic History of the Argentine Republic*, pp. 296–8.

27. *Censo Industrial* (1946).

28. Randall, *A Comparative Economic History of Latin America*, ch. 7.

29. For a discussion of this point, see Villanueva, "El Origen de la Industrialización Argentina."

30. Dudley Maynard Phelps, *Migration of Industry to South America* and Prebisch, *Conversaciones con el doctor Raúl Prebisch*, 1:1–4

31. Ferrer and Wheelright, *Industrialization in Argentina and Australia*, pp. 6–7. Ferrer served as Minister of Economía y Hacienda of the province of Buenos Aires.

32. Dudley Maynard Phelps, *Migration of Industry to South America*, p. 205; Jorge, *Industria y Concentración Económica*, p. 63.

33. *New York Times*, October 18, 1932.

34. Treaty quoted in U.S. Tariff Commission, *The Argentine Customs Tariff and Other Trade Restrictions*, p. 9; see also *Board of Trade Journal*, May 11, 1933, pp. 727–29; and Dudley Maynard Phelps, *Migration of Industry to South America*, pp. 209–10.

35. See Dudley Maynard Phelps, *Migration of Industry to South America;* Salera, *Exchange Control and the Argentine Market;* Wright, *Railways*.

36. Prebisch, Interview. The loan was provided for in the Roca-Runciman Treaty.

37. Ferns, *The Argentine Republic*, p. 119; and Villanueva, "El Origen de la Industrialización Argentina," p. 469.

38. CEPAL, *El Desarrollo Económico de la Argentina*, p. 109.

39. Rennie, *The Argentine Republic*, pp. 250, 329; Smith, *Politics and Beef in Argentina*, p. 144. Specific provisions protecting British shipping were adopted.

40. Smith, *Politics and Beef in Argentina,* p. 146.

41. Rennie, *The Argentine Republic,* p. 255.

42. *Ibid.,* p. 261; and Ferns, *The Argentine Republic,* p. 102.

43. CEPAL, *El Desarrollo Económico de la Argentina,* p. 109; Ferns, *The Argentine Republic,* pp. 101–2.

44. Conversations I had with Professors Tulchin, Carmagnani, and Haight.

45. Rennie, *The Argentine Republic,* p. 33.

46. *Ibid.* Yet their future profitability appeared to be limited by the 1936 Anglo-Argentine trade agreement, which stipulated that a minimum quota for the import of British rayon and cotton textiles would be established if Argentina placed quantitative import restrictions on these commodities (see chap. 8, note 20).

47. Díaz Alejandro, *Essays on the Economic History of the Argentine Republic,* pp. 224–25.

48. Ciria, *Partidos y Poder en la Argentina Moderna,* p. 47.

49. Villafañe, *El Atraso del Interior,* pp. 5–12. (Villafañe was governor of Jujuy.)

50. Argentine practice resembles French planning practice.

51. See infant mortality rates, for example, in Diaz Alejandro, *Essays on the Economic History of the Argentine Republic,* p. 427.

52. Blanksten, *Peron's Argentina,* p. 36.

53. Enrique Uriburu, "Exposición del Ministro de Hacienda sobre el Estado de las Finanzas Nacionales," *Revista Económica Argentina* (October 1931), 27:253.

54. Dorfman, *Historia de la Industria Argentina,* p. 203.

55. Murmis and Portantiero, *Estudios Sobre Orígines del Peronismo,* p. 84.

56. J. L. Romero, cited in Cantón, Moreno and Ciria, *Argentina: La Democracia Constitucional,* p. 195.

57. *Ibid.,* p. 196.

58. Rennie, *The Argentine Republic,* p. 248. See also Salera, *Exchange Control and the Argentine Market.* Note: The government was said to be trying to conserve its reserve position. See chap. 8.

59. Weil, *Argentine Riddle,* p. 24.

60. Prebisch, *Conversaciones con el doctor Raúl Prebisch,* p. 96.

61. Prebisch, lecture at Columbia University, February 3, 1971.

62. Peterson, *Argentina and the United States,* p. 408.

63. *Ibid.;* and Ferns, *The Argentine Republic,* p. 142.

64. Prebisch, *Conversaciones con el doctor Raúl Prebisch,* p. 43.

65. Ferns, *The Argentine Republic,* p. 143.

66. Peterson, *Argentina and the United States,* pp. 413, 425.

67. *Ibid.,* p. 438.

68. República Argentina: *Plan de Gobierno, 1947–1951,* p. 13.

69. Altimir, Santamaria, and Sourrouille, "Los Instrumentos de Promoción Industrial," pp. 96, 114.

70. *Ibid.*, pp. 472, 473.

71. *Ibid.*, pp. 474–75.

72. Gomez Morales, *Interviews,* p. 35.

73. Altimir, Santamaria, and Sourrouille, "Los Instrumentos de Promoción Industrial," pp. 470, 476.

74. Gomez Morales, *Interviews,* p. 78.

75. Altimir, Santamaria, and Sourrouille, "Los Instrumentos de Promoción Industrial," p. 479.

76. Gomez Morales, Interviews, p. 78.

77. *Ibid.*, p. 79.

78. These are: phenolic and ureic powder, formaldehyde, and hexametilentetramine (linked to petrochemicals).

79. Altimir, Santamaria, and Sourrouille, "Los Instrumentos de Promoción Industrial," pp. 481–82.

80. *Ibid.*, p. 115.

81. *Ibid.*, pp. 90, 97, 99–100, 105, 109, 115, 471.

82. *Ibid.*, pp. 116–17.

83. *Ibid.*, p. 903.

84. *Ibid.*, p. 905.

85. *Ibid.*, pp. 90, 91, 723, 894–901.

86. Schwartz, *The Argentine Experience with Industrial Credit and Protection Incentives, 1943–1958,* pp. 77–82.

87. *Ibid.*, pp. 122–23.

88. Blanksten, *Perón's Argentina,* pp. 255–56.

89. Detailed information on industrial growth is available, beginning with 1950. The published census classifications are broader than the national interest industry descriptions. Output by value added by these categories has not been published. The procedure used was to take BCRA estimates, which most closely correspond to the national interest industry mentioned. Note that the BCRA 1960 price weights are close to world average. The BCRA classification printed in January 1971 is closer to that in the national interest industry decrees than that used by the census.

Because of the classification problem mentioned above, BCRA data were used. However, in most cases, BCRA indices of manufacturing output are the lowest available. In the case where broad classifications are available, manufacturing growth as a whole was 2.9 times as rapid as the BCRA estimates. Thus, the Perón program was probably more effective than the minimum estimates published here; but I do not have exact data to prove this point.

For a detailed evaluation of varying estimates of manufacturing output, see Randall, "Lies, Damn Lies and Argentine G.D.P."

90. Macario, "Protectionism and Industrialization in Latin America," pp. 73–74.

91. Dagnino Pastore, "Productos Exportables: Resultados de Encuestos" (Documento de Trabajo), Instituto Torcuato di Tella (1964), cited in Felix, "Comment on Barend A. DeVries, International Price Comparisons," p. 358.

92. The cost of transition from statist to free competition was great, and the attempt to shift was abandoned.

93. Schwartz, *Argentine Experience with Industrial Credit,* pp. 84–7.

94. The detailed reasoning behind this statement is as follows: for Argentina, the assumption that the domestic price is equal to C.I.F. import price plus the nominal tariff on both the inputs and the output is a dubious one, because the levels of protection on many import substitutes were set at prohibitively high levels. The actual domestic prices were in such cases usually well below the import price plus the nominal tariff rate. On the other hand, many imports were allowed in under special dispensations; for example, in 1959–63 roughly 50 percent of all imports came in duty-free, most under regimens which exempted such goods from the normal import duties and surcharges. Again, unless adjustments are made for this, the import price plus the nominal tariff rate for such goods overestimates their domestic price. This argument is based on private communication with David Felix.

95. Much of the analysis in this suggestion is based on comments from David Felix, and his articles listed in the bibliography. Any errors are mine.

96. Salazar-Carrillo, *Price Purchasing Power and Real Product Comparisons,* indicates that the rate was undervalued 9 percent in June (p. 123); Loser's study was carried out from October to December. Domestic inflation from June to December was 5.5 percent. There was no change in the exchange rate during this period. Little, Scitovsky, and Scott note in *Industry and Trade* that Balassa's estimates of Argentine protection are based on nominal tariffs rather than direct price information, and are probably too great; Chenery used the Balassa estimates in his study of comparative development strategies (p. 431).

97. "Results of the Survey on Production and Investment Expectations of Industrial Enterprises," Table 3 (CONADE, March 1965). Cited in Schydlowsky, "Industrialization and Growth," p. 135.

98. de Janvry, *A Model Case of Economic Stagnation.*

99. "Allocative Efficiency vs. 'X-Efficiency,'" *American Economic Review* (June 1966), p. 392.

100. Felix, "Did Import Substitution Industrialization Save Foreign Exchange in 1953–1960?" pp. 5, 6, 20, 22. Older import substitution industries were also heavily protected; textiles, for example, had a higher nominal protection rate than did newer industries.

101. Loser, *The Intensity of Trade Restrictions in Argentina,* pp. 46–49. Loser finds significant rank correlations between protection and growth. Note that Loser's study used a variety of countries, alternatively, to determine world price, and various goods for exportables. The results are similar in all cases. The main trends have been reported here.

102. *Ibid.,* pp. 267–68.

103. Although the difference in demand for bank credit is in part attributed to the difference in the size of internal cash flows between industries, and to investment financing needs, both are largely influenced by prospective product demand. I have

shown about that this is the weakest of the elements influencing growth under Perón, and that it was heavily influenced by government policy; it is not an independent factor of sufficient force to weaken the above argument.

104. Pinedo, Interview, *Esto Es.*

105. Gomez Morales, *Interviews*, p. 76.

106. Cited in Altimir, Santamaria, and Sourrouille, "Los Instrumentos de Promoción Industrial," p. 122.

107. *Ibid.*, pp. 110–11.

108. *Ibid.*, p. 112.

109. *Ibid.*, pp. 104–8; and Randall, "Economic Development Policies and Argentine Economic Growth," p. 132.

110. Altimir, Santamaria, and Sourrouille, "Los Instrumentos de Promoción Industrial," p. 142.

111. *Ibid.*, pp. 122–23.

112. CONADE, *Plan Nacional de Desarrollo y Seguridad, 1971–75* (República Argentina, 1971), p. 18.

113. O'Donnell and Linck, *Dependencia y Autonomía*, p. 101. The section on economy was written by Linck.

114. For a list of nontraditional exports by volume and percentage growth, see Guillermo S. Edelberg and Osvaldo Baccino, *Definición e identificación de las exportaciones no tradicionales de la República Argentina, en base a las estádisticas oficiales 1938–1963*, Documento de Trabajo, Instituto Torcuato Di Tella, Centro de Investigaciones Economicas, 2d ed. (Buenos Aires, 1966).

115. O'Donnell and Linck, *Dependencia y Autonomía*, p. 105.

116. *Ibid.*, p. 140. A .81 (sig. 1 percent) correlation was found between bank nationality and amount of foreign capital in the sector to which a loan was made. The percentage distribution correlation was $r = .44$ (sig. 1 percent), for percent percentage of portfolio by activity compared to foreign investment. Ribas et al., "Las Inversiones Extranjeras en la Argentina," pp. 152–3.

117. O'Donnell and Linck, *Dependencia y Autonomía*, p. 117.

118. *Ibid.* Note: Skupch, "Concentración Industrial en la Argentina," p. 6, gives slightly different figures which show the same trend.

119. Skupch, "Concentración Industrial en la Argentina," p. 10.

120. See, for example, Zuvekas, "Argentine Economic Policy, 1958–1962: The Frondizi Government's Development Plan," pp. 45–74.

121. O'Donnell and Linck, *Dependencia y Autonomía*, pp. 122–23.

122. Baccino, Bajraj, and Di Tella, "La Industria Manufacturera en Argentina."

123. Thompson, "Argentine Economic Policy under the Onganía Regime," p. 73.

124. Note: poster merely gave name to party. Policy implicit.

125. CONADE, *Plan Nacional*, p. 24.

126. Brodersohn, *Regional Development and Industrial Location Policy in Argentina*, pp. 46–7.

127. *Ibid.*, p. 38.

128. Ministerio de Hacienda y Finanzas, Dirección Nacional de Programación e Investigación, *Inversión del Sector Público Argentino por Regiones, Años 1968–1971,* pp. 4, 5, 35.

129. For a discussion of this point, see Schydlowsky, "Industrialization and Growth," pp. 131–32.

Chapter Seven: Railroads and Oil

1. Bunge, *Los Ferrocarriles Naciones,* pp. 19, 116.

2. Alberdi, *Bases y Puntos de Partido para la Organización Pólitica de la República Argentina,* translated by and cited in Wright, *British Owned Railways in Argentina,* pp. 15–16.

3. Legón and Medrano, *Las Constituciones de la República Argentina,* pp. 42–43.

4. Wright, *British Owned Railways in Argentina,* p. 22; Randall, *A Comparative Economic History of Latin America,* chap. 7.

5. Wright, *British Owned Railways in Argentina,* pp. 20–23.

6. *Ibid.,* pp. 26–30; Randall; *A Comparative Economic History of Latin America,* chap. 7.

7. Bunge, *Los Ferrocarriles Nacionales,* pp. 40–56.

8. Wright, *British Owned Railways in Argentina,* p. 57; Randall, *A Comparative Economic History of Latin America,* chap. 7.

9. Wright, *British Owned Railways in Argentina,* p. 60–61.

10. *Ibid.,* pp. 66–67.

11. *Ibid.,* pp. 67–68; Randall, *A Comparative Economic History of Latin America,* ch. 7.

12. Wright, *British Owned Railways in Argentina,* p. 80.

13. Income from railroads owned by the government disappeared from the general government budget as a separate item around 1911. Major improvements in the railroads owned by the government were made in 1908 by financing imports of equipment and construction of repair shops. *Message of the President of the Republic Opening the Session of the Argentine Congress,* p. 44.

14. Salera, *Exchange Control and the Argentine Market,* pp. 133–4; Wright, *British Owned Railways in Argentina,* pp. 85–87, 119–20.

15. Bunge, *Ferrocarrilles Nacionales,* pp. 292–93.

16. Scalabrini Ortiz, *Historia de los Ferrocarriles Argentinos,* pp. 320–21.

17. Cited in Cuccorese, *Historia de los Ferrocarriles,* pp. 130–31.

18. Ortiz, *Historia Económica de la República Argentina,* vol. 2.

19. *Ibid.,* p. 261.

20. *Diputados,* (1909), 2:122–24, cited in Wright, *British Owned Railways in Argentina,* p. 103.

21. Wright, *British Owned Railways in Argentina,* pp. 100–4.

22. Bunge, *Ferrocarriles Nacionales,* pp. 254–66.

23. Two preceding paragraphs based on Wright, *British Owned Railways in Argentina,* pp. 110–119.

24. Wright, *British Owned Railways in Argentina,* p. 125. In this instance, the British loan proposal was made through the Department of Overseas Trade without consulting the Foreign Office.

25. Felix Luna, *Alvear,* cited in Wright, *British Owned Railways in Argentina,* p. 126.

26. Wright, *British Owned Railways in Argentina,* p. 128.

27. *Ibid.,* pp. 128–29.

28. *Ibid.,* p. 135.

29. *Ibid.,* pp. 141–42.

30. Roca-Runciman Treaty, Protocol, Article 1.

31. Salera, *Exchange Control and the Argentine Market,* p. 160.

32. Wright, *British Owned Railways in Argentina,* p. 144; Salera, *Exchange Control and the Argentine Market,* p. 132.

33. Salera, *Exchange Control and the Argentine Market,* p. 135. This was provided for in confidential notes to the 1936 renewal of the Roca-Runciman Treaty. Wright, *British Owned Railways in Argentina,* pp. 191–95.

34. Wright, *British Owned Railways in Argentina.*

35. A sum rising to £12 million after interest charges. *Ibid.,* pp. 198–209.

36. "We find that to the original sterling cost, less depreciation, was added accrued interest plus the difference between the peso value of the pound during the periods in which sections of the road were constructed, and the ruling sterling rate. Apart, of course, from the host of difficulties (known to all students of public utility valuation) associated with the original cost reckonings, it is interesting to note that the exchange depreciation provision departed very materially from the treatment accorded to the railways. Whereas the special remittance rate of 15.75 pesos to the pound reduced the "exchange loss" by approximately 23 percent, the (retroactive) application of the 15 peso rate to the Córdoba Central valuation involved cutting down the effect of peso depreciation by about 38 percent. In view of these circumstances, there can be no doubt that the transaction was immeasurably more favorable to the investors than any scheme that might have been offered in the absence of London's unquestioned bargaining advantage (the exchange loss is the fraction which the remittance saving of 1.25 pesos to the pound bears to the difference between the old sterling parity and the official selling rate)." Salera, *Exchange Control and the Argentine Market,* p. 162.

37. Wright, *British Owned Railways in Argentina,* p. 151. The government began to include special provision in its budget for the conservation and improvement of roads in 1927. In 1931, a surtax was placed on gasoline; the proceeds of this tax were earmarked for road expansion. República Argentina, vol. 2, *Vialidad Nacional, Parques Nacionales, Obras del Riachuelo.*

38. Wright, *British Owned Railways in Argentina,* pp. 156–57.

39. Hobsbawm, *Industry and Empire.*

40. Wright, *British Owned Railways in Argentina,* p. 150.

41. *Ibid.,* chap. 8.

42. Cited in Wright, *British Owned Railways in Argentina,* p. 208.

43. *Ibid.,* p. 219. See also Skupch, "Nacionalización, Libras Bloqueadas y Substitución de Importaciones," pp. 477–93.

44. Prebisch, lecture at Columbia University, February 23, 1971.

45. Wright, *British Owned Railways in Argentina,* chap. 11; Skupch, "Nacionalización, Libras Bloqueadas y Substitución de Importaciones."

46. Hernandez Arreguí, *La Formación de la Conciencia Nacional,* p. 285.

47. Wright, *British Owned Railways in Argentina,* p. 180.

48. *Ibid.,* pp. 181–182.

49. Cited in Wright, *British Owned Railways in Argentina,* p. 232.

50. The company's capital was written down from 326,875,000 to 169,927,000 pesos. Rennie, *The Argentine Republic,* pp. 231–34, 241, 261, 301–4, 332, 347, 351.

51. Wright, *British Owned Railways in Argentina,* pp. 250–51.

52. *Times* (London), September 18, 1946, p. 3.

53. *Economist,* p. 236.

54. Paz and Ferrari, *Argentina's Foreign Policy,* p. 160; see also Skupch, "Nacíonalización, Libras Bloqueadas y Substitución de Importaciones."

55. Wright, *British Owned Railways in Argentina,* p. 257; Skupch, "Nacionalización, Libras Bloqueadas y Substitución de Importaciones."

56. Santa Cruz, *Ferrocarriles Argentinos,* p. 31.

57. *Ibid.,* pp. 22–23.

58. John Brook, ed., *The South American Handbook,* 1975, Trade and Travel Publications, 51st ed. (Bath, England, 1975), p. 33; and Robert T. Brown, *Transport and the Economic Integration of South America* (Washington, D.C.: Brookings Institution), p. 172.

59. Randall, "Economic Development Policies and Argentine Economic Growth."

60. Santa Cruz, *Ferrocarriles Argentinos,* p. 33; Ferrocarrilles Argentinos, *Memoria,* p. 30; Randall, "Economic Development Policies and Argentine Economic Growth," p. 135.

61. In this section of the chapter, where several sources give the same information, reference is made only to Frondizi, which is the most readily available of the books. Frondizi, *Petróleo y Política,* pp. 44–45.

62. *Ibid.,* pp. 45–46.

63. *Ibid.,* pp. 53 ff.

64. Cited in Frondizi, *Petróleo y Política,* p. 54.

65. *Ibid.,* pp. 55, 57.

66. *Ibid.,* p. 69.

67. *Ibid.*, pp. 57, 64.

68. *Ibid.*, p. 79.

69. *Ibid.*, p. 92.

70. *Ibid.*

71. *Ibid.*, p. 101.

72. *Ibid.*, p. 106.

73. *Ibid.*, p. 159.

74. *Ibid.*, p. 160.

75. *Ibid.*, p. 161.

76. *Ibid.*, p. 154.

77. *Ibid.*, p. 155.

78. *Ibid.*, p. 156.

79. Peterson, *Argentina and the United States,* pp. 348–49.

80. *Ibid.*, p. 349; and Frondizi, *Petróleo y Política,* p. 248.

81. *Ibid.*, pp. 170–71.

82. *Ibid.*, p. 241; and Diz, "Money and Prices in Argentina," p. 136.

83. Frondizi, *Petróleo y Política,* pp. 242, 251–53, 330.

84. *Ibid.*, pp. 233, 276.

85. *Ibid.*, pp. 330–42, 379.

86. *Ibid.*, pp. 353–57.

87. Kaplan, *Economía y Política del Petróleo Argentino,* pp. 24–5.

88. Frondizi, *Petróleo y Política,* pp. 361–63.

89. Gonzalez Clement, cited in Kaplan, *Económia y Política del Petróleo Argentino,* p. 45. Cafiero states that in 1948, the United States detained shipments to Argentina of oil equipment that had already been paid for, *Cinco Años Después,* p. 405.

90. Minister Barro, Chamber of Deputies, 1949, pp. 2734, 2758. Cited in Kaplan, *Economía y Política del Petróleo Argentino,* pp. 44–47, and Silenzi de Stagni, *El Petróleo Argentino,* p. 100

91. Silenzi de Stagni, *El Petróleo Argentino,* pp. 85–87. In 1950, The Dirección Nacional de la Energía was replaced by the Empresas Nacionales de Energía. See also Kaplan, *Economía y Política del Petróleo Argentino,* pp. 51–55.

92. Cited in Kaplan, *Economía y Política del Petróleo Argentino,* p. 38, 94. See also Frondizi, *Petróleo y Nación,* p. 8: and Cámara de la Industria del Petróleo, *El Desarrollo de Petróleo en la República Argentina,* p. 26.

93. Cafiero states that a contract was signed with California Oil because EXIMBANK and other United States banks refused to grant credit if private sources were not tapped. *Cinco Años Después,* p. 405.

94. Frondizi, *Petróleo y Nación,* pp. 8, 9.

95. Kaplan, *Economía y Política del Petróleo Argentino,* p. 41.

96. Levin, unpublished manuscript.

97. Cámara de Petróleo, *El Desarrollo de Petróleo en la República Argentina,* p. 26; Díaz Alejandro, *Essays on the Economic History of the Argentine Republic,* pp. 467, 480, 514.

98. Levin, unpublished manuscript; Kaplan, *Economía y Política del Petróleo Argentino;* Silenzi de Stagni, *El Petróleo Argentino.*

99. *New York Times,* May 16, 1964.

100. UN, *Yearbook of International Trade Statistics,* several issues; BCRA, *Origen del Producto y Distribución del Ingreso.*

Chapter Eight: Argentine Economic Dependence and Independence in the Twentieth Century

1. Kuznets, *Modern Economic Growth,* pp. 64–65.

2. Randall, "Argentina and the World Economy," paper presented at Columbia University, October 1975.

3. Cited in Randall, *A Comparative Economic History of Latin America,* ch. 7.

4. Complete information on size distribution of firms by owner or otherwise is not published in censuses.

5. Jorge, *Industria y Concentración Económica,* p. 47; and Ferrer, *United States-Argentine Economic Relations,* pp. 43, 47.

6. This relationship is weak and significant for 1909–54 as a whole, but the foreign- and domestic-influenced policy variables are only occasionally significantly correlated for subperiods. The relationship between real money supply and real government spending is inconsistent between 1909 and 1939, and significant and positive from 1940 onward. The results for 1909–39 and 1940–54 are highly similar. The result for the period for which multicollinearity is not a problem supports the same hypothesis as do the results for which multicollinearity might be important; I therefore believe that the latter results are not significantly affected by possible multicollinearity, and they should be given the benefit of the doubt.

7. The correlation coefficients are .99 and .94, respectively.

8. The correlation between United Kingdom imports from Argentina and Argentine gross domestic product during this period is .39.

9. In fact, the government virtually always—in boom or recession—resorted to borrowing, usually from the banking system. Moreno, "La Politica Economica que conviene al país en las actuales circumstancias," p. 281.

10. The correlation between real money supply and real gross domestic product is .95.

11. Pinedo served as economy minister from 1933 to 1935, 1940 to 1941, and in 1962; Gomez Morales from 1949 to 1955, and 1973 to 1975.

12. In 1914, before Yrigoyen's presidency, the export of coal, wheat, and flour was prohibited. Soares, *Economia y Finanzas de la Nación Argentina,* p. 29.

13. The Argentine president takes office in the middle of the year; to account for lags between the giving of an order and its execution, the presidency is assigned to the year following that in which the president first took office.

14. *Primera Plana,* July 13, 1965.

15. Ferrer, *United States-Argentine Economic Relations,* p. 218.

16. *Ibid.,* pp. 219–20.

17. *Ibid.,* p. 204; see also Jorge, *Industria y Concentración Económica.*

18. The correlation between Argentine and British real income is −.64 for 1918–24 and .85 for 1925–29.

19. Similar movements in United Kingdom imports and Argentine gross domestic product are reflected in the fact that in 1930–32 United Kingdom imports from Argentina were more strongly correlated with Argentine real gross domestic product (.99) than were real government spending (−.97) or real money supply (.88).

20. United States officials were understandably unhappy at Argentine pro-British, anti-United States policy. Describing the 1936 Anglo-Argentine customs agreement, an American official, A. J. Poirier, stated that the new agreement "continued in force the Argentine tariff concessions made in the earlier agreement. However, new concessions were made in trade matters by Argentina, including an agreement to maintain the Argentine market for British coal, protection of British shipping in case it became necessary to establish a meat-export control, and the establishment of minimum quotas for British rayon and cotton piece goods if quantitative import restrictions on these commodities were put in operation by Argentina. Argentina further agreed to cooperate in proposals to regulate beef supplies to the British market through an international conference. The principal changes by the United Kingdom from the preceding arrangement were the imposition of duties on certain meats imported from non-Empire countries and the establishment of minimum quotas for Argentina." "Argentina and Its Tariff," p. 10.

21. Salera, *Exchange Control and the Argentine Market,* p. 150.

22. *Ibid.,* p. 154.

23. From 1932 to 1937, United Kingdom imports from Argentina correlate only moderately (.43) with Argentina real gross domestic product. World business conditions correlate (.97), followed by real government expenditure (.93).

24. Salera, *Exchange Control and the Argentine Market.* The national government took over the debt of the provinces in 1936 by exchanging provincial for national bonds which had been sold abroad and took over some provincial revenues in compensation.

25. Gomez Morales, *Interviews,* pp. 19, 32.

26. Gomez Morales, *Política Económica Peronista,* pp. 23–24.

27. *Ibid.,* and Peterson, *Argentina and the United States,* p. 468.

28. Gomez Morales, *Interviews,* p. 78.

29. Peterson, *Argentina and the United States,* p. 476; *New York Times,* August 5, 1948. In July 1948, the Economic Cooperation Administration (ECA) representative, Struve Hensel, announced that Argentina was off its list for 1948. At the close of 1948, ECA had authorized purchases of $3 million from Argentina, of which only $512,000 were shipped in that year. Early in 1949, the State Department list of alleged discrimination "included deals between Argentina and various European countries, where it was argued that the ECA had advised the other country along lines tending to force down Argentine prices." In October 1948, "the State Department intervened to keep ECA policymakers in Washington from passing on to Paris

the idea that Argentina must sell at the equivalent of United States prices even where the deal was for soft currency; and without a return guarantee that Argentina would be able to obtain desired imports on the same deal at United States prices," *New York Times,* June 11, 1949. A partial exception is the case of rubber, previously obtained as "patriotic contraband" from Brazil; a treaty regulating this trade was signed in 1945. "História del Peronismo," *Primera Plana,* June 22, 1965, p. 50.

30. Gomez Morales, *Interviews,* pp. 38–40.

31. *New York Times,* June 16, 1949; June 18, 1949; and *Times* (London), October 20, 1949.

32. Gomez Morales, *Política Económica Peronista,* pp. 43–45.

33. I am indebted to Professor H. Finch for information on Uruguay's agricultural policies and performances.

34. On another occasion, Peronist economy minister Cafiero noted that European nations had government food purchasing agencies, so that Argentina needed a sales monopoly to redress the balance in bargaining. Cafiero also cited United States, Canadian, and Australian government sales agencies. Cafiero, *Cinco Años Despues,* p. 227.

35. Gomez Morales, *Interviews,* pp. 32–33.

36. *Ibid.,* pp. 80–81.

37. October 14, 1949. See also the *Times* (London), October 20, 1949. Although no U.S. oil companies had apparently objected to tying Argentina to British oil supplies, Acting Secretary of State James E. Webb felt that this part of the pact was of concern to the State Department. *New York Times,* June 16, 1949. For a different point of view, see "História del Peronismo," *Primera Plana,* June 22, 1965, which argues that oil treaties were signed so that Argentina would be admitted to the San Francisco Conference. The series "História del Peronismo," *Primera Plana,* 1965–67, provides a wealth of political detail for a history of decision making from 1943 through the Perón years.

38. *Times* (London), April 15, 1950.

39. Gomez Morales, *Interviews,* pp. 82–86.

40. *Ibid.,* p. 84.

41. Title: Secretario de Relaciones Económicas y Sociales de la Presidencia de la Nacion, 1958.

42. Gomez Morales, *Interviews,* p. 85.

43. *Ibid.,* pp. 75–85.

Appendix A: The Regression Model Used in Chapter Two

1. Nerlove, *Dynamics of Supply.*

2. Nerlove and Reca use past prices to estimate producers' expectations which determine desired output. I believe that changes in real unit profits provide a better estimate of producers' expectations and have therefore used them instead of prices in equation (2). See pp. 9–10 for an analysis of the reason for doing so.

3. Reca, *The Price and Production Duality within Argentine Agriculture,* p. 95.

Bibliography

The bibliography is restricted to items cited in the text, as the Social Science Research Council is publishing an annotated bibliography of the economic history of Argentina.

Alberdi, Juan Bautista. *Bases y Puntos de Partido para la Organización Política de la República Argentina.* Buenos Aires: n.p., 1952.

Altimir, Oscar, Horacio Santamaria, and Juan Sourrouille. "Los Instrumentos de Promoción Industrial en la Postguerra," *Desarrollo Económico,* nos. 21–25, 28, 29 (1966–68).

Andruchowicz, Eugenio W. *Use and Productivity of Resources in the Corn Producing Area of Argentina,* M.A. thesis, Texas Agricultural and Mechanical University, 1970.

Anuario del Comercio Exterior.

"Argentina and Its Tariff," *Foreign Commerce Weekly,* 12, 19, and 26 August 1944.

Arkes, Hadley. *Bureaucracy, the Marshall Plan, and the National Interest.* Princeton, N.J.: Princeton University Press, 1972.

Baccino, Oswaldo, N. Bajraj, and G. Di Tella. "La Industria Manufacturera en Argentina," *Economía,* 1970.

Balassa, Bela. "Effective Protection in Developing Countries." In Jagdish Bhagwati, Ronald Jones, Robert Mundell, and Jaroslav Vanek, eds., *Trade, Balance of Payments, and Growth.* New York: American Elsevier, 1971.

—— "Tariff Protection in Industrial Countries: An Evaluation," *Journal of Political Economy,* 73.

Banco Central de la República Argentina (BCRA). *La Evolución de la Balanza de Pagos.* Buenos Aires, 1955.

—— *Memória Anual.* Buenos Aires, 1935–73.

—— *Annual Report.* Buenos Aires, 1938–43.

—— *Origen del Producto y Distribución del Ingreso, Años 1950–1969. Suplemento del Boletín Estadístico no. 1, enero de 1971.* Buenos Aires.

—— *Transacciones Intersectoriales de la República Argentina.* 1950; 1953; 1963.

Banco de la Nación Argentina. *El Banco de la Nación en su Cincuentenario.* Buenos Aires, 1941.

Basevi, Giorgio. "The United States Tariff Structure: Estimates of Effective Rates of Protection of United States Industries and Industrial Labor," *Review of Economics and Statistics* (May 1966), vol. 48, no. 2.

BCRA, *see* Banco Central de la República Argentina.

Biggs, Huntley Hedges. *Devaluations, Inflation, and Relative Price Changes for Agricultural Exports: Argentina, 1959–1967.* Ph.D. dissertation, Vanderbilt University, 1970.

Blanksten, George. *Peron's Argentina.* Chicago: University of Chicago Press, 1953.

Brodersohn, Mario. "Historical View of Regional Implications in National Development." Mimeographed.

—— *Regional Development and Industrial Location Policy in Argentina.* Buenos Aires: Instituto Torcuato Di Tella, 1967.

Bunge, Alejandro. *Los Ferrocarriles Nacionales.* Buenos Aires, n.p., 1918.

—— *Las Industrias del Norte,* Buenos Aires: n.p., 1922.

Burmeister, Edwin and Paul Taubman. "Labour and Non-Labour Saving Propensities," *Canadian Journal of Economics* (February 1969), vol. 2, no.1.

Cafiero, Antonio. *Cinco Años Despues.* Buenos Aries: n.p., 1961.

Cantón, D., J. L. Moreno, and A. Ciria. *Argentina: La Democracia Constitucional y Su Crisis.* Buenos Aires, n.p., 1972.

Cámara de la Industria de Petroleo. *El Desarrollo de Petroleo en la República Argentina.* Buenos Aires, n.p., 1967.

CEPAL, *see* Comisión Económica para América Latina.

CIDA, *see* Comité Interamericano de Desarrollo Agrícola.

Ciria, Alberto. *Partidos y Poder en la Argentina Moderna, 1930–1946.* Buenos Aires, n.p., 1969.

Comisión Económica para América Latina (CEPAL). *El Desarrollo Económico de la Argentina.* 3 vols. México, 1959. The mimeographed appendix is identified as E/CN.12/429/Add.4.

Comité Interamericano de Desarrollo Agrícola (CIDA). *Tenencia de la Tierra y Desarrollo Socio-Económico del Sector Agrícola Argentina*. Washington, D.C.: Pan American Union, 1965.

CONADE, see República Argentina, Consejo Nacional de Desarrollo Económica.

Coní, Emilio A. "Apuntes para la Historia de la Colonización en la Argentina," *Revista Económica Argentina* (January 1919).

Cortés Conde, Roberto. "Régimen de la Tierra en Argentina," *Anuario* no. 7 (1964), Instituto de Investigaciones Históricas, Rosario. Universidad del Litoral, Facultad de Filosofia y Letras.

Cortés Conde, R., H. Gorostegui de Torres, and T. Halperín Donghi. *Evolución de las Exportaciones Argentinas*. Buenos Aires: planillas (galleys, never published), n.d.

Cuccorese, Horacio Juan. *Historia de los Ferrocarriles en la Argentina*. Córdoba: Macchi, 1969.

Dagnino Pastore, José María. *Ingreso y Dinero, Argentina, 1935–1960*. 3 vols. Buenos Aires: n.p., 1966.

Defilpe, Bruno. *Geografia Económica Argentina*. Buenos Aires: n.p., n.d.

Díaz Alejandro, Carlos F. *Essays on the Economic History of the Argentine Republic*. New Haven: Yale University Press, 1970.

Dieguez, Hector L. "Crecimiento e inestabilidad de las exportaciones," *Desarrollo Económico* (July–September), vol. 12, no. 46.

Diz, Adolfo. "Money and Prices in Argentina, 1935–1962." In D. Meiselman, ed., *Varieties of Monetary Experience*. Chicago: University of Chicago Press, 1970.

Dorfman, Adolfo. *Historia de la Industria Argentina*. Buenos Aires: Solar Hachette, 1970.

ECLA, see United Nations, Economic Commission for Latin America.

The Economic Review.

The Economist (Feb. 18, 1947), vol. 152.

Edel, Matthew. "Regional Integration and Income Distribution: Complements or Substitutes?" In Ronald Hilton, ed., *The Movement Toward Latin America Unity*. New York: Praeger, 1969.

Elias, Victor Jorge. *Estimates of Value Added, Capital and Labor in Argentine Manufacturing, 1935–1963*. Ph.D. dissertation, University of Chicago, 1969.

Eshag, Eprime and Rosemary Thorp. "Economic and Social Consequences of Orthodox Economic Policies in Argentina in the Post-War Years," *Bulletin of the Oxford University Institute of Economics and Statistics* (February 1965), vol. 27, no. 1.

Esto Es. 27 July 1954.

Farmsworth, A. and C. Kevarkian. *Argentina, Competitor of United States Agriculture.* U.S. Dept. of Agriculture. Foreign Agricultural Reports, no. 101, September 1957.

Felix, David. "Comment on Barend A. De Vries' International Price Comparisons of Selected Capital Goods Industries." In National Bureau of Economic Research, *International Comparisons of Prices and Output.* New York: NBER, 1972.

—— "Did Import Substitution Industrialization Save Foreign Exchange in 1953–1960? A Report on Some Findings." Buenos Aires: Instituto Torcuato Di Tella, Centro de Investigaciones Económicas, Doc. no. 7, 1965.

Ferns, H. S. *Britain and Argentina in the Nineteenth Century.* Oxford: Clarendon Press, 1960.

—— *Argentina.* London: Ernest Benn, 1969.

—— *The Argentine Republic.* New York: Barnes and Noble, 1973.

Ferrer, Aldo and E. L. Wheelwright, *Industrialization in Argentina and Australia: A Comparative Study.* Buenos Aires: Instituto Torcuato Di Tella, Centro de Investigaciones Economicas, Doc. no. 23, n.d.

Ferrer, Jr., James. *United States–Argentine Economic Relations, 1900–1930.* Ph.D. dissertation, University of California, 1964.

Ferrocarriles Argentinos. *Memoria Y Balance, 1970.*

Fienup, Darrell F., Russell H. Brannon, and Frank A. Fender. *The Agricultural Development of Argentina.* New York: Praeger, 1969.

Financial Times (London), 14 October 1949.

Friedman, Milton. *A Theory of the Consumption Function.* Princeton: Princeton University Press, 1957.

Friend, Irwin. *The Propensity to Consume and Save in Argentina.* Buenos Aires: Instituto Torcuato Di Tella, Working Doc. no. 30, 1965.

Frondizi, Arturo. *Petróleo y Nación.* Buenos Aires: n.p., 1963.

—— *Petróleo y Política.* Buenos Aires: Raigal, 1955.

Gallo, Ezequiel. *Agrarian Expansion and Industrial Development in Argentina, 1880–1930.* Buenos Aires: Instituto Torcuato Di Tella, Doc. no. 70.

Ganz, Alexander. "Problems and Uses of National Wealth Estimates in Latin America." In Raymond Goldsmith and Christopher Saunders, eds., *The Measurement of National Wealth*. Income and Wealth, Series 8. London: Bowes and Bowes, 1959.

Giberti, Horacio. "El Desarrollo Agropecuario," *Desarrollo Económico* (April–June 1962), vol. 1, no. 4.

Gomez Morales, Alfredo. *Interviews*. Transcript on deposit at Columbia University and Instituto Torcuato Di Tella.

—— *Política Económica Peronista*. Buenos Aires: n.p., n.d.

Gravil, R. "La intervención estatal en el comercio de exportación Argentino entre las dos guerras," *Desarrollo Económico* (October–December 1970; January–March 1971), vol. 10, no. 39–40.

Gupta, Syamaprasad. *An Economic Model for Argentina*. Washington, D.C.: International Bank for Reconstruction and Development, Staff Working Paper no. 177, April 1944.

Halperín, Ricardo. *The Behavior of the Argentine Monetary Sector*. Ph.D. dissertation, Columbia University, 1968.

Heilbroner, Robert. *Understanding Macroeconomics*. Englewood Cliffs, N.J.: Prentice-Hall, 1972.

Hernandez Arregui, Juan José. *La Formación de la Conciencia Nacional, 1930–1960*. Buenos Aires: Hachea, 1970.

Herschel, Federico J. and Samuel Itzcovitch. "Fiscal Policy in Argentina," *Public Finance* (1957), vol. 12, no. 1.

Hobsbawm, Eric. *Industry and Empire*. Baltimore: Penguin Books, 1969.

Horowitz, Morris. "High Level Manpower in the Economic Development of Argentina." In Frederick Harbison and Charles Myers, eds., *Manpower and Education*. New York: McGraw-Hill, 1965.

Hueyo, Alberto. *La Argentina en la Depresión Mundial, 1932–1933. Discursos, Conferencias*. Buenos Aires: El Ateneo, 1938.

International Monetary Fund. *Balance of Payments Yearbook*.

de Janvry, Alain. *A Model Case of Economic Stagnation, The Role of Agriculture in Argentine Economic Development*. May 1971. Mimeographed.

Jarvis, Lovell Stuber. *Supply Response in the Cattle Industry. The Argentine Case. 1937–8 to 1966–7*. Ph.D. dissertation, Massachusetts Institute of Technology, 1969.

Jorge, Eduardo. *Industria y Concentración Económica*. Buenos Aires: Siglo Veinte Uno, 1971.

Kaplan, Marcos. *Economía y Política del Petróleo Argentino, 1939–1956*. Buenos Aires: Praxis, 1957.

Komiya, Ryutaro. "The Supply of Personal Savings." In R. Komiya, ed., *Postwar Economic Growth in Japan*. Berkeley: University of California Press, 1966.

Kuznets, Simon. *Modern Economic Growth, Rate Structure and Spread*. New Haven: Yale University Press, 1966.

—— "Quantitative Aspects of the Economic Growth of Nations," Part VIII, "Distribution of Income by Size," *Economic Development and Cultural Change* (January 1963, part II).

Legón, F. and S. Medrano. *Las Constituciones de la República Argentina*. Buenos Aries: Cultura Hispanica, 1953.

Leibenstein, Harvey. "Allocative Efficiency vs. 'X-Efficiency,'" *American Economic Review* (June 1966),vol. 56, no.3.

Little, Ian, Tibor Scitovsky, and Maurice Scott. *Industry and Trade in Some Developing Countries: A Comparative Study*. London: Oxford University Press, 1970.

Loser, Claudio. *The Intensity of Trade Restrictions in Argentina, 1938–1968*. Ph.D. dissertation, University of Chicago, 1971.

Lucas Jr., R. "Some International Evidence on Output-Inflation Tradeoffs," *American Economic Review* (June 1963), vol. 63, no. 3.

Macario, Santiago. "Protectionism and Industrialization in Latin America," *Economic Bulletin for Latin America* (March 1964), vol. 9, no. 1.

Mallon, Richard D. and Juan Sourrouille. *Economic Policy Making in a Conflict Society: The Argentine Case*. Xerox. 1973. (Subsequently published by Harvard University Press, 1975.)

Martinez, A. B. and M. Lewandowski. *The Argentine in the Twentieth Century*. London: n.p., 1911.

Mathias, Peter. *The First Industrial Nation, An Economic History of Britain, 1700–1914*. New York: Scribners, 1969.

Ministerio de Educación, Universidad Nacional de Buenos Aires, Facultad de Ciencias Económicas. *Regimen Bancario Argentino*. Buenos Aires, 1951.

Moreno, R. "La política económica que conviene al país en las actuales circunstancias," *Revista de Ciencias Económicas* (November 1917), vol. 5, no. 53.

Morley, Samuel A. and Gordon W. Smith, *The Effect of Changes in the Distribution of Income on Labor, Foreign Investment, and Growth in Brazil*, Program of Development Studies Paper No. 15, Rice University (Summer 1971).

Moyano Llerena, Carlos. "La Devolución de los Depositos," *Panorama de la Economía Argentina*, vol. 1.

Mulhall, M. *Handbook of the River Plate*. Buenos Aires: n.p., 1892.

Murmis, M. and J. Portantiero. *Estudios Sobre Orígenes del Peronismo.* Buenos Aires: Siglo Veinte Uno, 1972.

Nerlove, Mark. *The Dynamics of Supply.* Baltimore: Johns Hopkins University Press, 1958.

New York Times, 5 August 1948; 11, 16, and 18 June 1949.

de Obchatko, E. Scheinkerman. *Factores Limitantes a la Introducción del Cambio Tecnológico en el Sector Agropecuario.* Tésis, Escuela de Graduados, n.d.

O'Donnell, Guillermo and Delfina Linck. *Dependencia y Autonomía.* Buenos Aires: Amorrotu, 1973.

Olivera, Julio H. G. "Aspectos Dinámicos de la Inflación Estructural," *Desarrollo Economico* (October–December 1967), vol. 7, no. 27.

—— "El Dinero Pasivo," *El Trimestre Económico* (October–December 1968), vol 35, no. 4.

—— "A Note on Passive Money, Inflation, and Economic Growth," *The Journal of Money, Credit, and Banking* (February 1971).

——— "On Structural Inflation and Latin American 'Structuralism,'" *Oxford Economic Papers* (October 1964), new series, vol. 16, no. 3.

Organization for Economic Cooperation and Development. *Education, Human Resources and Development in Argentina.* Paris: 1967.

Ortiz, Ricardo. *História Económica de la República Argentina.* 2 vols. Buenos Aires: Pampa y Cielo, 1964.

Paz, Alberto and Gustavo Ferrari. *Argentina's Foreign Policy, 1930–1962.* Notre Dame: University of Notre Dame Press, 1966.

Peters, Harold E. *The Foreign Debt of the Argentine Republic.* Baltimore: Johns Hopkins University Press, 1934.

Peterson, Harold F. *Argentina and the United States, 1810–1960.* Buffalo: State University of New York, 1964.

Phelps, Dudley Maynard. *Migration of Industry to South America.* New York and London, McGraw Hill, 1936.

Phelps, Vernon S. *The International Economic Position of Argentina.* London: Oxford University Press, 1938.

Pinedo, Federico. *Interviews.* On deposit at Columbia University and Instituto Torcuato Di Tella.

—— *Nuestro Problema Monetario,* 2 vols. *Revista del Colegio Libre de Estudios Superiores.* Vol. 1: no. 1, July 1931; no. 2, August 1931.

—— *Siglo y Medio de Economía Argentina.* México: Fundo de Cultura Económica, 1971.

—— *En Tiempos de la República*. Buenos Aires: Mundo Forense, 1946.

Pla, Alberto J. "La Propiedad Rural en América Latina," *Anuario* no. 7 (1964). Instituto de Investigaciones Históricas, Rosario. Universidad del Litoral, Facultad de Filosofia y Letras.

Powelson, John. "The Terms of Trade Again," *Inter-American Economic Affairs* (Spring 1970), vol. 23, no. 4.

Prebisch, Raúl. *Conversaciones con el doctor Raúl Prebisch en el Banco de México, S.A. 15 April 1944*. Transcription.

—— *The Economic Development of Latin America and Its Principal Problems*. New York: United Nations, 1950.

—— Interviews. Spring 1971.

—— Lectures at Columbia University. Spring 1971.

Primera Plana.

"Public Enterprises: Their Present Significance and Their Potential in Development," *Economic Bulletin for Latin America* (January–June 1971), vol 16, no.1.

Quintana, C., ed. *Development Problems in Latin America*. Austin: University of Texas Press, 1970.

Ramos Mexia, Ezequiel. *A Programme of Public Works and Finance for the Argentine Republic*. London: Waterlow, 1913.

Randall, Laura. *A Comparative Economic History of Latin America: Argentina, Brazil, Mexico, and Peru, 1500–1914*. 4 vols. Ann Arbor: University Microfilms International, 1977.

—— "Economic Development Policies and Argentine Economic Growth." In Laura Randall, ed., *Economic Development: Evolution or Revolution?* Boston: D. C. Heath, 1964.

—— "Inflation and Economic Development in Latin America, 1950–1960," *Social and Economic Studies* (1967), vol. 16, no. 4.

—— "Inflation and Economic Development in Latin America: Some New Evidence," *Journal of Development Studies* (January 1973), vol. 9, no. 2.

—— "Lies, Damn Lies, and Argentine Gross Domestic Product," *Latin American Research Review* (Fall 1977), vol. 12, no. 3.

Reca, Lucio Graciano. *The Price and Production Duality Within Argentine Agriculture, 1923–1965*. Ph.D. dissertation, University of Chicago, 1967.

Rennie, Ysabel Fisk. *The Argentine Republic*. New York: Macmillan, 1945.

República Argentina. Congreso. *Message of the President of the Republic Opening the Session of the Argentine Congress, 1909*.

—— Consejo Nacional de Desarrollo Económico (CONADE). *Plan Nacional de Desarrollo y Seguridad, 1971–1975*. Buenos Aires, 1971.

—— Dirección Général de Comercio e Industria. *Censo Industrial y Comercial de la Repúblic Argentina, 1908–1914*. Buenos Aires, 1915.

—— Ministerios de Hacienda y Agricultura de la Nación. *El Plan de Acción Económica Nacional, 1934*. Buenos Aires, 1934.

—— Ministerio de Hacienda y Finanzas. Dirección Nacional de Programación e Investigación. *Inversión del Sector Público Argentino por Regiones, años 1968–1971*. Buenos Aires, 1972.

—— *Plan de Gobierno, 1947–1951*. Buenos Aires, 1946.

—— Poder Ejecutivo Nacional. *Período 1932–1938*, 12 vols. Buenos Aires, n.d.

—— Poder Ejecutivo Nacional, Secretaria de Asuntos Economicos. *Producto e Ingreso de la República Argentina en el Período 1935–1954*. Buenos Aires, 1955.

Revista de Ciencias Economicas.

Revista Económica Argentina.

Ribas, Arzac, Klurfan, and De Pablo. "Las Inversiones Extranjeras en la Argentina," *Fiel*, no. 68.

Salazar-Carillo, Jorge. *Price, Purchasing Power, and Real Product Comparisons in Latin America*. Technical Series T-004. Washington, D.C.: Brookings Institution, 1974.

Salera, Virgil. *Exchange Control and the Argentine Market*. New York: Columbia University Press, 1941,

Santa Cruz, Juan María. *Ferrocarriles Argentinos*. Santa Fe: Universidad Nacional del Litoral, 1966.

Scalabrini Ortiz, Raúl. *Historia de los Ferrocarriles Argentinos*. Buenos Aires: Devenir, 1958.

—— *Los Ferrocarriles Deben Ser Argentinos*. Buenos Aires: Pena Lillo, 1965.

Schwartz, Hugh H. *The Argentine Experience With Industrial Credit and Protection Incentives, 1943–1958*. 2 vols. Ph.D. dissertation, Yale University, 1967.

Schydlowsky, Daniel M. "Industrialization and Growth." In Luigi R. Einaudi, ed., *Beyond Cuba: Latin America Takes Charge of Its Future*. New York: Crane, Russak, 1974.

Scobie, James R. *Argentina: A City and a Nation*. New York: Oxford University Press, 1971.

—— *Revolution on the Pampas: A Social History of Argentine Wheat, 1860–1910*. Austin: University of Texas Press, 1964.

Shackle, G. L. S. "Keynes and Today's Establishment in Economic Theory: A View," *Journal of Economic Literature* (June 1973), vol. 11, no. 2.

Sidrauski, Miguel. "Davaluación, Inflación y Desempleo," *Economía* (January–August 1968), vol. 11, no. 1–2.

Silenzi di Stagni, A. *El Petróleo Argentino*. Buenos Aires: Problemas Nacionales, 1955.

Skupch, Pedro. "Concentración Industrial en la Argentina, 1956–1966," *Desarrollo Económico* (April–June 1972), vol. 11, no. 41,

—— "Nacionalización, Libras Bloqueadas y Substitución de Importaciones," *Desarrollo Económico* (October–December 1972), no. 47.

Smith, Peter. *Politics and Beef in Argentina*. New York: Columbia University Press, 1969.

Soares, Carlos. *Economía y Finanzas de la Nación Argentina 1903–1913*. Buenos Aires: Grau y Soulés, 1913.

Sociedad Rural Argentina (SRA). *Anuario, 1928; 1929; 1949*.

Solberg, Carl. "Rural Unrest and Agrarian Policy in Argentina, 1912–1930," *Journal of Inter-American Studies and World Affairs* (January 1971), vol. 13, no. 1.

—— "The Tariff and Politics in Argentina, 1916–1930," *Hispanic American Historical Review* (May 1973), vol. 53, no. 2.

SRA, *see* Sociedad Rural Argentina.

Solís, Leopoldo M. and Sergio Ghighliazza, "Estabilidad económica y política monetaria," *El Trimestre Económico* (April–June 1963), vol. 30.

Taylor, Carl C. *Rural Life in Argentina*. Baton Rouge: Louisiana State University Press, 1948.

Techint. *Boletin Informativo* (June 1962), no. 128 ("Las Crisis Económicas"), and (October–November 1964), no. 143.

Thiriot, Luis F. *Estudio Sobre Los Presupuestos de la República y Las Provincias y los Municipios Argentinas*. Buenos Aires: Sudamericana de Billetes de Banco, 1901.

Thompson, John. "Argentine Economic Policy Under the Onganía Regime," *Inter-American Economic Affairs* (Summer 1970), vol. 24, no. 1.

Times (London), 18 September 1946; 20 October 1949; 15 April 1950.

Tornquist E., and Co. *The Economic Development of the Argentine Republic in the Last Fifty Years*. Buenos Aires: n.p., 1919.

Tulchin, Joseph, Kenneth Hardy, and Carl Hoffman. "Agricultural Credit and Politics in Argentina, 1910–1930," *Research Reviews* (April 1973), vol. 20, no. 1. Institute for Research in Social Science, University of North Carolina at Chapel Hill.

United Nations. Economic Commission for Latin America (ECLA). *Economic Development and Income Distribution in Argentina.* New York: UN, 1969.

—— *Statistical Bulletin for Latin America,* vol. 9. New York: UN, 1972.

—— *Yearbook of International Trade Statistics.*

—— *Yearbook of National Income Account Statistics.*

United States Tariff Commission, *The Argentine Customs Tariff and Other Trade Restrictions on Imports from the United States Since January 1, 1922.* Washington, D.C. Mimeographed.

Vásquez-Presedo, Vicente. *El Caso Argentino: Migración de Factores: Comercio Exterior y Desarrollo 1875–1914.* Buenos Aires: Eudeba, 1971.

Villafañe, Benjamin. *El Atraso del Interior: Documentos Oficiales del Gobierno de Jujuy Pidiendo Amparo Para las Industrias del Norte.* Jujuy: n.p., 1926.

Villanueva, Javier. "El Origen de la Industrialización Argentina," *Desarrollo Económico* (October–December 1972), vol. 12, no. 47.

Wall Street Journal, 16 July 1975.

Weil, Felix. *Argentine Riddle.* New York: John Day, 1944.

White, John W. *Argentina: The Life Story of a Nation.* New York: Viking, 1942.

Williams, John H. *Argentine International Trade Under Inconvertible Paper Money, 1880–1900.* Cambridge: Harvard University Press, 1920.

Wright, Winthrop. *British-Owned Railways in Argentina: Their Effect on the Growth of Economic Nationalism, 1854–1948.* Austin: University of Texas Press, 1974.

Zuvekas, Clarence Jr., "Economic Growth and Income Distribution in Postwar Argentina," *Inter-American Economic Affairs* (Winter 1966), vol. 20, no. 3.

Index

Index of Time Periods